International Commercial Rivalry

*Produced with generous financial
assistance from William J. Klausner*

International Commercial Rivalry in Southeast Asia in the Interwar Period

edited by

SUGIYAMA SHINYA

and

MILAGROS C. GUERRERO

Monograph 39/Yale Southeast Asia Studies
Yale Center for International and Area Studies

Library of Congress Catalog Card Number: 9361623
International Standard Book Number: paper 0938692-51-8
cloth 0938692-52-6

© 1994 by Yale Southeast Asia Studies
New Haven, Connecticut 06520-8206

Distributor:
Yale University Southeast Asia Studies
P.O. Box 208206
New Haven, Connecticut 06520-8206
U.S.A.

Printed in U.S.A.

Contents

List of Tables

List of Figures

Contributors

BENJAMIN A. BATSON, Senior Lecturer in History, National University of Singapore

ANNE E. BOOTH, Professor of Economics, School of Oriental and African Studies, University of London

IAN G. BROWN, Lecturer in Economic History, School of Oriental and African Studies, University of London

MILAGROS C. GUERRERO, Professor of History, University of the Philippines

SUMIO HATANO, Associate Professor in Diplomatic History, University of Tsukuba, Ibaragi

HIDEMASA KOKAZE, Associate Professor in History, Ochanomizu Women's University, Tokyo

HAJIME SHIMIZU, Professor of Economics, Graduate School of Economics, Nagasaki Prefectural University, Nagasaki

SHINYA SUGIYAMA, Professor of Economic History, Keio University, Tokyo

Introduction

Sugiyama Shinya

The main object of this book is to present an overall picture of the international economic rivalry which arose in Southeast Asia in the 1920s and 1930s, and to evaluate in a wider historical perspective the significance of Japan's southward advance into the area. A related aim is to shed light on the historical background for Southeast Asia's present international economic and political position and the course of industrialization in the region. Methodologically the book attempts to produce "inter-area studies," by linking Japanese and Southeast Asian studies in order to examine international commercial rivalry from a variety of different perspectives.

The book is organized around the dynamic inter-relationships linking three key factors: the advance of Japan into Southeast Asia; the response to this advance from existing Western political and economic interests in the area; and the rise of nationalism—both political and economic—in Thailand and in the countries of the region which were under Western colonial control. It consists of eight case studies which examine these factors as they determined international commercial rivalry. Part 1 deals with Japan's advance into Southeast Asia (chapters 1–4) and Part 2 with the responses of Western colonial powers in the region and of Thailand (chapters 5–8).

Except for Thailand, Southeast Asia was under the control of four different Western colonial powers: Britain in Malaya (including

Singapore) and Burma, the Netherlands in Indonesia, France in Indochina, and the United States in the Philippines. The political and economic interests of the four powers in the region were by no means identical, but their ruling structure can be described as relatively stable. In this sense, Southeast Asia in the interwar period was a microcosm of the state of international relations in the period after the Washington Conference of 1921–22. Japan's advance into the area, first economic and then political and military, disturbed this equilibrium, and eventually forced a fundamental readjustment in the position of the Western colonial powers in Southeast Asia.

World War I had changed the structure of both world politics and the world economy. It had also had a crucial effect on the Japanese economy, although, or rather because, Japan was not directly involved. After 1915, Japan enjoyed an economic boom brought about by the expansion of her exports into the vacuum left by Western countries whose energies were being taken up by the war. Two points are important here in relation to the trade conflicts that were to occur in the next decades: first, Japan's exports of manufactured goods to Asian countries increased, replacing Western ones; secondly, there was a rapid expansion in her shipping industry, with sharp increases in the total tonnage of ships. Japan shifted from a debtor to a creditor nation, and Japan's commercial interests in Asian countries became much greater.

Chapter 1, by Shimizu Hajime, deals with the intellectual background to Japan's advance into Southeast Asia. He sees World War I as crucial in the sense that arguments for Japan to advance southward (*Nanshinron*) began to acquire expansionist and pan-Asian dimensions which had previously characterised only the arguments for northward advance (*Hokushinron*). This tendency became stronger as commercial rivalry with the West intensified in the 1930s.

Japan's export trade fell in the 1920s with the return of Western goods to the Asian market. The Japanese domestic economy experienced a series of long recessions interspersed with short periods of prosperity. Throughout this decade and into the early 1930s, the two main Japanese political parties put forward basically contrasting combinations of financial and foreign policy as solutions to the country's problems. The Seiyukai favoured an inflationary financial policy through the issue of loans and advocated expansion into China; the Kenseikai (which became the Minseito in 1927) preferred a deflationary financial policy and cooperation with the Western powers, as exemplified by the policies of Shidehara Kijuro, Foreign Minister from 1924 to 1927 and 1929 to 1931. The logical outcome to the latter combination was Japan's return to the gold standard. The Great Kanto Earthquake of September 1923 had allowed the (Seiyukai) government to adopt an expansionary policy in order to reconstruct the economy. But, this had postponed the reorganisation of the swollen war-boom economy and led to a financial crisis in 1927. Japan found herself gradually isolated from the international economy as the Western powers, one by one, returned to the gold standard in the 1920s, while she still hesitated over what action to take.

It was the Minseito cabinet, formed in 1929 with Inoue Junnosuke as Finance Minister, that finally made the decision to return to the gold standard in January 1930. Unfortunately this made Japan acutely vulnerable to the effects of the economic collapse of 1929 and the depression that followed. The outflow of gold increased, and rural areas were badly hit by a fall in agricultural prices. In September 1931 the Manchurian Incident occurred; three days later Great Britain left the gold standard. These events led to speculation that Japan would reimpose an embargo on gold exports. The continuing economic recession and the increasing atmosphere of militarism cost the Minseito its national support and brought in a Seiyukai cabinet that promptly suspended gold exports from Japan in December 1931.

The need to recover from the depression meant that the developed countries were preoccupied with domestic economic issues rather than with the pursuit of international cooperation. This was also the case in Japan. The government adopted a more interventionist role in the economy; in particular, Takahashi Korekiyo, Finance Minister of the new Seiyukai government, adopted a spending policy.

He increased military expenditure and boosted exports by allowing the depreciation of the yen. The annual average exchange rate of the yen against the US dollar declined rapidly, from 49.375 dollars per 100 yen during the period from 1930 to 1931 to 26 dollars in 1932.

During her recovery from the depression, Japan's interest in Southeast Asia grew in economic as well as political and military terms. Her advance into this area greatly increased the suspicion with which she was regarded by Western countries such as Britain. Not only did this become a cause of conflict in the 1930s, but the counter-measures which the Western powers adopted as a result had significant repercussions, both direct and indirect,throughout Southeast Asia.

By 1933, Japan had been able to bring production levels back to their predepression rates, the only advanced country to manage such a quick recovery. This feat had been accomplished by increasing exports, particularly of cotton textiles, at relatively low selling prices which were aided by the rapid depreciation of the yen. Since Japan's main overseas markets were India and the Dutch East Indies, the increasing exports from Japan forced those areas to take protective measures such as the introduction of import quotas and increased import duties on Japanese goods.

Japan attempted to remove these restrictions by opening bi-lateral trade negotiations, for example, with Britain, India, and the Dutch East Indies in 1933 and 1934. Chapter 2, by Sugiyama Shinya, traces this process by examining the internal and external backgrounds to the growing exports of Japanese cotton textiles in this period. Chapter 6, by Anne Booth, investigates the dramatic growth of Japanese imports to the Dutch East Indies in the early 1930s in the context of the developing Indonesian economy and the changing economic policy of the Dutch East Indies government. After 1934 the government took a more active role in the colony's economic development.

Although the Philippines was not a major market for Japanese cotton textiles, Milagros Guerrero shows in chapter 7 how the increase in imports of Japanese cotton goods influenced the relationship between the Philippines and the United States and caused conflicts of interest at various levels, both domestic and bi-lateral. Japan's push to increase exports of her cotton textiles to world markets, regardless of the effect on other producer countries, provoked protective measures against major Japanese exports from the Dutch East Indies and elsewhere (chapter 2).

Shipping rivalry was another major issue in the trade disagreements between Japan and Western countries. Chapter 3, by Kokaze Hidemasa, examines the competition between the Dutch firms of the Java-China-Japan Line and the Royal Dutch Shipping Company (KPM) and the Japanese firms of Nanyo Yusen, Osaka Shosen (OSK), Nippon Yusen (NYK), and Ishihara Sangyo Kaiun. The four Japanese firms differed among themselves about the shipping agreements between the Netherlands and Japan. As a result, Ishihara Sangyo Kaiun was finally excluded from Nanyo Kaiun, the shipping line which united the other three Japanese firms under government auspices.

Throughout Southeast Asia the rapid Japanese economic advance produced disagreements and conflicts of interest among Western policymakers and businessmen, as they pondered its significance and the countermeasures which they should take. Chapter 5, by Ian Brown, shows that the British merchant community in Singapore responded in two contrasting ways to Japanese commercial expansion. It reacted particularly strongly to imports of Japanese textiles and to the fact that exports of crude rubber through Singapore for the United States were being carried increasingly by Japanese ships. This split demonstrated the diversified interests of the Singapore merchant community.

The increasing Japanese interests in Southeast Asia had a significant influence on the political and economic situation in Thailand also. The only independent state in Southeast Asia at that time, Thailand found itself caught between Japan and the Western powers. In chapter 8, Benjamin Batson gives a vivid description of the Thai position and puts the Thai perception of Japan into historical perspective. The establishment of the constitutional monarchy in 1932 was the crucial turning point in Thai relations with Japan. After this, "Siam and Japan ... sought to challenge and ultimately overturn the established order in Southeast Asia" (chapter 8).

The growing tendency towards militarism in Japan was exacerbated by the attempted coup by young army officers of 1936, known as the February 26 Incident. As a result, economic policies were aimed at increasing military production by promoting cooperation between military and business interests. While the army was interested in Manchuria and North China, the navy stressed the significance of Southeast Asia. In chapter 4, Hatano Sumio analyses the serious conflicts which, nevertheless, existed within the navy. The need to ensure fuel supplies made the southward expansion inevitable. This was strongly advocated by the group which opposed the naval reductions agreed upon at the Washington naval conference of 1922 and affirmed military expansion in China.

The outbreak of the Sino-Japanese War in 1937 led to a further increase in direct government control of political and economic activities. Even so, the country faced steadily increasing inflation, a growing shortage of strategically significant materials, and the stagnation of its basic industries. While Japan was becoming more influential in Southeast Asia, Southeast Asia was becoming more important to Japan. The increasing hostility of the international community was making her more dependent on that region both as a market for her exports and as a source of such essential raw materials as iron ore, rubber, and petroleum.

This book examines only the principal aspects of commercial rivalry in Southeast Asia in the interwar period. It has therefore had to omit analysis of the links between Southeast Asia and China/Manchuria in Japanese overseas expansion, the French presence in Indochina, and the impact of commercial rivalry on the political and economic positions of the Western powers and their colonies. Nevertheless, it makes an important contribution to both Japanese and Southeast Asian studies.

This book is the result of a joint research project on "International Commercial Rivalry in Southeast Asia in the Interwar Period" which was carried out from 1985 to 1988. The essays are revised versions of papers presented at the project workshop, held from 12 to 15 April 1988 in Shimoda, Japan. The Japanese version of this book has already been published under the title *Senkanki Tonan Ajia no Keizai Masatsu* (Tokyo: Dobunkan, 1990).

I would like to express my gratitude to the Japan Society for Promotion of Sciences and the Fukutake Science and Culture Foundation for their generous assistance. I would also like to thank those who took part in the workshop as discussants and/or helped the project in various ways: Dr Yuen Choy Leng, Dr Howard Dick, Professor Saruwatari Keiko, Mr Takahashi Hisashi, Dr Helen Ballhatchet, and Mrs Fushimi Yukari.

Note: All Japanese names in this book are in the usual Japanese order of family name followed by given name.

PART I

Japan's Advancement into Southeast Asia

1

Japanese Economic Penetration into Southeast Asia and the "Southward Expansion" School of Thought

Shimizu Hajime

Introduction

Penetration into the Pacific region south of Japan was a frequent topic among Japanese from 1870 to 1940. The various ideas that were discussed over those seventy years have been loosely classified into what is known as *nanshin–ron*, or views on southward expansion, the series of calls for a doctrine proclaiming that the South Seas were vital not just to Japanese economic development but to Japan's very existence as a nation.[1]

Nanshin-ron, which first appeared in the 1880s and 1890s, was presumably influenced by the rampant imperialism occurring in the world in those days. However, it should be noted that the *nanshin-ron* that developed during this period was not necessarily expansionist in nature. Rather, it had a modest character based on a realistic assessment of the limited national power that Japan possessed at that time and on a prudence not to impinge on the vested interests of the Western imperial powers in Southeast Asia and the Pacific. The advocates of *nanshin-ron* at this time were interested primarily in the islands of the Pacific and not in Southeast Asia, which had already fallen under the colonial domain of the Western powers. The *nanshin-ron* was a set of views that the state had to have strong foundations that were built through prosperity in international trade, that the establishment of free trade was a long-term goal of the state, and that sea power was a major means of achieving that goal. The main substance of *nanshin-ron* was a call for international trade and economic advance into the Pacific islands, Australia, and, subsequently, into North and South America into what we know today as the Pacific Rim.

It should be pointed out that, although the *nanshin-ron* of this period was not entirely devoid of expansionist ideas, it was directed mainly towards a peaceful economic advance into the Pacific region and not at territorial gains through aggression.[2] In addition, it should be noted that the Asiatic nature of *nanshin-ron* that assumed predominance in later periods, as exemplified by such slogans as "Asia for Asians" and "Asian solidarity," had not yet surfaced during this period. The thrust of the argument was that Japan needed Southeast Asia and the Pacific as places in which to pursue a long-term policy of developing manufacturing industries and commercial exchange based upon "free trade."

The turning point in Japan's southward advance during World War I

The turning point for *nanshin-ron* was brought about by the outbreak of World War I in 1914.[3] The war provided favorable circumstances for Japan's southward expansion, since it curtailed trade between the Western countries and Southeast Asian markets and provided an opportunity for Japan to move in and fill the vacuum by selling food, textiles, and sundry other items. As a result, full-scale economic relations began between Japan and Southeast Asia. Japanese import and export trade and investment in the area increased rapidly, although there were some variations depending on business fluctuations. For example, between 1914 and 1925, exports from Japan to Southeast Asia increased eightfold, and imports from

Southeast Asia increased more than fivefold. There was a doubling (from 11,845 in 1913 to 23,967 in 1918) of the Japanese population in the area in the five years following the outbreak of the War.[4]

It is also notewothy that various Japanese organizations for promoting economic ties and facilities for the local Japanese communities were rapidly established and developed in many parts of Southeast Asia during World War I and in the 1920s. After the war, new Japanese consulates were opened in such places as Haiphong, Davao, Surabaya, Saigon, Hanoi, and Medan, in addition to those in Manila, Singapore, Bangkok, and Batavia, which had already been established before the war. Moreover, the Yokohama Species Bank and the Bank of Taiwan opened branches in many parts of Southeast Asia, and, at the same time, Japanese Chambers of Commerce, Japanese Associations, Japanese elementary schools, as well as Japanese-language newspapers and magazines also sprang up. These organizations were indispensable for unity and cooperation and for cultivating a sense of belonging and distinct consciousness among subjects of the Japanese Empire. Newspapers and elementary schools were expected to be particularly instrumental in nurturing nationalistic patriotism.[5]

At home, on the other hand, Nan'yo Kyokai (The South Seas Society) was founded in January 1915 with financial support from the Governor-General's Office of Taiwan and with the cooperation of both the Ministry of Foreign Affairs and the Ministry of Agriculture and Commerce.[6] The South Seas Society established branches in places such as Singapore, Taiwan, Java, the Pacific or South Seas Islands, Manila, Davao, Sumatra, and Bangkok. Of these, the Singapore branch, with the help of the Ministry of Agriculture and Commerce, set up the Singapore Exhibition House of Japanese Goods, which served as an intermediary between Japan and Southeast Asia, facilitating subsequent Japanese economic penetration into Southeast Asia.[7]

One of the major reasons for these moves was the belief that the success of the Chinese in Southeast Asia was attributable to the unions, mutual aid groups, social-help associations, and guilds and clubs that united members from the same provinces and the same clans. The Japanese, therefore, felt it was necessary to devise their own versions of these organizations so that they could make a systematic advance into Southeast Asia that was in no way inferior to what the Chinese had accomplished. In order to facilitate the achievement of those ends, they would use the concepts of state and nation that the Chinese seemed to lack.

What was it that propelled Japan to become economically involved in Southeast Asia during World War I and in the following decade? It was the increasingly urgent need to secure raw materials for the development of heavy and chemical industries, which were considered vital to the Japanese economy at that time. Because she was technologically inferior to the West, it was imperative that Japan obtain raw materials from geographically proximate Southeast Asia in order to achieve the development of her heavy and chemical industries in competition with the West. The idea of looking to Southeast Asia as well as China as a supplier of raw materials appeared quite early during this period.[8]

The need to secure raw materials for the development of heavy and chemical industries created another reason for further economic involvement in Southeast Asia. The import of raw materials produced a perennial excess of imports and aggravated Japan's balance of payments. A solution to this problem called for a vigorous export drive and diversification of export markets in order to acquire foreign currencies. In this context, Southeast Asia emerged as an important market for Japanese cotton textiles.

Another opportunity was afforded under the guise of the Anglo-Japanese Alliance. This allowed Japan to enter the war against Germany and, by 12 October 1914, to seize the German Pacific island possessions of the Marianas, Marshalls, and the East and West Carolines to establish an effective bridgehead in the South Seas. The two events gave a new angle to the *nanshin-ron*. They established the basic principle of southward expansion in which Southeast Asia became the most important objective. Japan now had bases for southward advance by way of the central Pacific islands and Taiwan. For the first time, this created the idea of expansion into Southeast Asia, including into the Dutch East Indies.

It was around this time, much in advance of the West, that the Japanese began to use the term "Tonan Ajia" (Southeast Asia) to indicate the region as it is today.[9] The standard state geography textbook for elementary education published in February 1919 contains a chapter entitled "Southeast Asia," which treats insular and peninsular Southeast Asia as one. That was a significant change from previous texts which treated peninsular Southeast Asia as part of Asia and insular Southeast Asia as part of Oceania, as was the usage in the West. From then on, the ministry of education made "Southeast Asia" the common term in geography texts.

The description in this textbook is only about 440 words long, a curt examination of resources of trade with Japan that stands in stark contrast to previous discourses on regional topography, climate, natural features, customs, and industries. The short article about rice in Indochina, rubber in Malaya, sugar in Java, petroleum in Sumatra and Borneo, and manila hemp in the Philippines concludes: "A gradually increasing number of Japanese are going to Malaya and ships of our country have recently begun scheduled service to Malayan destinations. That means that our trade with that area is also increasing."[10] The description clearly indicates growth in economic relations with Southeast Asia after World War I, and provides some clue as to how the concept of Southeast Asia as a regional market and resource supplier to Japan was formed.

Just as Japan had used World War I to good advantage to begin acquiring rights and interests in the South Seas, she also began to advance economically and politically into Southeast Asia. This was certain to provoke a confrontation with the Western powers that still ruled the region.

Moreover, the seizure of the South Seas islands was instrumental in forming the clique within the navy that was responsible for the thought and practice of the southward expansion of the navy that would gain momentum in the 1930s. The clique consisted of such young naval officers as Nakahara Yoshimasa, who was later called "the king of the South Seas;" Konishi Tatehiko, who was appointed as the director of the Institute of the South Seas Economies in the early 1940s; Ishikawa Shingo, an anti-American hardliner at the outbreak of the Pacific War, and Chudo Kan'e. They had graduated from the Naval Academy in Japan and shared an experience travelling through the South Seas islands and Southeast Asia in an expedition after their graduation. This trip convinced them that expansion into these areas would be vital for Japan's survival, and that the navy should actively support the idea. The argument put forward by these officers, who were to play a pivotal role in the formulation of the navy's southward advance policy in the 1930s, was based on their opposition to the Washington Conference treaty system, and it had an element of expansionism about it. It was undoubtedly influenced by their trip through the South Seas islands and their exposure to the discussions during this period about Southward expansion.

Nanshin-ron took on expansionist tendencies in this period, as expressed by the slogan "the entire world as one family." Such tendencies were logical because expansionist ideas had become more widely accepted and were no longer limited to southward advance. The *nanshin-ron* became part of the discussions that called for expansion to the north, south, east, and west; its advocates became especially aware of the theory's complementarity and coexistence with the *hokushin-ron* (northward expansion theory).[11] Thus, "south" was no longer the only appropriate direction of expansion. For all practical purposes, the dichotomy that had existed between *nanshu-hokushin-ron* (hold fast in the south, advance in the north) and *hokushu-nanshin-ron* (hold fast in the north, advance in the south) logically disappeared. This led inevitably to a loss of the ideological and political coloring that was intrinsic in *nanshin-ron* as long as it had remained the antithesis of *hokushin-ron*.

Nanshin-ron became strongly infused with the Asiatic ideology that had been the hallmark of *hokushin-ron*. The Asiatic theme, *i.e.*, Japan's mission as the self-professed leader of the Orient in liberating Asians or members of the same race who shared a similar culture and allegedly used similar writing systems, pervaded every aspect of the *nanshin-ron* at this time. To the *nanshin-ron* advocates, Japan's duty was to lead those living under uncivilized conditions, as it had done in China, to liberate Asia from Western colonial control and promote Asian development.[12] Japan's reasons for assuming this duty were to be found in the common cultural and racial bonds of the Japanese and Southeast Asian peoples and Japan's confidence in her status as an advanced country.[13] The *nanshin-ron* advocates believed that Japan and Southeast Asia were quite similar; however, Japan was modernized and Southeast Asia was underdeveloped, and it was the responsibility of a more advanced country to bring light to the less advanced.

It is noteworthy that these two aspects effectively infused moral principles into the ideology of expansionism that the Japanese called "Imperialism" and the "Greater Japan Policy" (*Dai-Nipponshugi*). These concepts also served to justify the distinction the Japanese made between their expansionism and imperialism and that of the West. Propriety and morality in Japanese expansionism were declared under the pretentious slogans of "moral imperialism" and the "righteous path of greater Japan"; Europe and America were branded the "white clique" as Japan sought to prevent their advance into Southeast Asia.[14]

Despite its spirit of confrontation with Europe and America and its insistence on the morality of Japanese imperialism and the injustices of Europe and American imperialism, the *nanshin-ron* in this period refrained from encouraging actual expansion into Southeast Asia. Although it made the liberation and development of Southeast Asia its great causes: the *nanshin-ron* stressed trade and industrial development for Japan's sake more than for the sake of the people living in the region. On behalf of the political liberation of Southeast Asia, Japan tried to understand its nationalism and gave passive support to its independence from its Western masters. The Japanese considered it wise to avoid competition and friction with Europe and America as much as possible. Soejima Yasoroku, a supporter of the *nanshin-ron* at this time, demonstrates well the huge gap between Japan's exaggerated sense of mission, its ideology of expansionism, and its meager expression of concrete advances when he proclaims in the introduction to his *Teikoku nanshin saku* [An imperial southward expansion policy] Japan's mission as leader and peacekeeper of the Orient:

> I have in mind a great ideal. I hope that the people of Japan in their true power shall bring about expansion and development and, at the same time, that they lead and awaken the other peoples of the Orient. With them, we can contribute to a new future civilization.[15]

But his main text does a complete about-face; it discusses only what is in the Japanese interest: "The main reason I am concerned about India and the South Seas area is their rich resources. An important topic from now on will be how Japan is going to take advantage of those resources."[16] The book fails to make any mention of liberating Southeast Asia for its own sake.

That the *nanshin-ron* would make profiteering the main element of the Japanese southward expansion was inevitable. The Japanese interest in Southeast Asia was concerned only with exploiting rich resources. Interestingly, the Japanese called those resources "heaven's blessings" (*tenkei*) or "heaven's riches" (*tenpu*); *ten*, the word for heaven, implied that the resources were given equally to all people under heaven. But these words also had another meaning: "unowned land with no one on it," "undeveloped," or "land which the owner hopes someone else will come to develop" and, as such, they expressed the self-deceiving belief and hope that Southeast Asia was an unclaimed land without owners and open to anybody. Needless to say, this kind of notion of Southeast Asia was used to justify advances into the area as a Japanese prerogative.[17]

This gap between an expansionist, Asianist ideology and the benefits of exploiting Southeast Asia was the remarkable feature of the *nanshin-ron* of this period. This gap arose out of a psychological defence mechanism based on Japanese doubts about the nation's real power. Expressions such as moral imperialism, genuine greater Japan policy, righteous way, and leader of the Orient represented the pained hopes of a country forced to compete with Europe and America and of a country trying to become a first-class nation despite the lack of adequate power.

The Conference on Japanese Trade with Southeast Asia and the Idea of "Southward Expansion" in the 1920s

However, such *nanshin-ron* with a strong expansionist and Asiatic ideology was on the wane in the 1920s after the War, although a large number of books and articles about the South Seas area, especially Southeast Asia, were published. In fact, most of these publications were official reports and business books on the economies, resources, and industries of the region, rather than discussions advocating policies or ideologies of southward advance. Generally speaking, the full-scale development of Japanese-Southeast Asian economic relations transformed discussions about the region to more pragmatic and businesslike ones. In particular, the solutions for more urgent economic problems in Southeast Asia, including measures for the relief of rubber planters who were heavily damaged by the depression after World War I, and the establishment of a special financial institution for promoting exports and imports with the region, took precedence over ideological discussions. Moreover, it should also be noted that the international line of disarmament and non-expansion under the "Washington Treaties System" of 1921 and 1922 functioned as a brake on the expansionist version of *nanshin-ron*.

Japanese views on Southeast Asia during the period were reflected in discussions at the Conference on Japanese Trade with Southeast Asia, held in Tokyo from 13 to 23 September 1926 under the auspices of the Ministry of Foreign Affairs.[18] The conference was held against the backdrop of Japan facing an urgent need to improve the worsening balance of payments that had resulted from declining exports in the aftermath of the post World War I recession and rising imports of reconstruction materials following the Great Kanto Earthquake of September 1923. A solution to this problem required a vigorous export drive, for which the markets of India and Southeast Asia attracted considerable attention. The two markets were expected to compensate for the gradually declining exports to the United States and China. Almost all government ministries, private business circles, and public economic organizations were represented at the Conference. They included Ministries of Foreign Affairs, Commerce and Industry, Agriculture and Forestry, and Finance; the six biggest chambers of commerce; export firms such as Mitsui Bussan and Mitsubishi Shoji; manufacturers; the Yokohama Specie Bank and the Bank of Taiwan; shipping interests such as Nippon Yusen and Osaka Shosen; insurers; and the South Seas Society.

The conference was ostensibly held to seek solutions for the urgent economic problems with Southeast Asia, but the Ministry of Foreign Affairs wished also to change its diplomatic policy using the conference as a lever. If the promotion of Japanese exports and investment in Southeast Asia had been its only objectives, the conference could instead have been sponsored by the Ministry of Commerce and Industry. As a matter of fact, there had been rivalry about its sponsorship between the two ministries before the conference. The Ministry of Foreign Affairs expected the conference to mark the opening of a new phase in Japanese diplomacy, one which would spell the end of the traditional diplomatic role that it had adopted since the conclusion of the Russo-Japanese War in 1905. Apart from wishing to stop covering up the "continental policy" of the army, the Ministry of Foreign Affairs sought also to promote the policy of peaceful economic diplomacy and international cooperation espoused by Foreign Minister Shidehara. In effect, the Ministry of Foreign Affairs wished to convert its foreign economic policy, which had been devoted exclusively to China under the influence of the military "continental policy," into a more comprehensive one, based upon free trade and including Southeast Asia. Shidehara's opening address at the conference indicates clearly that his diplomatic principles guided the conference throughout.[19] He made it clear that the conference was devoid of political ambitions, but was held for purely commercial and economic motives, advocating the efficacy of international trade in promoting the interests of all parties concerned.

How did the other participants respond to the stance of the Ministry of Foreign Affairs based upon Shidehara's diplomatic principles? A heated controversy arose over free trade or protective trade. The Ministry of Foreign Affairs took a firm stand for free trade and against protective duties, while the Ministry of Commerce and Industry insisted on protectionism including an increase in import tariffs for the purpose of protecting domestic industries. There were also heated debates among the representatives of private enterprises over this issue, as their interests were more directly at stake. The proponents of free trade, opposed to levying protective duties, included such major exporting firms as Mitsui Bussan Company and associations of manufacturers of textiles for export such as the Japan Federation of Knitted Goods Manufacturers Associations.[20] On the other hand, advocates of protectionism who were opposed to indiscriminate free trade included the dyestuff and sugar industries that were vulnerable to imported goods, in addition to heavy industry which required governmental protective policies. With the Furukawa Mining Company taking the lead, these groups objected to free trade, citing the cause of national defence.[21]

How was the controversy resolved? When the conference closed on 23 September 1926, a tendency prevailed among the partcipants towards an international cooperation policy based upon the principle of free trade over "protectionism in the name of national defence." It could be said that this was the natural and logical outcome in view of Japan's economic needs at that time. As mentioned above, one of the most important motives of the conference had been the improvement of the worsening balance of payments. It is usually the case that there is an inclination towards protectionism and the restriction of imports when the balance of payments is worsening. However, because Japan was dependent mainly on the export of articles manufactured from imported materials, she had no alternative but to conduct an export drive to cope with the situation. Therefore,the principle of free trade, which would more easily facilitate exports, held sway at the conference, suppressing various arguments for protectionism.

It is important to note that the final outcome, which represented the interests of export trading firms and associations, coincided with the diplomatic principles that the Ministry of Foreign Affairs, and particularly Foreign Minister Shidehara Kijuro, were trying to pursue. In other words, because the 1920s were a time of pragmatic business relations with Southeast Asia, discussions about the region during the period were inevitably oriented towards international cooperation based upon economic interests, instead of southward expansionism.

International Economic Frictions in Southeast Asia and the Revival of Nanshin-Ron in the 1930s

The conclusions reached by the conference on Japanese trade with Southeast Asia, however, rapidly lost their effectiveness with the rise of protectionist ideas and the trend towards bloc economies in the 1930s. In the process of emerging from the economic collapse of 1929 and the depression that followed, the formation of economic blocs by the advanced countries of the world increased and brought international economic and political tensions to the surface. As part of this process, Japan began to advance extensively into Southeast Asian markets to acquire a sufficient fund of foreign currencies to construct a Japan-Manchuria-China economic bloc. This was considered vital, given the frailty of international trade generally and the declining volume of business carried on with the United States and China specifically after the Manchurian Incident of 1931. While

Western trade with Southeast Asia declined, Japanese goods, mainly cotton products, aided by the devalued exchange rate of the yen, streamed into Southeast Asian markets where primary products had been seriously damaged by the economic crisis and purchasing power had been lowered. This rapid increase of exports changed the Japanese trade structure with Southeast Asia from one of deficit into one of surplus. These phenomena made Southeast Asia the scene of international economic frictions between Japan, the Western colonial powers, and the local economies.

Japan's advance into Southeast Asia greatly increased the suspicion with which she was regarded by Western countries such as Britain. Not only did this become a cause of conflict, but it also had great influence on the colonies in Southeast Asia both directly and indirectly.

Great Britain had had a sense of impending crisis for Indian and Southeast Asian markets since around 1925, and now began to devise measures through bilateral agreements for protecting its cotton products' market in the region in the 1930s. But these had little effect, and it found its market share reduced more rapidly. The three trade negotiations between Britain and India, Japan and India, and Japan and Britain, held in 1933 and 1934, were the culmination of trade frictions over cotton products.

Greater trade frictions occurred in the Dutch East Indies, where the influx of Japanese products, especially cotton goods, began to make inroads into the Western share of the market. The Japanese penetration at the expense of the Dutch in the early 1930s happened because Holland had not altered its traditional free trade policy towards the East Indies. In spite of the fact that the British had formed a pound-sterling bloc at the British Imperial Economic Conference held in Ottawa in August 1932, the Dutch did not resort to such measures as tariff barriers to protect their products.

In view of the fact that the Dutch East Indies was thus the only major market left for Japan, the first round of Japanese-Dutch negotiations, which took place sporadically between June and December 1934, was considered a test of Japan's accommodating economic policy. Failure in the negotiations would mean that all doors in the world market would be closed to future Japanese economic penetration. Indeed, having failed to persuade the Dutch to ease newly-imposed restrictions on imports, Japan searched in vain around the world for a market comparable in size to India and the Dutch East Indies. This left no alternative for Japan but to seek a closed market in its own Japan-Machukuo-China economic bloc.

The trade friction with Holland over the Dutch East Indies originated in the textile-producing areas that felt endangered by the large-scale inroads into the market made by Japanese products. Responding to the pleas of the textile manufacturers, the Dutch cabinet that came into office in May 1933 gradually drifted towards protectionism, as reflected in its annoucement of the introduction of an import quota system. However, the population in the Dutch East Indies did not necessarily give full support to this policy shift toward protectionism. Many, including general consumers with lower purchasing power as a result of the Great Depression, cotton planters who wanted to keep wages down, import merchants dealing in Japanese goods, and batik producers using Japanese materials found cheap Japanese cotton textiles desirable.

The conflict between the Dutch East Indies and Japan was intensified because of the rapid increase in the number of Japanese merchants there in the 1930s.[22] For the Japanese, the increasing number of Japanese merchants was merely the result of their endeavor to develop new outlets for Japanese goods that had thus far been neglected by most of the Dutch merchants. But, in the eyes of Dutch merchants, it was perceived as a threat to their share of the market. In an effort to monopolize the market, the Dutch merchants created conditions in which import restriction acts played a key role in their favor. A number of such acts, directed mainly against Japan, were implemented from June 1933. Many of them stipulated not only that import volume should be restricted, but also that importers should be licenced.

To cope with these measures to restrict imports, Japan began to press for negotiations. There were two possible Japanese responses to these measures: accommodation or a hard-line policy toward the Dutch East Indies. Those favoring the former argued that Japan should have the ban on its exports lifted in return for increasing its purchase of products, particularly sugar, from the Dutch East Indies.[23]

On the other hand, those, including Matsue Haruji, advocating hard-line policies against the Dutch argued that Japan should compete with Holland by rallying to its side the support of the indigenous nationalist movement. Moreover, some local Japanese newspapers even carried articles which proposed the principle of "Japanese goods by the Japanese." In other words, the import, transport, storage, and sale of Japanese products should be handled only by the Japanese themselves.[24]

This attitude made the Dutch strongly distrustful of and belligerent towards the Japanese. In the East Indies, the Dutch began to suspect that the Japanese, with ambitions that were even political, were systematically invading the entire economy of the colony. These suspicions were confirmed in the following statement by Nagaoka Shun'ichi, the chief representative of the Japanese delegation to the trade negotiations, on his arrival in Batavia on 3 June 1934.

> Japanese products, both in terms of quality and prices, are the most suitable for the general public in the Dutch East Indies. ... Japan and the Dutch East Indies are inseparably connected by natural law. ... Therefore, I would have to say that trying to sever this natural relationship is like disobeying the order of God. ... If Japanese goods impaired the welfare and prosperity of the Dutch East Indies, Japan would not hesitate to give due consideration to this matter. ... I believe that because Japan's trail-blazing development of untapped lands and the increase in the number of Japanese shops are being appreciated by the indigenous people, this means that the Japanese are being welcomed by the general public in the East Indies.[25]

The statement asserted that the restrictions on imports in the Dutch East Indies were intended to serve only the interests of the Dutch in the colony, not those of the native people in general. Japan did not originally intend to display an attitude that essentially challenged and criticized Dutch colonial policy. However, the sudden announcement of this statement reflected the impatience and desperation of the delegates to proceed with the negotiations to suit their own convenience, coupled with the emerging hard-line attitude among the Japanese. The statement may have been effective in appealing to the native people, but it added fuel to the flames of anti-Japanese sentiments among the Dutch and handicapped the Japanese delegation in proceeding with the negotiations. It also had the unintended effect of providing justification for the concerns that the Dutch community in the colony had harbored about Japanese political and territorial ambitions toward the East Indies. Not surprisingly, the negotiations, which had originated from this kind of misunderstanding, did not go well. The first round was adjourned after the last discussion between the two chief delegates on 21 December 1934 with no declaration or communiqué being issued. Four days later, the Japanese delegation left the Dutch East Indies empty-handed.

The first Dutch-Japanese trade negotiations in 1934 were a turning point from the conciliatory approach which both countries had thus far adopted toward each other. After the breakdown of the negotiations, political and ideological antagonism between the two countries intensified. Various anti-Japanese measures, such as the "Emergency Act of Import Restriction" and the "Operation Restriction Act" in which the targets of restriction were exclusively Japanese goods and merchants, were implemented in the Dutch East Indies. On the other hand, hard-liners increased in number among the Japanese affected by these measures, and local Japanese newspapers loudly advocated the principle of "Japanese goods being handled by the Japanese."[26] The Dutch felt a strong hostility and vigilance towards the movement; they recognized that the Japanese were systematically undermining Dutch interests in the East Indies' economy, aided and abetted by the sponsorship of the Japanese government.

Various economic frictions, including the recurrent Davao land problems, had also developed in the Philippines,[27] which had the greatest number of Japanese in Southeast Asia at the turn of the decade. A series of anti-Japanese movements in this period was originally caused by the rise in the number of Japanese immigrants from the late 1920s. There were two reasons for this change in public opinion in the Philippines: firstly, the Filipinos were suspicious of Japanese farmers in Davao, who comprised the majority of the Japanese community in the Philippines; and, secondly, they opposed Japanese expansionist policies as evidenced by the Manchurian Incident. The growing suspicion toward the Japanese community in Davao was not only because of the rise in the Japanese population, but also because there had been a fundamental change in the pattern of Japanese immigration, from migrant workers leaving their families behind to permanent settlers bringing their families with them. A glimpse of this situation is provided by a local newspaper article reporting the fact that the Japanese Association in Davao tried to act as an agent to introduce brides to Japanese farmers in the region.[28] The article commented that the problem should not be regarded merely as a Japanese economic advance, but as one with social and political implications. It is important to note that the issue of Japanese farmers in Davao was not discussed as a purely economic problem, but also as a political one which made many Filipinos more conscious of the shadow of the Japanese Empire.

Moreover, the Manchurian Incident in September 1931 heightened further the Filipinos' suspicions and apprehension about Japan, as they discerned a tangible sign of Japanese expansionism in the incident. For instance, in October 1931, the Haro City Council in Iloilo province adopted a resolution calling on the authorities involved to settle the Davao problem as soon as possible, because they were afraid that failure to do so would result in an incident in the Philippines similar to the Manchurian Incident.[29] There was also a rumor that some Japanese landowners in Davao were reserve officers in the Japanese army or relatives of high officials in the Japanese government.[30] The sense of crisis manifested by these examples often led Davao province to be referred to as the "New Japanese State'[31] or "Davaokuo" following the pattern of "Manchukuo".[32] This name vividly portrays the Southeast Asian suspicions and vigilance toward Japanese military and political ambitions in Asia after the Manchurian Incident.

Similarly, the United States, the suzerain of the Philippines, had expressed a growing anxiety about the rise in the number of Japanese residents in the colony. In January 1933 in one of his last Presidential messages, the U.S. President Hoover referred to the danger of "peaceful infiltration" and "forcible entry" of a great number of neighbors into the Philippines.[33] Significantly, the word "infiltration" suggested a sort of military invasion without arms.

During the 1930s, therefore, peoples in Southeast Asia became increasingly conscious of the shadow cast by the Japanese state over the economic problems that they faced. Many suspected that these contentious issues could no longer be treated only through economic means. In fact, from this time onward, Japan began to strengthen her commitment to Southeast Asia in economic as well as political and military terms. The fact that *nanshin-ron*, which had been frozen in the 1920s, began to be reactivated in the early 1930s is evidence of this tendency. Particularly, with the emergence of the problem of national defence resources, including petroleum from the Dutch East Indies, the *nanshin-ron* of the Japanese navy erupted.[34] At this time, the naval *nanshin-ron* refrained from confronting and criticizing the "Continental Policy" of the army (that had been traditionally a very important aspect in the naval *nanshin-ron*). In addition, the navy changed their defence policy to one based upon approval of the "defence of the continent." This was because a new group of *nanshin-ron* supporters in the navy (the above-mentioned clique of naval officers formed after World War I) grasped the idea that the claims for independent armament and the Manchurian problem were integral parts of the Japanese "right to survive." This meant in effect that this group affirmed its support for the Manchurian Incident. The group had lived through the Washington treaty era with prudence and endurance. In the 1930s, it had rapidly gained power, mainly in the "Policy Study Committee for the South Seas Area" organized in July 1935, as the hard-line element speaking out against England and the United States. The group tried to provide a practical formula for the navy's southward advance and started to discuss how to penetrate into Southeast Asia, especially into the Dutch East Indies.[35]

Thus, not only had *nanshin-ron* been revived against the backdrop of a tightening net of economic sanctions against Japan since the breakdown of the Indian- and Dutch-Japanese trade negotiations, but this was also its heyday. It involved a variety of discussions about the desirability or otherwise of bloc economies or large economic spheres, ideas which later resulted in the "Greater East Asian Co-prosperity Sphere" concept.

A notable characteristic of the *nanshin-ron* that reappeared at this time was that the South Seas, and especially Southeast Asia, became an official area of projected Japanese development and concern. In other words, for the first time *nanshin-ron* became a national policy. This trend is apparent in the document, *Kokusaku no Kijun* (Fundamentals of National Policy), approved on 7 August 1936 by the Five Ministers' Conference of the Hirota Cabinet (March 1936–February 1937). This official decision in favor of a policy of southward expansion was made on the initiative of the navy. By about 1935, the navy, which had been oriented traditionally towards southward expansion, began to formulate a clear-cut policy on this issue. This was done against a background of denunciation of both the Washington and London Naval Limitation Treaties and of the perceived threat of expansion by U.S. naval forces. In April 1936, naval headquarters reached a decision called the "General Principles of National Policy" in which the policy of southward expansion had been successfully integrated into Japan's policy on Manchuria, China, and Russia in the north.

The Manchurian Incident marked a watershed in *nanshin-ron*'s transformation in the same way that it had brought about the integration of southward expansion into a national policy. The Incident was also a turning point for *nanshin-ron* in public discussion. For example, Ishihara Hiroichiro, president of the Ishihara Industry Company engaged in iron mine development in Malaysia since 1920, referred to the outbreak of the Manchurian Incident as a "godsend opportunity to advocate *nanshin-ron*," which he did after hurriedly returning to Japan. Eleven years later in July 1942, looking back upon those days, he contributed an article entitled "To the Malay People" to one of most influential Japanese newspapers in which he said:

> The time has finally come. The solving of the Manchurian problems should be accompanied by a solution of the southern problems. I have made up my mind to devote myself to this aim. ... I had a farewell dinner with a few Malays. On that occasion, I told them, "I am going back to Japan. Next time I return here, our imperial army will also be here." I left there, asking them to wait for that day to come.[36]

The major characteristic of revised *nanshin-ron* in the 1930s, advocated by many people including Ishihara, was the open expression of belligerence towards the West against the backdrop of increasing economic friction over the Southeast Asian market. As is well-known, Ishihara was in the vanguard of advocating hard-line policies in dealing with the trade friction with the Dutch East Indies.[37]

In 1936, the same year in which the "Fundamentals of National Policy" was adopted, a book symbolically entitled *Nanshinron* was published. The author, Murobushi Takanobu, a famous jounalist and an opinion leader of the time, forcefully presented the theme of "southward expansion" as if it were the be-all and end-all of Japan's existence. At the same time, he treated it as Japan's destiny, as if it were an inevitable mission and an historical necessity. Such determinism or fatalism were important characteristics of *nanshin-ron* in this period.[38]

Murobushi repeatedly advocated stringent anti-Western, especially anti-British policies in response to the trade friction and the resolutions denouncing Japan at the League of Nations. According to him, Japan was forced by the cunning manipulation of British diplomacy to adopt the policies of northern expansion, and to end up making China—which should have been its friend—its enemy. He argued as follows:

> The Manchurian Incident is the culmination of these developments. However, Japan should use this as a great opportunity to alter its external policy into one in which southern advance will be pursued, and emancipate the colonies in Southeast Asia and break the Western monopoly of natural resources and markets. In this sense, Japan's southward expansion ought to be interpreted not as an invasion or aggresion, but as an act of justice in the name of liberation.

We can read into this an element of fatalism that Japan's southward expansion is a natural or historical necessity. It is a prominent feature of the revised *nanshin-ron* that the southward expansion came to be regarded as a destiny or fate, that is, that the element of fatalism was its culminating feature.[39]

The idea of regarding the Japanese southward expansion as "a destiny that nature orders" led naturally to an emphasis on fatal destiny and an emotional identification of Japan with the southern areas. For example, Shinmura Izuru, a linguist, rather naively wrote in his book *Nanpo-ki* (Southern Areas) that "Japan's southward expansion is based upon an unconscious nostalgia for our beloved motherland."[40] These ideas emphasizing the identity between Japan and the southern areas were ultimately absorbed into a meaningless, even tinged with incantation, concept of "Sumara Ajia" (The Emperor's Asia), advocated by Kanokogi Kazunobu, a philosopher of the Imperial Way and a Pan-Asianist.[41]

Amid the growing belligerence toward the West that the public *nanshin-ron* assumed, the war in Europe broke out in September 1939. Japan was economically dependent on the West, and naturally became concerned about the possibility that the flow of vital materials would be terminated. This in turn propelled Japan to make attempts to shed her dependence on the West. The Abe Nobuyuki Cabinet, in power at the time, formulated *Taigai shisaku hoshin yoko*

(The Outlines of External Policies) in December 1939, in which it was declared that peaceful southward advance would be pursued in order to establish a self-sufficient economic sphere for defence. Seizing this opportunity, a faction of the navy started insisting again that Japan be restored as a sea power.[42]

Moreover, the success of the German blitzkrieg on the Western front in Europe between April and June 1940 added another dimension to *nanshin-ron*, namely the emergence of an opportunistic *nanshin-ron*, both in the army and the navy, which insisted on taking advantage of this chance to move south. Worthy of special mention is the fact that the army suggested southward expansion for the first time, and even the use of force in expanding southward. This was to secure natural resources for the conduct of the war in China and to eliminate the possibility of Britain forming a strong Anglo-American bloc in Southeast Asia, since Europe was now in the hands of Germany.

This opportunistic *nanshin-ron* proposed by the army manifested itself in the way it dealt with the French Indochina problem by capitalizing on the French defeat in Europe. It is important to note that the use of force was mooted in order to cut off the supply route supporting Chiang Kai-Shek. On 4 July 1940, the army submitted to the navy the idea of forcible expansion into the South. The navy accepted this in principle, and took the stand that the use of force would be possible if a solution could not be found to the likelihood of a U.S. oil embargo as a sanction against Japan, about which the navy was very concerned.[43]

The second Konoe Cabinet, which was formed in July 1940 following the Yonai Cabinet, fully accepted the army's conception of "armed expansion into the South," and decided on two major policies. These were incorporated in the 26 July 1940 *Kihon kokusaku yoko* (General Principles of National Policy) and the 27 July *Sekai josei no suii ni tomonau jikyoku shori yoko* (General Principles for Dealing with the Political Situation in Response to the Changing World Situation). The former enunciated the idea for constructing a "Greater East

Asian New Order" in which Southeast Asia was, for the first time, included with the Japan-Manchuria-China bloc; the latter clearly reflected the army's opportunism and willingness to use force in expanding southward.[44] The announcement of these policies spelled out in the two documents signalled an end to the earlier version of *nanshin-ron*, which had called for peaceful economic expansion into the South Seas.

These ideas came to be known as the "Greater East Asian Co-prosperity Sphere" concept after the statement made by Foreign Minister Matsuoka Yosuke at a press conference held on 1 August 1940. In order to fulfill this grand scheme, Japan subsequently escalated its aggression. It occupied the northern part of French Indochina on 22 September 1940 and the southern part on 28 July 1941, ultimately plunging into the Pacific War.

However, the concept of a "Greater East Asian Co-prosperity Sphere" was not a well thought out scheme elaborated in detail. Rather, it was an ad hoc set of emergency measures that had been implemented successively since the Manchurian Incident (1931) and the China Incident (1937). It lacked a consistent plan. More importantly, it was not created through dialogue with other Asian countries. Furthermore, this concept, which incorporated the South Seas area as a sub-system of a policy mainly oriented toward the continent of China, meant the end of the tendency to see the South Seas area as an independent oceanic region separate from the continent. It suggested instead a transformation of the South Seas into a mere southern extension of the continent. In other words, the concept of a "Greater East Asian Co-prosperity Sphere" neglected the accumulated history of Japanese relationships with the South Seas area—commercial and peaceful relationships. It degenerated into a simplistic idea focused on the conduct of a possible war and the exploitation of the resources of the region by Japan.

The aims of establishing the "Greater East Asian Co-prosperity Sphere" were professedly to achieve the liberation and independence of the Southeast Asian colonies, but it seems from various documents that these motives were much less important than a sense of rivalry with the West and a desire to establish a self-sufficient economic sphere for Japan.[45] It must be said that the idea was nothing more than a plan for rearranging colonies that reflected Japan's desire to exercise sole domination in Southeast Asia.

Notes

1   Surveys of the development and transformation of *nanshin-ron* in modern Japan can be found in Shimizu Hajime, *Southeast Asia in Modern Japanese Thought: The Development and Transformation of "Nanshin-ron"* (Canberra: Australian National University, 1980) and Yano Toru, *Nihon no nan'yo-shikan* [A historical view of South Seas in Japan] (Tokyo: Chuo koron-sha, 1980).

2   On the *nanshin-ron*, see Kida Jun'ichiro, "Nangoku ki" [The southern countries], in vol. 6 of *Meiji no gunzo* [Figures of the Meiji period], Hanzawa Hiroshi (ed.), *Ajia e no yume* [A dream towards Asia] (Tokyo: San'ichi shobo, 1970).

3   On the transformation of *nanshin-ron* during the World War I period, see Shimizu Hajime, "Nanshin-ron: Its turning point in World War I," *The Developing Economies* vol. 25, no. 4 (December 1987).

4   On the rise of Japanese population in Southeast Asia, see *Ajia keizai* vol. 26, no. 3, special issue: *Pre-war Japanese Advance into Southeast Asia* (by Shimizu Hajime, Hashiya Hiroshi, and Murayama Yoshitada), March 1985.

5   Nakai Kinjo, *Nan'yo dan* [An account of the South Seas] (Tokyo: Togyo-kenkyukai, 1914), pp. 48–49.

6   "The Prospectus of the South Seas Society" (30 January 1915) says the following about the purpose of the Society:

> The vast South Seas is an inexhaustible treasure house, where Java, Sumatra, Borneo, the Celebes, the Malay peninsula, and the Philippines alone occupy about a million square miles. In particular, there have been the closest relations between the South Seas and Japan in terms of geography, history and economy. As Japan directs its attention to the very large labor force in the region, our relations with the South Seas will develop more and more in the future. The objective of the Society is to study extensively about the conditions of the region, and to endeavor to develop it. Thereby, our Society intends to contribute to the increase of welfare among both the peoples of Japan and of the Southeast Asian nations, and to the progress of world civilization.

7   The objective of the Singapore Exhibition House of Japanese Goods was as follows:

> The objective of our Exhibition House is to serve as a guide and an intermediary facilitating Japanese economic development directed

towards the southern areas. … The exhibition of Japanese goods is a mere means to attain the goal of our House. We in fact intend to devote ourselves to research and correspondence in order to understand various conditions in the southern areas, on the one hand, and to facilitate expansion of our market, improvement of our goods and development of our industry, on the other. (*Toyo keizai jiho* [Current news of oriental economies] vol. 1, no. 1, 25 January 1919), p. 1.

8   For example, the "Resolution on the Mining Industry" by the Economic Study Commission in 1916 states as follows:

> To compensate for our lack of ore, we would be better off turning to the geographically proximate areas of the East and South Seas such as Siberia, China, French Indochina, Burma, and Australia for supplies. Therefore, the government's support regarding the acquisition of ore would be most helpful for developing the mining industry.

9   On this point, see Shimizu Hajime, "Kindai Nihon ni okeru Tonan Ajia chi-iki gainen no seiritsu" [The emergence of the regional concept of "Southeast Asia" in modern Japan], Part I and Part 2., *Ajia keizai*, vol. 28, no. 6 and no. 7 (June and July 1987). It is conventional knowledge among Southeast Asia specialists in the West that the name and geographical concept of Southeast Asia trace back to the "Southeast Asia Command" set up by the Allied Forces in 1943 in Columbo, Ceylon to regain the Southeastern part of Asia occupied by Japan. Before this period, the area now known as Southeast Asia was subsumed under such terms as Monsoon Asia, the East Indies, Further India, Tropical Asia, and the Far East. The term "Southeastern Asia," which sounds quite similar to Southeast Asia, was also used in the nineteenth century. However, it differed considerably from the area now known as Southeast Asia as it did not generally cover insular Southeast Asia, and as far as the continental part was concerned, it covered a wider geographical entity as part of India and the southern part of China were also included.

10   *Jinjo shogaku chiri sho* [Geography textbook for ordinary elementary schools] vol. 2 (February 1919), p. 75.

11   Soejima Yasoroku, *Teikoku nanshin saku* [An imperial southward expansion policy] (Tokyo: Min'yu-sha, 1916), p. 30.

12   Tsurumi Yusuke, *Nan'yo yuki* [Travel sketches of the South Seas] (Tokyo: Dai-Nihon yubenkai-kodan-sha, 1917), p. 653.

13   Inoue Masaji, *Nan'yo* [The South Seas] (Tokyo: Fuzanbo, 1915), p. 18.

14   Tsurumi, *Nan'yo yuki*, p. 36.

15   Soejima, *Teikoku nanshin saku*, pp. 29–30.

16   *Ibid.*, p. 43.

17   Yamada Kiichi, *Nanshin saku to Ogasawara Gunto* [The policy of southward expansion and the Bonin Islands] (Tokyo: Min'yu-sha, 1916), pp. 49–50.

18   For their discussions, see Shimizu Hajime, "The Conference on Japanese Trade with Southeast Asia (September 1926) and the Idea of "Southward Expansion" in the 1920s," in Shimizu Hajime (ed.), *Ryo-taisenkanki Nihon*

Tonan-Ajia kankei no shoso [Japanese-Southeast Asian relations during the interwar period] (Tokyo: Institute of Developing Economies, 1986).

19 Foreign Minister Shidehara Kijuro, Opening Address at the Conference on Japanese Trade with Southeast Asia, 13 September 1926. In the address he states:

> This conference has been held purely out of our concern for improving commercial relations, and has no political motive behind it. Needless to say, international commerce is mutually complimentary to all parties concerned. It should bring benefits not only to our country, but also to other countries, and is therefore something we must strive for. Commercial activities based upon entirely selfish interests would be extremely foolhardy and we would be digging our own graves if we pursued that, just like a company spending its capital only to increase its dividends. The basic tenet of our foreign policy has traditionally been the principle of co-existence and co-prosperity with other powers. We must not deviate from this policy, in order to secure true lasting benefits for ourselves. I believe that it is also the most effective and safest policy regarding our external trade.

20 For example, see a statement made by Yasukawa Yunosuke, the managing director of Mitsui Bussan, at the meeting of the import section, 17 September 1926.

> While it must be fully acknowledged that Japanese industries will be threatened following the abolition of tariffs on the import of raw materials and therefore they need protection, Japan must import raw materials from abroad at low cost in order that we can make the promotion of exports our national policy in the future. Being complicated in procedure, the existing tax rebate system fails to meet the expectations of merchants. We must abolish our tariffs on raw materials. If we raise the tariffs indiscriminately, others will do the same. The debate over free trade vs. protectionism will take a long time to come to an end and cannot be settled overnight, but being extremely poor in natural resources, Japan has no alternative but to take the path of free trade.

21 For example, Nakagawa Suekichi, Director of the Furukawa Mining Company, spoke as follows:

> In order to develop and expand our markets abroad, we must shake off the bonds of convention, namely we must think about problems from a national point of view. It goes without saying that those engaged in the same business must strive to promote it, discarding their own private interests. I believe that the time has come for both the government and the private sector to make concerted efforts to achieve this purpose. ... At the moment, what little protection is being provided by the nation is only in a few cases of some kinds of barriers for imported goods and tax exemption for exports. It is a great pity that as far as the active encouragement and protection of exports are concerned, the nation's involvement is virtually nil. It is our urgent task to call on the nation to provide protection ... to implement policies of thorough protectionism and export encouragement.

"Fundamental Policies of Promoting Exports" (10 September 1926).

22 See Murayama Yoshitada, "Dai-ichiji Nichiran kaisho" [The first Dutch-Japanese trade negotiations], in Shimizu (ed.), *Japanese-Southeast Asian Relations.*, p. 96.

23 A personal letter addressed to the managing director of the Mitsui Bussan from the branch manager in Surabaya, 6 March 1934, reads as follows:

> I propose that we should hold a general trade negotiation with the Dutch after formulating a concrete plan on the purchase of products of the Dutch East Indies in accordance with the spirit of reciprocity which they desire, and seek to turn the situation in our favor.

Diplomatic Record Office Archive, Ministry of Foreign Affairs of Japan, E.3.7.0 X1–N2 (6 March 1934).

24 Matsu Haruji is quoted in "The Japanese-Dutch Trade Negotiations and the Liberation of the Dutch East Indies" as follows:

> In view of the fact that it is the attitude of the native people numbering sixty million in the Dutch East Indies that ultimately restrains the Dutch stance in the Japanese-Dutch trade negotiations, I therefore believe that the last resort to turn the negotiations in our favor can only be to manipulate the nationalist movement surging forth throughout the Dutch East Indies. Diplomatic Record Office Archive, Ministry of Foreign Affairs of Japan, B.2.0.0 J/N 2–1–8 (April 1934).

25 The Diplomatic Record Office Archive, Ministry of Foreign Affairs of Japan, B.2.0.0 J/N 2–1–9 (February 1935).

26 The Diplomatic Record Office Archive, Ministry of Foreign Affairs of Japan, E.3.7.0 X1–N2 (22 March 1934).

27 See Hashiya Hiroshi, "1930-nendai zenhanki Filipin ni taisuru Nihon no keizaiteki shinshutu" [Japanese economic advance into the Philippines in the early 1930s], in Shimizu (ed.), *Japanese-Southeast Asian Relations*, pp. 119–54.

28 *La Vanguardia*, 23 May 1931.

29 Dispatch No. 184 (7 November 1931), from Vice Consul Kaneko in Davao to Foreign Minister Shidehara, in the Diplomatic Record Office Archive, Ministry of Foreign Affairs of Japan, "Miscellanea on emigration: The Philippines."

30 *Manila Herald*, 25 May 1932.

31 Dispatch No. 192 (24 November 1932), from Vice Consul Kaneko in Davao to Foreign Minister Shidehara, in the Diplomatic Record Office Archive, Ministry of Foreign Affairs of Japan, E3.3.0. J/X1, "The Philippines."

32 Goodman, G.K., *Four Aspects of Philippine-Japanese Relations, 1930–40* (New Haven: Yale University Press, 1967), p. 103.

33 *Ibid.*, p. 7.

34 On the *nanshin-ron* of the Japanese navy, see Hatano Sumio, "Nihon kaigun to 'nansin'" [The Japanese Navy and southward advance], in Shimizu (ed.), *Japanese-Southeast Asian Relations*, pp. 213–14.

35 The address by the chairman of the "Policy Study Committee for the South Seas Area," 15 July 1935, stated: "From the viewpoint of national defence

as well as national policies related to it, the Committee is intended to conduct various researches and studies on Southeast Asia, and thereby be conducive to the formulation of the navy's authoritative policies towards Southeast Asia."

36 *Asahi Shimbun*, 1 July 1942.

37 See the Diplomatic Record Office Archive, Ministry of Foreign Affairs of Japan, E.3.7.0. X1–N2.

38 See Murobushi Takanobu, *Nanshin-ron*, (Tokyo: Nihon Hyoron-sha, 1936), pp. 254–56.

39 *Ibid.*, p. 161, pp. 175–77, and pp. 248–51. Also see Murobushi Takanobu, *Senso to heiwa* [War and peace] (Tokyo: Chikura-shobo, 1937), pp. 294–97.

40 Shinmura Izuru, *Nanpo-ki* [Southern areas] (Tokyo: Meiji-shobo, 1943), p. 29.

41 Kanokogi Kazunobu, *Sumera Ajia* [The Emperor's Asia] (Tokyo: Dobun-shoin, 1938), p. 119.

42 Nakahara Yoshimasa, "Vice Admiral Nakahara's Diary," 15 January 1940:

No matter how you put it, it is important to bring Japan back as a sea power and focus our efforts on developing our navy. This would help us to establish a new order in East Asia and settle the problems arising from the China Incident. (In order to achieve these purposes, we shall not be hesitant even to wage war against Britain and the U.S.). However, the order of things must be, first, solving the China Incident, followed by the establishment of a new order in East Asia, and then finally the construction of our sea power. We cannot simply ignore the China Incident now.

43 The Naval Command Office, "A Study of Policies toward French Indochina," August 1940, stated that,

It has the above-mentioned advantages for settling both the China Incident and the Southern problem to achieve the goals of the military policy toward French Indochina. Therefore if we can prevent the United States from imposing an embargo or if we can have the prospect of overcoming it, the use of force should be possible and there should be no problem in attaining our purposes.

44 "Sekai josei no suii ni tomonau jikyoku shori yoko" [General principles for dealing with the situation in response to the changing world situation], 27 July 1940, reads as follows:

1. If a settlement of the China Incident seems close at hand, we should seize the opportunity and use force to solve the problems in the southern areas, in so far as all circumstances, both domestic and external, permit.

2. If the China Incident remains unsettled, we should make it our policy that war should not be made against a third power. But in the case things develop in our favor, force could be used to solve problems in the southern areas.

3. The extent and method of using armed force should be decided according to the situation.

4. In using force, we should endeavor to restrict our opponent to Great Britain alone. Nevertheless, we should take every possible precaution to

prepare for a war against the United States, because such a war may be inevitable.

45 For example, "Nanpo keizai taisaku yoko" [An outline of economic policy in the southern areas] stated,

A main point of economic policy should be an urgent filling of the demand for essential strategic resources to make possible the prosecution of the war. At the same time, policy should aim to establish a self-sufficient system of the "Greater East Asian Co-prosperity Sphere," and should try to strengthen and increase Imperial economic power. *Gendaishi shiryo* [Documents of contemporary history], vol. 43 (Tokyo: Misuzu-shobo, 1970), p. 195.

2

The Expansion of Japan's Cotton Textile Exports into Southeast Asia*

SUGIYAMA SHINYA

The Japanese Cotton Industry and Trade in the Interwar Period

The development of the Japanese cotton industry in the nineteenth and twentieth centuries is a typical case of import substitution. Its rapid development in the 1880s ousted both domestic hand-spun yarn and imported machine-spun yarn from the Japanese market; by the outbreak of World War I, machine-spun Japanese cotton yarn and cotton fabrics were being exported to China and Manchuria, where they successfully competed with Indian yarn and British and American cotton manufactures. World War I gave Japanese products the opportunity to advance into India and Southeast Asia to supplement for the decreasing supply from the West. Japan was able to take advantage of her proximity to the market to compete successfully with British goods.[1] In order to adapt to the increased overseas demand, there was a shift in the type of cotton product manufactured, from narrow goods to plain goods.[2]

After World War I the return of foreign cotton goods to the market, the development of the Chinese cotton industry, and the rising export prices of Japanese cotton goods all produced difficulties for Japan. In China, foreign cotton mills, including those under Japanese ownership, were able to produce cotton goods at low cost due to the abundant supply of cheap labour and the easy access to raw cotton and a large consumer market. This hindered imports of Japanese cotton yarn into China. The high Japanese export prices resulted from the rise in the domestic price of cotton goods caused by the increase in domestic demand and wages. This combination of factors weakened the overseas competitiveness of Japanese cotton goods; particularly affected were the coarser types of cotton yarn under no. 20, and textiles such as shirting, sheeting, and drills. It was therefore necessary for Japan to shift production from coarse to medium and fine yarn, and from coarse to finer fabric, through technological improvements.[3] As competition in the China market increased, India and Southeast Asia became more important as outlets for Japanese cotton products. Exports to Southeast Asia were primarily the domain of locally based small- and medium-sized manufacturers. Product development was required in areas where demand was different from China in terms of quality, size, and pattern.[4]

In September 1926, at a conference on Japan's external trade which had been convened under the auspices of the Ministry of Foreign Affairs, representatives of the Japan Cotton Spinners' Association (*Dai-Nihon Boseki Rengokai*) pointed out the importance of India, the Dutch East Indies, and other regions such as the Straits Settlements, the Philippines, and Siam, and stressed the need for counter measures in response to tariff barriers imposed by India and Indo-China. They also emphasized the importance of market research by government officials into overseas demand and technology, the improvement of commodity exhibition centres abroad, and better terms of foreign exchange for exporters.[5]

Tables 1, 2 and 3 give basic figures for the state of Japanese cotton mills and for cotton yarn and textile production during the interwar period. Japanese mills had been able to build up their financial strength during World War I, to the point where they were financing raw cotton purchases from their own funds without recourse to advances from cotton merchants. 60–70% of the production costs for cotton yarn were accounted for by purchases of raw cotton; the price of the latter therefore had a crucial affect on prices of cotton

Table 2.1. *Development of Japanese cotton mills, 1919–1939*

Year	Number of firms*	Number of mills*	Paid-up capital*	Reserved funds*	Net profits**	Av. dividend rates**
			(mil. yen)	(mil. yen)	(mil. yen)	%
1919	54	190	166	139	129	50.5
1920	56	198	277	166	142	37.5
1921	61	217	296	182	93	24.7
1922	64	235	317	203	101	24.3
1923	70	241	376	217	60	18.9
1924	69	247	398	219	70	16.3
1925	64	243	383	224	64	16.7
1926	64	247	391	231	57	15.1
1927	64	257	392	238	59	14.6
1928	72	259	420	250	66	13.9
1929	70	258	429	260	62	13.7
1930	74	263	425	252	5	8.3
1931	72	263	399	241	45	8.9
1932	71	265	398	246	51	9.8
1933	69	268	404	255	63	10.7
1934	72	275	439	273	73	12.5
1935	74	281	459	283	71	12.1
1936	74	282	484	292	70	11.3
1937	82	291	596	310	98	12.2
1938	82	294	643	326	99	12.4
1939	79	248	660	343	105	12.3

Sources: Menshi Boseki Jijo Sankosho [Statistics of the Japanese cotton industry], corresponding years.

Notes: * for 31 December, each year.
      ** for cotton mills belonging to the Japan Cotton Spinners' Association only.

yarn and cloth. Since cotton mills usually needed to purchase enough raw cotton for six months' forward consumption, they were anxious to obtain raw cotton as cheaply as possible, and were willing to buy a range of types (Chinese, Indian, American, and Egyptian) in order to reduce their risks. This situation inevitably encouraged developments in technology for blending various types of cotton.[6] The shift to spinning medium and finer counts of yarn, in order to avoid competition with the coarse yarn produced in China, took place very slowly, however. To produce the medium and finer

Table 2.2 *Japan's cotton yarn production, 1919–1939*

Year	Raw cotton consumption	Production	Exports	Productivity per worker	Productivity per spindle	Average spindles in operation	Spindles per worker	Number of workers	Average price of left 20s	Average price of raw cotton
	mil. lb.	mil. lb.	mil. lb.	thou. lb.	thou. lb.	thousand		thousand	yen	yen
1919	898	768	92	5.8	0.24	3,180	24.1	132	510	78
1920	852	727	122	5.0	0.23	3,192	22.2	144	411	64
1921	861	725	117	5.1	0.23	3,162	22.4	141	247	37
1922	1,048	891	158	5.2	0.22	3,968	22.9	173	220	52
1923	1,020	868	99	5.4	0.21	4,080	25.5	160	249	65
1924	969	829	108	5.4	0.20	4,116	26.9	153	328	84
1925	1,134	975	124	5.6	0.21	4,670	26.8	174	320	75
1926	1,237	1,043	82	5.7	0.21	5,003	27.3	183	228	49
1927	1,189	1,012	47	6.0	0.21	4,831	28.4	170	218	51
1928	1,149	981	29	6.4	0.20	4,844	31.5	154	231	64
1929	1,314	1,117	27	7.0	0.19	5,784	36.2	160	231	62
1930	1,180	1,010	24	7.3	0.17	5,898	42.4	139	145	41
1931	1,211	1,027	9	8.4	0.19	5,904	48.4	122	124	28
1932	1,303	1,124	36	8.9	0.18	6,308	49.7	127	151	39
1933	1,430	1,240	19	9.6	0.18	6,738	52.2	129	206	52
1934	1,610	1,389	26	9.9	0.19	7,503	53.2	141	214	64
1935	1,669	1,424	39	9.3	0.17	8,197	53.6	153	206	64
1936	1,689	1,443	44	9.6	0.17	8,392	55.6	151	208	65
1937	1,846	1,586	52	9.6	0.18	8,973	54.1	166	253	69
1938	1,319	1,307	42	8.7	0.16	8,243	54.6	151	213	54
1939	1,227	1,219	83	9.1	0.15	8,118	60.6	134	205	56

Sources: Nihon Mengyo Kurabu, *Naigai Mengyo Nenkan* [Cotton industry yearbook]; Dai-Nihon Boseki Rengo-kai, *Menshi Boseki Jijo Sankosho*, for corresponding years.

Note: Average prices for raw cotton are spot prices for Indian broach/American middling.

counts, American cotton of better quality was required. In the 1920s
Indian raw cotton accounted for 55% on average of Japanese consumption and American raw cotton 37%; American cotton increased
from the late 1920s and superseded Indian cotton in the early 1930s.
Even in the mid-1930s, however, 60% of the total cotton yarn produced consisted of under no. 20.[7]

Low wages and long working hours had been a major factor in
the development of the Japanese cotton industry in the period before
World War I. Night work by female and child labour in particular
became a focus of social concern in Japan, and was discussed at the
Washington Conference of the International Labour Organization in
1919. Under external and internal pressure, a Factory Law was
passed prohibiting night work by women and by children under 16.[8]
Cotton firms were originally given three years to prepare for the new
situation, but the Great Earthquake of 1923 led to a further post-
ponement of the actual enforcement, until July 1929. This gave the
large cotton mills ample time to adjust, so that the abolition of night
work had little adverse effect. The 15% reduction in total working
hours which the law would bring about was partly offset by the suspension of official curtailments on production which had been fixed
by the Japan Cotton Spinners' Association.

In addition, cotton firms carried out "rationalization."[9] The low
selling price of cotton yarn and the relatively higher quotations for
raw cotton led to a decrease in the profitability of cotton spinning in
the late 1920s (Tables 1 and 2). For this reason too, owners of cotton
mills were compelled to reduce production costs through rationalization, and to expand into weaving the yarn which they had spun.
These changes were achieved through the introduction of higher
technology such as the application of hydraft and symplex methods
in spinning, the introduction of automatic weaving machines in
weaving, and increases in the speed of machinery in both sectors,
which permitted intensification of labour and prevented rises in
labour costs. During the period from 1926 to 1933, the number of
spindles per worker increased by 91% and productivity per worker

by 68%. Despite the increasing speed at which spindles were able to revolve, the shift to medium and finer yarn production meant a 14% decline in productivity per spindle. Substantial wages increased gradually up until 1930, but decreased rapidly in the early 1930s.

In the 1920s Japanese cotton spinning firms expanded their production to weaving. Rationalization took place much faster in weaving than in spinning, and the decrease in the number of workers was correspondingly greater. During the period from 1926 to 1931, while productivity per spindle increased by only 12%, productivity per worker increased by 118%, and the number of looms per worker by 96%. From 1927 automatic stop motion devices were attached to ordinary looms, and automatic looms came into wide use. The number of power looms for plain goods increased from 161,833 in 1928 to 220,310 in 1933, while the number of power looms for narrow goods decreased from 109,594 in 1928 to 83,244 in 1933 and the number of manual looms from 98,520 in 1928 to 59,312 in 1933. As a result there was a shift in production from coarse to finer fabrics, and 82% of the total value of cotton textile production was now accounted for by plain goods.[10]

The figures for weaving in Table 3 are taken from cotton mills belonging to the Japan Cotton Spinners' Association, which represented 90% of the large cotton mills. It should be borne in mind, however, that there existed a large number of small- and medium-sized manufacturers which specialized in weaving only and belonged to different associations. In 1933 91% of the total number of 53,531 cotton weaving factories were equipped with less than ten weaving machines, and the average number of looms per factory came to about 5 as against 785 for establishments belonging to the Japan Cotton Spinners' Association. In 1934 these smaller manufacturers owned 72% of all weaving machines and accounted for 68% of the total production of 950 million yen in value.[11]

Table 4 shows Japan's cotton trade during the period from 1919 to 1939. Cotton yarn was a major export article before World War I, but in terms of value was exceeded by cotton piece goods from 1917.

Table 2.3 *Japan's cotton textile production, 1919–1939*

Year	Average looms in operation	Production (mil. sq. yds.)	Cotton yarn consumption (mil. lb.)	Number of workers	Number of looms per worker	Productivity per worker (hundred yds.)	Productivity per loom (hundred yds.)
1919	40,969	739	180	44,675	0.92	16.5	18.0
1920	44,635	762	190	47,053	0.95	16.2	17.1
1921	44,109	701	179	39,260	1.12	17.9	15.9
1922	51,033	869	214	45,959	1.11	18.9	17.0
1923	52,972	1,001	241	48,511	1.09	20.6	18.9
1924	56,351	1,031	241	51,235	1.10	20.1	18.3
1925	62,976	1,180	274	55,726	1.13	21.2	18.7
1926	65,699	1,278	294	57,393	1.14	22.3	19.5
1927	66,733	1,295	293	50,527	1.32	25.6	19.4
1928	70,606	1,382	303	43,705	1.62	31.6	19.6
1929	68,640	1,538	336	42,692	1.61	36.0	22.4
1930	65,169	1,388	297	35,352	1.84	39.3	21.3
1931	64,392	1,405	301	28,836	2.23	48.7	21.8
1932	68,028	1,533	326	30,394	2.24	50.4	22.5
1933	73,966	1,674	362	34,309	2.16	48.8	22.6
1934	79,630	1,794	385	35,954	2.21	49.9	22.5
1935	82,397	1,843	393	37,188	2.22	49.6	22.4
1936	85,974	1,802	384	38,459	2.24	46.9	21.0
1937	90,197	1,891	407	43,587	2.10	43.4	21.0
1938	86,582	2,017	450	45,166	1.92	44.7	23.3
1939	88,925	3,166	725	44,412	2.00	71.3	35.6

Sources: Nihon Mengyo Kurabu, *Naigai Mengyo Nenkan*; Dai-Nihon Boseki Rengo-kai, *Menshi Boseki Jijo Sankosho*, for corresponding years.

After this the significance of cotton yarn as a part of Japan's export trade decreased rapidly. Exports of cotton textiles, however, continued to account for nearly 20% of Japan's total exports throughout the 1920s and 1930s. 1932 saw the industry recover from the world-wide depression, and exports reached a peak of 2,725 million square yards in 1935. It can therefore be said that the Japanese cotton industry in the interwar period was dependent on the export of cotton piece goods for its development.

Table 5 shows the main export markets for Japanese cotton textiles in the years 1921, 1929, and 1937. The increase during the 1920s

Table 2.4 *Japan's cotton trade, 1919–1939*

Year	Raw cotton imports		Cotton yarn exports		Cotton textile exports		
	Quantity (mil. lb.)	Value (mil. yen)	Quantity (mil. lb.)	Value (mil. yen)	Quantity (mil. sq. yds.)	Value (mil. yen)	Av. price per 100 sq. yds.
1919	1,068	675	92	122	—	351	—
1920	1,054	727	122	155	—	352	—
1921	1,168	438	117	81	—	204	—
1922	1,161	428	158	115	—	222	—
1923	1,179	513	99	79	—	234	—
1924	1,083	605	108	110	—	327	—
1925	1,459	923	124	123	—	433	—
1926	1,553	726	82	71	—	416	—
1927	1,707	625	47	39	—	384	—
1928	1,302	550	29	26	1,419	352	24.8
1929	1,439	573	27	27	1,791	413	23.1
1930	1,276	362	24	15	1,572	272	17.3
1931	1,488	296	9	9	1,414	199	14.1
1932	1,699	447	36	22	2,032	289	14.2
1933	1,665	605	19	16	2,320	383	16.5
1934	1,807	731	26	23	2,577	492	19.1
1935	1,638	714	39	36	2,725	496	18.2
1936	2,028	850	44	38	2,710	484	17.9
1937	1,835	851	52	55	2,644	573	21.7
1938	1,250	437	42	40	2,181	404	18.5
1939	1,335	462	83	71	2,446	404	16.5

Sources: Nihon Mengyo Kurabu, *Naigai Mengyo Nenkan*; Dai-Nihon Boseki Rengo-kai, *Menshi Boseki Jijo Sankosho*, corresponding years.

resulted from expansion into India, China, Egypt, and the Dutch East Indies. China, including Manchuria, Kwantung Province, and Hong Kong, was the most important market, followed by India and the Dutch East Indies. These three areas took 85% of the total value of Japanese exports of cotton piece goods in 1921, and 77% in 1929. In the 1930s, exports to China proper drastically decreased in the face of the Chinese boycott of Japanese goods and a decrease in Chinese purchasing power; in Manchuria and Kwantung Province, however, Japanese goods flourished under the protection of Japanese military rule. India and the Dutch East Indies remained important

Table 2.5 *Main export markets for Japanese cotton textiles, 1921, 1929, 1937*
(in thousand yen)

Market	1921		1929		Contribution rate to increase	1937		Contribution rate to increase
	thousand yen	%	thousand yen	%	%	thousand yen	%	%
China	100,987	(49.6)	150,115	(36.4)	23.5	11,295	(2.0)	-86.6
Kwantung Province	15,536	(7.6)	15,342	(3.7)	-0.1	29,425	(5.1)	8.8
Manchuria						55,748	(9.7)	
British India	30,465	(15.0)	109,124	(26.4)	37.6	63,040	(11.0)	-28.7
Straits Settlements	3,841	(1.9)	5,787	(1.4)	0.9	12,230	(2.1)	4.0
Dutch East Indies	25,571	(12.6)	42,269	(10.2)	8.0	85,603	(14.9)	27.0
Philippines	3,779	(1.9)	5,615	(1.4)	0.9	12,056	(2.1)	4.0
Siam	609	(0.3)	3,799	(0.9)	1.5	16,148	(2.8)	7.7
South Africa	—		3,043	(0.7)	1.5	10,214	(1.8)	4.5
Egypt	—		24,398	(5.9)	11.7	10,509	(1.8)	-8.7
Australia	2,857	(1.4)	2,917	(0.7)	0.0	13,527	(2.4)	6.6
Argentine	280	(0.1)	4,154	(1.0)	1.9	29,294	(5.1)	15.7
Total (with others)	203,673	(100.0)	412,706	(100.0)	—	573,064	(100.0)	—

Sources: *Menshi Boseki Iijo Sankosho*, corresponding years. *Notes*: Korea is excluded. China does not include Hong Kong.

throughout the 1920s and 1930s. Exports to India enjoyed a consistent average of 18%, reaching a peak of 85.2 million yen (556 million square yards) in 1935. The Dutch East Indies took 12% in the 1920s and 14% in the 1930s, increasing in line with the fall in exports to China. The Straits Settlements, the Philippines, and Siam each purchased at most 3%. The overall trend in the 1930s was towards a diversification in the export markets for Japanese textiles, with a shift to the more neutral markets of Africa and Latin America, which imposed fewer restrictions.

Table 2.6 *Exports of cotton piece goods from Japan by category*
(in yen)

Year	Unbleached		Bleached		Printed and Dyed	
	yen	%	yen	%	yen	%
1920	244,500	(73)	n.a.		90,456	(27)
1924	205,762	(63)	n.a.		120,825	(37)
1929	157,942	(38)	29,650	(7)	225,115	(55)
1934	123,580	(25)	88,917	(18)	279,855	(57)
1939	110,860	(27)	79,506	(20)	213,580	(53)

Source: "Honpo boseki saikin junen-shi" [A history of the past ten years of the Japanese cotton industry], *DNBRG* 454 (June 1930); "Dai-Nihon boseki rengo-kai," *Menshi Boseki Jijo Sankosho,* corresponding years.
Notes: Cotton blankets, towels, and knitted goods are excluded.

Table 6 divides Japan's cotton textile exports into categories. It is clear that production shifted from coarse grey shirting to finer bleached, and to printed and dyed goods. Figure 1 shows the average export prices of Japanese cotton piece goods by market for the period after 1928, when figures for quantity as well as volume became available. The increase in average export prices reflects the rise in quality from coarse to finer goods. There were three types of market. China and Kwantung Province stand together as "high-price" markets. In 1929, 18% of the total value of exports to China was for grey shirting, 12% for bleached, and 70% for printed and

Figure 2.1 *Average export prices of Japanese cotton piece goods by market*
(per 100 square yards)

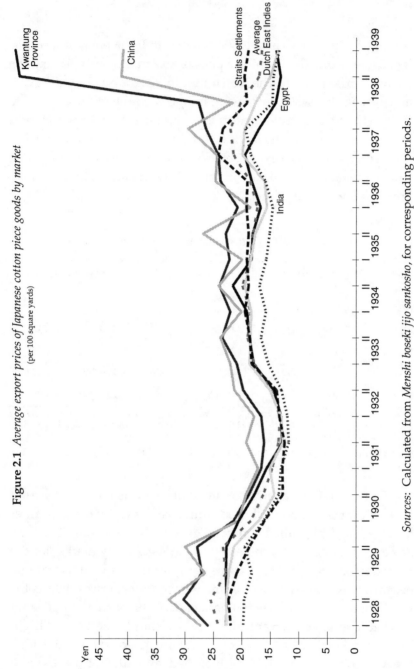

Sources: Calculated from *Menshi boseki jijo sankosho*, for corresponding periods.

dyed piece goods.[12] The Dutch East Indies, the Straits Settlements, the rest of Southeast Asia, and Egypt were "middle-price," and India was a "low-price" market, where unbleached goods were most in demand. The differences in export prices suggest that India and the Dutch East Indies could not act as substitute markets.

Table 2.7 *Export prices of Japanese textiles in relative terms*

Year	Average export price of cotton piece goods	Average exchange rates per 100 yen			Indices of export price in relative terms			
		US $	Rupee	Guilder	Export price	in $	in Rp.	in G.
	yen	dollar	rupee	guilder				
1928	24.83	46.50	126.75	116.13	100	100	100	100
1929	23.05	46.07	126.38	114.41	93	92	93	92
1930	17.31	49.37	136.32	122.42	70	74	76	74
1931	14.06	48.87	144.57	122.23	57	60	65	60
1932	14.21	28.12	104.84	69.01	57	34	47	34
1933	18.33	25.23	79.60	49.34	74	40	47	31
1934	19.10	29.51	77.72	43.51	77	49	47	28
1935	18.20	28.57	77.29	42.04	73	45	45	26
1936	17.85	28.95	77.18	44.98	72	45	44	28
1937	21.67	28.81	76.98	51.82	87	54	53	39
1938	17.42	28.50	77.74	51.75	70	43	43	32

Source: Nihon Ginko, Tokei-kyoku, *Honpo Shuyo Keizai Tokei* [A collection of major economic statistics for the Meiji period onwards] (Tokyo,1966), pp. 320–21; Gaimu-sho (ed.), *Tsusho Joyaku to Tsusho Seisaku no Hensen* [An official history of commercial treaties and trade policies of Japan] (Tokyo, 1951), pp. 1047–48.

Table 7 gives the average exchange rates of the Japanese yen and indices of relative export price, taking 1928 as the basic year. The overall decline in the value of Japanese currency in the 1920s did not have a noticeable effect on exports. The contrasting upward trend in the yen from 1928 to 1931 was largely compensated for by the decline in export prices achieved as a result of rationalization. Japan's departure from the gold standard in December 1931 helped the decline in relative export prices to continue despite an increase in export prices. In particular, the Japanese yen fell more quickly in value against the Dutch guilder than against the Indian rupee; this accelerated the increase in exports of Japanese cotton textiles to the Dutch East Indies after 1932.

Trade Negotiations: Britain, Japan, and India

Table 8 shows the annual average of world exports of cotton textiles for the period from 1909 to 1938. Japan's share in the textile market increased gradually, reaching 31% in the early 1930s, while Britain's share showed a steady decline. In the period from the late 1920s to the early 1930s, the decrease in the volume of British exports was greater than the increase in Japanese exports, largely because of the growing challenge Britain faced from the Indian and Chinese cotton industries and the rapid increase in exports of Japanese cotton textiles to the Asian market. There were also domestic factors at work, such as delays in both the expansion of productivity and the introduction of technological improvements, and inefficient marketing.[13]

During the 1920s Britain faced competition from Japanese textiles in all markets. At first, Lancashire did not feel seriously threatened, attributing Japan's advancement into the world textile market to a combination of low wages based on a low standard of living, and long working hours. In April 1925, however, the *Monthly Record* of the Manchester Chamber of Commerce remarked on the increasing competition from Japan in the world textile market and ascribed it to the growth of technical equipment and the existence of a stable financial and credit system.[14] This short article drew little attention, but it was a sign that the traditional understanding of Japan's rapid development was being seriously questioned. In this context two reports also seem worthy of mention: one by W.B. Cunningham, British Consul in Osaka, and the other by A.S. Pearse, General Secretary of the International Federation of Master Cotton Spinners' and Manufacturers' Associations.

Table 2.8 *Annual average of exports of cotton piece goods from the major producing countries*
(in million square yards)

	1909/13	1921/25	1926/28		1931/33		1936/38	
	%	%		%		%		%
Britain	(72.5)	(57.0)	3,939	(46.1)	1,981	(33.3)	1,741	(27.0)
Japan	(1.4)	(12.3)	1,442	(16.9)	1,845	(31.0)	2,511	(38.9)
U.S.A.	(4.6)	(7.4)	541	(6.3)	348	(5.9)	252	(3.9)
India	(1.0)	(2.2)	177	(2.1)	89	(1.4)	138	(2.1)
Others	(20.5)	(21.1)	2,451	(28.6)	1,687	(28.4)	1,808	(28.1)
Total	(100.0)	(100.0)	8,550	(100.0)	5,950	(100.0)	6,450	(100.0)

Source: "The position of the Lancashire cotton trade," Manchester Chamber of Commerce, *Monthly Record* (January 1927); Nihon Menpu Yushutsu Kumiai, *Nihon Mengyo Boeki-shi* [A history of Japan's cotton trade], p. 5.

Note: Only percentages are available for 1909/13 and 1921/25.

The Cunningham report was the most complete and detailed account of the Japanese cotton industry in English up to that date. He attributed the post-1918 development of the Japanese cotton industry to three elements: the fact that conditions were ripe for an extension of the industry, the excellent methods of organization and management, and the strong financial foundations of industrial firms. He discussed various factors, including the state of individual branches of the cotton industry, the production costs and conditions of firms, marketing, transportation, and legislation, and concluded: "The Japanese are a highly ambitious people and, having rendered themselves practically independent of foreign countries as regards their requirements of cotton goods, intend to have as large a share as possible of the trade in this direction in other parts of the world. Increased competition from Japan in cotton goods of all kinds, especially finished cloth, must therefore be anticipated."[15] Pearce pointed out both economic and non-economic factors which made the cotton industry in Japan different from that of Britain: the "group instinct" which was generated by the family system, the fact that there was little or no hedging in raw cotton, the strong financial foundations of industrial firms, the efficient organization of marketing, the technology for blending cotton, and the existence of lower wages than Britain alongside better labour conditions, particularly in terms of health and education.[16]

By the early 1930s, Japanese cotton textiles had penetrated both neutral markets and British spheres of influence. Up till now, Britain had been the dominant exporter, India being her single most important market. It is therefore not surprising that the increase in exports of Japanese textiles to the latter became a focus of Anglo-Japanese commercial conflict during this period. It was particularly irritating and unpleasant for Britain "because one is not able to retaliate in kind."[17] Three prime factors affecting the three-way interrelationship between Britain, Japan, and India were the development of the Indian cotton industry, the increasing Japanese competition on the Indian textile market, and the interdependence of Japan and India in the raw cotton trade.

In March 1930, faced with increasing imports of Japanese cotton textiles, the government of India increased the duties on cotton textiles originating in countries outside the British Empire from 11% to 20% *ad valorem* (compared with 15% for goods from the Empire) and set the minimum specific duty on plain grey goods at 3 *annas* per lb. In April and September 1931 and in August 1932 the duties were further increased, so that the minimum specific duty on plain grey goods reached 50% *ad valorem* or 5 *annas* per lb. In April 1933 the government of India issued the Safeguarding of Industries Act, and gave notice to Japan that it would terminate the Indo-Japanese commercial treaty of 1904; in June it increased the duties on all foreign cotton goods from 50% to 75% *ad valorem*. These measures were aimed primarily against Japan, and the Japan Cotton Spinners' Association reacted with a boycott against the purchase of Indian cotton. The Indian and Japanese governments therefore needed to meet in order to discuss their future economic relations.

Meanwhile in Britain, a "Special Committee on Japanese Competition" had been formed by the Manchester Chamber of Commerce in December 1932. Manchester's basic view with regard to Japanese competition was expressed in a draft memorandum on "Japanese competition and the British cotton and artificial silk export trade." The purpose of this draft was "to establish, namely, that Japanese competition in the world textile market presents the British industry and the British Government with a situation of crisis which demands in the first place emergency measures of a safeguarding character, and in the second place a long-view policy (if one can be found) which shall be calculated to preserve one of the greatest assets in the British economic position." Lancashire was faced with the choice of either advocating a policy of restrictions on Japanese exports or of waiting for Japan to exhaust herself. In the latter case, however, "before the Japanese attack exhausted itself the Lancashire industry, already weakened, would be so enfeebled as to be quite incapable of returning to the struggle and taking advantage of Japanese exhaustion." In particular, as it was the spiritual element of "almost religious and fanatical patriotism" which lent "to the Japanese assault on the world textile trade the real character of genuine menace," the conflict would be long and bitter. "The choice which British Statesmanship has to make is admittedly one between two evils," but "the Lancashire trade is convinced that the lesser evil must be chosen." Concerning the immediate measures to be taken, "In a general way tariffs, however high, are a more satisfactory method of safeguarding industry than any other procedure so far devised. Quota schemes and prohibitions are always excessively costly and troublesome to administer." The memorandum suggested finally that "It would seem impossible to invite the Colonies to adopt a policy which is not in force in the home market, and the industry therefore recommends that the Anglo-Japanese most-favoured-nation treaty be denounced so as to free our hands for a differential duty in the British market."[18]

In April 1933 the British government proposed a meeting of British and Japanese industrialists in London to discuss their competition in cotton textiles on the world scale. In May it gave notice to Japan that it was going to exclude British West Africa from the 1911 Anglo-Japanese commercial treaty. In the same month, the Manchester Special Committee on Japanese Competititon prepared a memorandum for submission to the government on the policy and procedures to be followed during the proposed Anglo-Japanese cotton trade conversations.[19] The Japanese side was doubtful as to whether Britain would be able to select a negotiating body to represent the cotton industry because "The Lancashire cotton industry ... is so ill-organised and comprises so many interests." T.M. Snow, British Ambassador to Tokyo, hoped that it would be possible to prevent the talks from offending the Japanese side by avoiding accusations about low standards of living, state subsidies, and "unfair trading" and "dumping," which were in any case largely not proven. He felt that the real solution would be to stabilize the political situation in China: this would provide an assured market for Japanese goods and diminish competition from them elsewhere.[20] In June the Foreign Office reached the following view on Japanese competition:

> The expanding volume of Japan's exports to all parts of the world has been due, not, as has been alleged, to "dumping," nor even to a policy of Government subsidies, but primarily to better organisation, coupled with a lower standard of living, lower wages, and, consequently, reduced costs of production. Latterly, too, the depreciation of the yen has been of considerable assistance, but the expansion referred to had begun before Japan's departure from the gold standard, and that event should not be given undue importance in any study of the problem. Something approaching a national unity of purpose and effort has inspired the rationalisation of Japan's industries, and given them an impetus which is lacking in countries whose industries have had a more gradual and haphazard growth. Progress on these lines has been particularly rapid in the various textile industries.[21]

Lancashire had warned that in the proposed Indo-Japanese negotiations "it would be dangerous if the Indians and the Japanese were to frame plans for their mutual trade regardless of British interests." There had also been anxiety on the side of the Indian mill owners "lest there should be any attempt in the proposed Anglo-Japanese conversations to deal with India in the absence of Indian representatives." This "alarm on both sides" led to the idea of presenting "a common front against Japan," and it was suggested that "it would be best to get an agreed front between India and Lancashire before either side met the Japanese." The Manchester Special Committee emphasised the need for unity between Britain and India, saying that "The Japanese seemed to think it important to drive a wedge between Indian manufacturers and the Indian cotton growers, and incidentally, between India and ourselves. If India and England were separated the Japanese would be able to bring force to bear on India. They would soon begin to dictate. The moral was that the United Kingdom and India must not be permitted to drift apart."[22] However, while India and Japan were interdependent in raw cotton and cotton textiles, the link between Britain and India was less strong, because Indian raw cotton exports were not dependent on the British market, and domestic production satisfied over 70% of the internal demand. As had been pointed out at the Ottawa Conference of August 1932, Britain needed to import increased amounts of Indian raw cotton in order to maintain cooperation and collaboration with India.[23]

British hopes of "tripartite conversations" on the world textile market between Britain, India, and Japan did not bear fruit, and the actual negotiations took place on a bi-lateral basis. In September 1933, official negotiations between India and Japan opened in Simla. The British Foreign Office instructed G.B. Sansom, then commercial counsellor at the British Embassy in Tokyo, to proceed to India as the adviser to the government of India, since the British government was responsible for India's international relations.[24] In November an informal meeting of Anglo-Japanese industrialists was also held in Simla. The British delegation pointed out three "abnormal" advantages enjoyed by Japan: the lower standard of living, less stringent working conditions, and lower currency standards. Japan's growth was being achieved "at the expense of other countries instead of forming part of a general upward movement throughout the world." It was therefore vital for Britain to take some measures to

protect her exports against the unfair Japanese competition. In reply
the Japanese delegation insisted that "the expansion of the Japanese
export trade was the natural result of their own honest and sincere
efforts." Such differences in their fundamental views produced an
anodyne resolution in which the two countries expressed the desire
to maintain good relations and hoped to engage in healthy and ami-
cable competition.[25] In late October the British delegation and the
Bombay Millowners' Association signed the Lees-Mody Agreement,
which stated that India was entitled to reasonable protective measures so long as duties were favourable to British goods, and that
any advantages which might be arranged for British goods should
be extended to Indian ones.[26]

The Indo-Japanese negotiations were completed early in January
1934, and an agreement was signed in London that July. The agreement, which was valid until March 1937, was on a barter basis:
Japan could export 400 million yards of cotton textiles to India, provided that she imported 1.5 million bales of Indian cotton in return.
45% of the total Japanese textile quota was to be allotted to plain
greys, 13% to bordered greys, 8% to bleached cottons and 34% to
coloured goods; variations of up to one tenth of the percentage in
any one category could be made up in other categories. The *ad valorem* duty on Japanese piece goods was to be reduced from 75% to
50%, and the minimum specific duty on plain greys reduced to 5
annas per lb.[27] The Japan Cotton Spinners' Association suspended its
boycott of Indian cotton, and, in March 1934, the Japan Export Association of Cotton Textiles to India was set up as a control organization to supervise the agreement.

Lancashire's verdict on the agreement was that "the Government of India has been rather more generous than the circumstances
really warranted in the terms granted in the India market to
Japan."[28] India drew from Britain the promise to purchase raw cotton, and the possibility of exporting her own cotton textiles to British
Empire markets in order to restrict Japanese competition. In fact,
India had used the conflict between Japan and Britain in order to

advance her own interests. On the one hand, by exploiting British hopes of reviving the Indian market for its cotton goods, she had managed to draw concessions in the form of openings for the sale of Indian raw cotton to Britain and the export of Indian cotton textiles to other parts of the Empire, while agreeing to impose higher duties on Japanese imports. From Japan, on the other hand, she had secured a "generous" quota system which did not endanger the Indian cotton industry, in exchange for guaranteed Japanese purchases of Indian raw cotton. By achieving restrictions in the imports of British as well as Japanese goods, India had been able to satisfy the expectations of both the Indian cotton industry and Indian cotton growers.

The Anglo-Japanese negotiations took place in February and March 1934 after five informal meetings starting in September 1933. From the beginning, however, Japanese cotton industrialists had no practical solutions to put forward, preferring a situation of free market competition without any agreements.[29] The fundamental difference in approach, which had already become clear in Simla, was simply a reflection of the different positions of Britain and Japan in the world economy.

Negotiations became deadlocked at the start on the question of the geographical area to be covered by the discussions. The primary object of the British delegation was to reach an agreement that would cover all areas outside India in order to bring stability to the world textile market. The Japanese side, however, wanted to confine discussions to the markets of Britain and her colonies. In practical terms, they said, any agreement that involved other markets would be worthless, since it would trespass on the sovereign rights of other nations. The British delegation emphasised that the increasing volume of low-priced Japanese exports was destabilizing the world market, preventing other countries from restoring their purchasing power, and, thus, recovering from the depression. They therefore asked Japan to limit the volume of Japanese exports, for at the longest three years. The Japanese side replied that the British proposal was "very one-sided" in suggesting a restriction on Japanese exports with no reciprocal obligation on the British side; Japan had made great efforts to reduce production costs in order to adjust to its reduced buying power, and any subsequent success was "the natural outcome of Japan's ability." The British proposal was "a noble one," but the economic stability of the world textile market could not be restored merely by restricting Japanese exports.

The British delegation had to admit that Britain's decrease in exports of 1,643 million square yards could not be explained totally by the 537 million square yards increase in Japanese exports; it had also recognized that Japan's success stemmed from a combination of factors such as efficiency in production. Therefore it was difficult for them to argue that restricting Japan's exports would directly increase the market for British goods. Early in March, Britain therefore made a modified proposal for separate discussions on six regional markets: Africa, Asia, the Near and Middle East, Europe, South America, and Central America. However, this was rejected on the grounds that "it simply divides the world markets into different regions instead of taking them as a whole." Negotiations broke down even before the basis for discussion had been agreed.[30]

The response of the Special Committee on Japanese Competition to this fiasco was to urge the government to introduce import quotas immediately. The Association of British Chambers of Commerce called upon the British government "to take whatever action may be open to it to secure stable markets for British export industries faced with Japanese competition."[31] Early in May Runciman, the President of the Board of Trade, announced that import quotas on foreign cotton and artificial silk textiles, based on the average imports of the years from 1927 to 1931, were to be introduced in British colonies and Protectorates.

Dutch-Japanese Trade Negotiations

The Dutch East Indies was the most important market for Japanese cotton goods in Southeast Asia, with the major economic inroads having been made first during World War I, and then in the early 1930s.[32] In the period from 1921 to 1930, the annual average exports from Japan to the Dutch East Indies were 67 million yen, reaching 160 million yen in 1933; on average from 1931 to 1933 49% of all exports were cotton textiles. The main export articles from the Dutch East Indies to Japan were raw materials—mainly sugar, mineral oil, and crude rubber. In 1929 the balance of payments shifted in Japan's favour.[33]

The main factors behind the increase in exports of cotton textiles were their low price, the open market policy of the government of the Dutch East Indies, and the absence of Indonesian competition. In the late 1920s bleached and printed or dyed goods began to replace sarongs and unbleached goods. As the importance of the market grew, producers made efforts to adapt by improving the quality and expanding production of the type of cotton textiles which were in strong demand. For example, in 1927 Toyo Boseki (Toyo Cotton Spinning Co.) started to produce cambric, a bleached fabric used for batik production.[34] Demand varied from area to area, however; for example, in the Batavia area finer goods were in favour, while in Surabaya the emphasis was on coarser bleached goods.[35]

Table 9 shows the market shares of cotton textile imports into the Dutch East Indies by type and country of origin for the years from 1928 to 1935. Japan had an overwhelming share in unbleached and printed and dyed fabrics, but in bleached goods the Netherlands maintained a strong position until 1931. This was mainly because it was able to supply bleached goods at competitively low prices at a time when the purchasing power of consumers in the Dutch East Indies was being weakened by the prolonged economic depression of the 1920s and the Great Depression which followed. Japan's re-embargo of gold exports in December 1931, and the subsequent depreciation of the Japanese yen, therefore facilitated a rapid increase in Japanese imports. Also important was the effect of increased import restrictions on Japanese cotton textiles in India, which forced them to find another market. In the case of unbleached

Table 2.9 *Types of imported cotton piece goods into the Dutch East Indies by country in quantity (%)*

Year	Unbleached				Bleached				Printed and dyed			
	Britain	Nether-lands	Japan	Total	Britain	Nether-lands	Japan	Total	Britain	Nether-lands	Japan	Total
	%	%	%	mil. yds.	%	%	%	mil. yds.	%	%	%	mil. yds.
1928	10	6	67	72	29	66	3	193	33	6	48	178
1929	10	5	70	69	25	68	5	194	27	7	55	196
1930	6	3	78	55	18	71	8	164	24	3	68	174
1931	2	5	82	57	11	70	16	137	14	4	78	169
1932	2	1	89	65	9	49	38	142	7	2	76	182
1933	1	0	90	67	4	14	78	163	3	1	85	186
1934	1	0	91	78	3	29	65	144	2	0	88	181
1935	0	0	98	71	3	46	49	118	2	0	94	182

Source: For 1928-31, "Ranryo-Indo no menpu yunyu ni oyoboseru fukyo no eikyo" [Effects of the depression on cotton textile imports into the Dutch East Indies] (Japanese consular report from Surabaya), *DNBRG* 476 (April 1932); for 1932–35, Nan'yo Kyokai, *Ranryo-Indo no Keizai Josei* [The economic condition of the Dutch East Indies], pp. 164-66.

goods, however, factors other than price, such as a superior distribution system, must also have been involved in giving Japan its lead, since British goods had little impact even though they were cheaper.

The distribution network which Japanese merchants built up parallel to the existing network of Chinese and Dutch merchants played a crucial role in increasing sales of Japanese goods. Trade with the Dutch East Indies had been started after the outbreak of World War I, mainly by large importers and exporters. The Bank of Taiwan, which opened branches in Surabaya in 1915, Semarang in 1917, and Batavia in 1918, made a vital contribution by financing small and medium-sized merchants in particular. It not only drew exchange bills and discounted bills of accounts receivable, but also sent money to Japan for emigrant workers.[36]

In the early 1930s, Japanese banks and major textile trading firms active in the Dutch East Indies generally had branches or offices at Batavia, Semarang, and Surabaya. Arima Yoko specialized in business in the Dutch East Indies, while the others were firms with overseas branches or offices all over the world. Goods were sold on a commission basis. In the period around 1932, sales of this kind amounted to 90% of the total exports of cotton textiles from Japan to the Dutch East Indies. Branches of Nichimen (the Japan Cotton Trading Co.) imported grey goods directly from Japan and developed the existing retail network of Japanese dealers such as Nan'yo Shokai, Nakamura Shoten, Meiji Shokai, and Nippu Yoko, all of which had branches in crucial towns in Java, Sumatra, and Borneo.[37] Toyo Menka (Toyo Cotton Trading Co.), which had been established in 1920 as an affiliate of Mitsui Bussan, sold the products of Kanegafuchi Boseki (Kanegafuchi Cotton Spinning Co.); Gosho Co. acted for Toyo Boseki; and Nichimen for Dai-Nihon Boseki (Dai-Nihon Cotton Spinning Co.). Toyo Menka, which handled 11% of Japan's total exports of cotton textiles, maintained a stong market position. It took advantage of its membership of the various Chambers of Commerce in the Dutch East Indies, and also reinforced its connection with Arima Yoko, the local specialist, and with a Dutch firm.[38]

Table 2.10 *The Japanese commercial population in the Dutch East Indies in 1933*

Area		Major cities	Number of whole-salers	Number of retailers	Total	Number of Japanese employers
Java	Eastern	Surabaya, Lumajang, Banyuwangi, Jember	30	227	257	543
	Middle	Semarang	14	77	91	288
	Western	Batavia	16	62	78	260
Sumatra		Medan	19	129	148	95
Borneo		Balikpapan	4	13	17	49
Eastern Islands		Makassar	8	32	40	61
Total			91	540	631	1,296

Source: "Ranryo Higashi-Indo ni okeru hojin shogyosha no chos" [A Survey of the Japanese commercial population in the Dutch East Indies], *Takumu Jiho* (September 1933).

Note: In original figures, total Japanese employers on Java were 1,037, totaling 1,296. They are corrected in this table.

Table 10 shows the number of Japanese wholesale dealers and retailers in the Dutch East Indies in 1933. There were 91 of the former and 540 of the latter. Every major commercial centre contained several large Japanese general stores and innumerable small shops. The cities and towns of Surabaya, Medan, Batavia, Semarang, Lumajang, Banyuwangi, and Jember each contained over twenty Japanese wholesale dealers and retailers.

By around 1933 Japanese shipping, banks, and wholesale dealers and retailers seem to have constructed a unified system of import and distribution. G.N. Carey, British Acting Commercial Agent at Batavia, described the trading situation as follows:

> The new factor in the import trade which has to be recognised is that the system of importing and distributing Japanese wares, through shipping, transport, wholesale and retail sales organisations, entirely under Japanese control, has become fairly well perfected during the year 1933. Deliveries *on a consignment basis*, from Japanese exporters to Japanese tokos, and from Japanese factories to their agencies in the Netherlands East Indies, coupled with sales to local retailers *on a cash*

basis, at prices defying all competition, has (sic) now become the rule.[39]
(Italics in original)

In the words of J. van Gelderen, one of the Dutch representatives in the Dutch-Japanese trade negotiations, "One Japanese chain ran from Yokohama to the native village."[40] Japanese textiles were sold "at prices defying competition, and which attract crowds of native buyers and guarantee large and rapid turnovers." Europeans had adopted "the time-honoured system of distribution through Chinese and wholesalers and retailers, on a three months' credit basis," but in 1933, as the increase in Japanese textiles at low prices brought about radical changes in the existing import trading methods, Dutch and other European importers began to show an interest in handling Japanese goods.[41] Japanese dealers had been accustomed to direct selling in large quantities on a cash basis with small margins, but the new competition from European dealers tended to force them to sell goods under cost.[42]

The main producing district of the cotton industry in the Netherlands was Truent, which had 50 cotton spinning and weaving firms with a total of 1.15 million spindles, 48,000 weaving machines, and 28,000 workers. It was therfore smaller than Toyo Boseki, which was equipped with 1,280,000 spindles. In the early 1930s one half of all Dutch cotton textile exports were bleached goods and 80% of these were exported to the Dutch East Indies. In 1933 it is clear that Japanese competition sharply reduced the market share of bleached goods from the Netherlands, from 49% in the previous year to a mere 14%.[43]

Not surprisingly, the increasing Japanese competition in this area was seen as a threat by Dutch manufacturers and formed the main reason for the proclamation by the East Indies government of an emergency import restriction ordinance in September 1933. Twice, in November and December 1933, local importers associations representing Batavia and other towns appealed to the government for protection from Japanese commercial penetration. While proposing to open trade negotiations with Japan in January 1934, the

government of the Dutch East Indies introduced an import quota
system, aimed at limiting imports of striped sarongs and bleached
cotton goods, which was to start in February 1934. This was obviously a move directed against Japan, since the restrictions would
apply to 80% of the total imports from Japan in value.[44] The new
quota system also gave Dutch importers the right to handle 60% of
all imported cambric. This provision created a conflict of interest
among the Japanese: the cotton firms considered that the ability to
sell their goods was more important than Japanese commercial
rights, while the shipping firms, exporters, and Japanese dealers resident in the Dutch East Indies felt that the latter were also crucial.[45]

In June 1934 trade negotiations between Japan and the Dutch
East Indies were held in Batavia.[46] However, immediately after their
arrival at Batavia the Japanese delegation, led by Nagaoka Shun'ichi,
former ambassador to the Netherlands, made an official statement
that the restrictions on imports of cheap Japanese goods into the
Dutch East Indies were against the general welfare of the people
there. This angered the Dutch East Indies' authorities. At the negotiations the Japanese delegation insisted on the removal of the
import restrictions, since they discriminated against Japanese goods
and therefore contravened the most-favoured nation clause. The
Dutch East Indies, however, insisted on the barter system, emphasizing their right to take appropriate measures against the increases
in Japanese imports since they mainly resulted from the depreciation
of the Japanese yen.

The main areas of disagreement concerned methods of import
restrictions, Japan's increasing purchases of raw sugar, and the
inclusion of a shipping agreement. From July 1934, the Dutch East
Indies government consecutively introduced restrictions on fifty-six
types of imported goods and put limits on the business activities of
Japanese firms. Dutch import-distributors, who had formed a group
called Batavia Importers, kindred trade associations, and local manufacturers, who were grouped under the Association for the Promotion of Netherlands East Indies Manufactures, continued to put

pressure on government commercial policy. Meanwhile Japanese importers, who were suffering from the depression of the local economy, the suspension of the trade negotiations, and the subsequent increasing restrictions on imports of Japanese goods, united to form the All Java League of Japanese Importers.[47]

In December 1934 the negotiations broke down without any substantial agreement, and all further discussions were held on an ad-hoc basis. Agreements on shipping were concluded in June 1936, and a provisional commercial treaty, known as the Ishizawa-Hart Agreement, was signed. According to the latter, Japanese firms in the Dutch East Indies were to handle a quarter of the total imports on the basis of the 1933 figures, and existing restrictions were removed. Japan promised to show a preference for the Dutch East Indies in its raw sugar purchases, and the Japan Export Association of Cotton Textiles to the Dutch East Indies was set up as a control organization to supervise the agreement.[48]

Conclusion

During the interwar period various changes occurred in the Japanese cotton industry. There was a shift in yarn production from coarser counts to medium and finer, and in textile production from coarse grey to finer printed and dyed goods. Piece goods replaced yarn as the main export, while India and the Dutch East Indies replaced China as the main export markets. Crucial factors in bringing these changes about were the progress of rationalization caused by internal and external pressure for the abolition of night work, and the rapid development of the Chinese cotton industry. From the late 1920s into the early 1930s, Japanese cotton mills carried out a successful programme of rationalization, introducing higher technology which made possible the intensification of labour. The lower selling prices of Japanese textiles which resulted from the reduction in production costs and the depreciation of the yen facilitated the increase in exports to India and the Dutch East Indies in the early 1930s.

The rapid increase in Japanese competition led to conflict with Britain and India, causing the latter to reinforce its restrictions against imports of Japanese textiles. Tension having reached a peak, 1933 to 1934 saw the summoning of the Indo-Japanese and Anglo-Japanese trade conventions. It was this combination of increasing Chinese competition in China, growing restrictions in India, and intensifying trade conflicts with Britain that encouraged Japan's vigorous commercial expansion into the Dutch East Indies, the last large market in Asia to continue a free-trade policy. However, the rapid increase in Japanese sales and business transformed the previous import trading system and forced the government to take some protective measures against Japan. Even if Japan's stand in the abortive negotiations with Britain and the Netherlands could be justified in principle, her understandable pride in the ability of her economy to adjust to changes in the global economic situation was unfortunate. It deflected her attention from the fact that the increased protectionism which she was encountering was only a natural response to the successful export drive which had brought her so rapidly out of the depression.

As of June 1936, Japanese goods were experiencing restrictions in some form or other in 56 markets out of the 106 markets listed in the official Japanese export statistics. In forty of these the restrictions were quantitative; in sixteen, more favourable rates were being given to her major competitor, Britain. In 1935, 67% of all Japanese exports of cotton textiles were affected by such measures.[49] While imposing controls on the amount of textiles exported through the Export Association Law, Japan experimented with bilateral trade negotiations as a way of winning outlets for Japanese goods in Egypt, Australia, the United States, and other countries. In this she was to achieve only limited success, becoming an increasingly isolated member of the world economy.

Japan's push to increase exports of Japanese cotton textiles to world markets, regardless of the effect on other producer countries, provoked protective measures against Japanese goods from the countries which formed her main markets. In time, therefore, the very vigour of her export drive paradoxically had the effect of limiting her exports.

Notes

* I am extremely grateful to Dr. H.J. Ballhatchet and Mrs. Y. Fushimi for their help in preparing this article.

1 "Honpo menpu menseihin no Nan'yo yushutsu ni tsuite" [On the exports of Japanese cotton piece goods to Nan'yo], *Dai-Nihon Boseki Rengo-kai Geppo* [Monthly report of the Japan Cotton Spinners" Association] (hereafter *DNBRG*) 267 (November 1914). The term "Nan'yo" was used in prewar Japan to refer primarily to Southeast Asia, although it sometimes included India and/or Australasia.

2 Yamazaki Hiroaki *et al.*, *Koza Teikokushugi Kenkyu* [Lectures on studies of imperialism], vol. 6 (Tokyo: Aoki shoten, 1973), pp. 33, 37–38. For case studies of the Japanese cotton industry in the interwar period, see, for example, Yamazaki Hiroaki, "Ryo-taisenkanki ni okeru Enshu men-orimonogyo no kozo to undo" [The structure and development of the cotton manufacturing industry in Enshu during the interwar period], *Keiei Shirin*, vol. 6, nos. 1, 2 (July 1969); Abe Takeshi, *Nihon ni okeru Sanchi-Orimonogyo no Tenkai* [The development of the local cotton manufacturing industry in Japan] (Tokyo: University of Tokyo Press, 1989), chap. 5.

3 "Yushutsu menshifu" [Cotton yarn and textiles for export], *DNBRG* 354 (February 1922).

4 "Wagaho menpu yushutsu ni tsuite" [On the export of cotton piece goods from Japan], *DNBRG* 370 (June 1923); "Nan'yo Indo-muke menseihin" [Cotton piece goods for the Nan'yo markets], *DNBRG* 388 (December 1924).

5 "Dai-ikkai boeki kaigi" [The first conference on Japan's external trade with Nan'yo], *DNBRG* 409 (September 1926). For this conference, see Shoda Kenichiro, "Senzenki Nihon shihonshugi to Tonan-Ajia" [Japanese capitalism and Southeast Asia in the pre-war period], pp. 151–57, in Shoda (ed.), *Kindai Nihon no Tonan Ajia-kan* [Southeast Asia in modern Japanese thought] (Tokyo: Institute of Developing Economies, 1978); Shimizu Hajime, "1920-nendai ni okeru 'Nanshin-ron' no kisu to Nan'yo Boeki Kaigi no shiso" [The trend towards "southward expansion" in the 1920s and the intellectual background to the Conference on Japan's external trade with Nan'yo], pp. 23–36, in Shimizu Hajime (ed.), *Ryotaisenkan-ki Nihon Tonan-Ajia Kankei no Shoso* [Aspects of the relationship between Japan and Southeast Asia in the interwar period] (Tokyo: Institute of Developing Economies, 1986). An essential work on Japan's trade with the Nan'yo during this period is Mitsubishi Keizai Kenkyujo, *Toyo oyobi Nan'yo Shokoku no Kokusai Boeki to Nihon no Chii* [Asian international trade and the position of Japan] (Tokyo, 1935).

6   Toyo Boseki Kabushiki Kaisha, *Hyakunen-shi: Toyo-bo* [A hundred year history of the Toyo Cotton Spinning Co.] (Osaka, 1986), pp. 237–39.

7   Nihon Boseki Kyokai (ed.), *Nihon Mengyo Tokei* [Statistics of the Japanese cotton industry] (Tokyo, 1951).

8   The Factory Law in September 1916 prohibited night work by women and children under 15, but it was not applied to factories which employed a two-shift operation system until fifteen years after it was originally passed.

9   For "rationalization" in the cotton industry, see "Bosekigyo ni okeru gorika no shinko" [The progress of rationalization in the cotton spinning industry], *Toyo Keizai Shinpo* [The Oriental Economist], no. 1611 (28 July 1934); for the effect of the abolition of night work, see "Shin'yagyo kinshi no eikyo chosa" [Survey of the effect of the abolition of night work], *DNBRG* 463 (March 1931) and 464 (April 1931).

10 Mitsubishi Keizai Kenkyujo, *Nihon no Sangyo to Boeki no Hatten* [The development of Japanese industry and trade] (Tokyo, 1935), p. 254.

11 *Ibid.*, pp. 253, 258–59. See also "Men-Ko-Ren no soshiki to jigyo" [The organization and practices of the Federation of Cotton Manufacturers of Japan], (1)(2), *Toyo Keizai Shinpo*, nos. 1651 (4 May 1935) and 1652 (11 May 1935).

12 "Honpo boseki saikin junen-shi" [A history of the past ten years of the Japanese cotton industry], *DNBRG* 454 (June 1930), p. 10.

13 For the British cotton industry in the interwar period, see F. Utley, *Lancashire and the Far East* (London, 1931); B. and H. Ellinger, "Japanese competition in the cotton trade," *Journal of the Royal Statistical Society*, vol. 93, Pt.1 (1930). For a recent survey of the British cotton industry which includes comparison with Japan, see W. Mass and W. Lazonick, "The British cotton industry and international competitive advantage: The state of the debates," *Business History*, vol. 32, no. 4 (October 1990), pp. 37–50. See also A.J. Robertson, "Lancashire and the rise of Japan," in the same issue.

14 "Growth of Japanese industries," Manchester Chamber of Commerce, *Monthly Record* (hereafter *MR*) (April 1925), p. 101.

15 W.B. Cunningham, *Report on the Cotton Spinning and Weaving Industry in Japan, 1925–26* (London: Department of Overseas Trade, 1927), p. 74. See also "Cotton Spinning and Weaving Industry in Japan," *MR* (March 1927).

16 A.S. Pearce, *The Cotton Industry of Japan and China* (Manchester, 1929), pp. 141–44; "The cotton industry of China and Japan," *MR* (September 1929); also "Nihon bosekigyo hatten no gen'in" [Factors in the development of the Japanese cotton industry], *DNBRG* 443 (July 1929). For criticism of these reports, see F. Utley, *op. cit.*, pp. 189 ff.

17 T.E. Gregory, "Japanese competition in world market," *International Affairs*, vol. 13, no. 3 (May 1934), p. 333.

18 "Japanese competition and the British cotton and artificial silk export trade," 22 December 1932 (*Manchester Chamber of Commerce Archives* (hereafter MCC

Archives), M8/5/18). See also A. Redford, Manchester Merchants and Foreign Trade, vol. 2 (Manchester, 1956), pp. 249–62.

19 Joint Committee of Cotton Trade Organizations, "Japanese competition," 12 May 1933 (MCC Archives M8/5/18).

20 T.M. Snow to J. Simon, Tokyo, 13 May 1933 (FO 410/95).

21 "Memorandum respecting Japanese Trade Competition," Far East Department, Foreign Office, 12 June 1933 (FO 410/95). See also "Extract from the Round Table," received in Foreign Office, 21 December 1933 (FO 410/95).

22 "Report given by the Secretary to the India Executive Committee," 14 July 1933 (MCC Archives M8/5/18).

23 "Ottawa Conference," *MR* (September 1932); "Lancashire and India" (Half-Yearly Meeting), *MR* (July 1933).

24 R. Vansittart to T.M. Snow, Foreign Office, 10 August 1933 and 21 August 1933 (FO 410/95).
    The firm stand against India and Britain taken by Japanese cotton mill owners is clear from speeches. See "Nichi-In tsusho joyaku haiki mondai to mengyo jinkengyo taisaku zadankai" [A round-table talk on the abolition of the Indo-Japanese commercial treaty and possible responses by the cotton and artificial silk industries], *Toyo Keizai Shinpo*, no. 1550 (20 May 1933).
    For the trade negotiations between India and Japan, see Gaimusho (ed.), *Tsusho Joyaku to Tsusho Seisaku no Hensen* [An official history of the commercial treaties and trade policies of Japan] (Tokyo: Sekai keizai chosa-kai, 1951) (hereafter *Tsusho Joyaku*), pp. 900–24; O. Ishii, *Cotton-Textile Diplomacy* (New York: Arno Press, 1981), pp. 114–46. See also the recollections of Sawada Setsuzo, the chief Japanese representative at the negotiations, in Sawada Toshio (ed), *Sawada Setsuzo Kaisoroku* [The memoirs of Sawada Setsuzo] (Tokyo: Yuhikaku, 1985), pp. 160–81.

25 "Documents used in conversations with the Japanese industrial delegation" (MCC Archives M8/5/18); "British textile mission to India," *MR* (November 1933).

26 "British textile mission to India," *MR* (November 1933).

27 Gaimusho (ed.), *Tsusho Joyaku*, pp. 917–20.

28 "Negotiations with Japan," *MR* (January 1934).

29 F.O. Lindley to J. Simon, Tokyo, 6 April 1934 (FO 410/95). See also C. Dodd to J. Simon, 25 May 1934 (FO 410/95).

30 See the minutes and other confidential documents relating to "Anglo-Japanese textile conference" (MCC Archives M8/5/22); "Anglo-Japanese textile conferences," *MR* (March 1934); Gaimusho (ed.), *Tsusho Joyaku*, pp. 843–48. See also the relevant diary entries of Raymond Streat, then Secretary of the Manchester Chamber of Commerce, in M. Dupree (ed.), *Lancashire and Whitehall: The Diary of Sir Raymond Streat*, vol. 1 (Manchester: Manchester University Press, 1987), pp. 294–304, 306–9, and the reminiscences of Okada Gentaro, the chief Japanese representative, in Ando Yoshio (ed.), *Showa*

Keizaishi e no Shogen [Eye witness accounts of prewar Japanese economic history] (Tokyo: Mainichi Shinbunsha, 1965).

31 "Quotas: Memorandum on present policy of the Special Committee on Japanese Competition" (MCC Archives, M8/5/22); "Association of British Chambers of Commerce," *MR* (April 1934).

32 H.W. Dick, "Japan's economic expansion in the Netherlands Indies between the First and Second World Wars," *Journal of South East Asian Studies*, vol. 20, no. 2 (September 1989).

33 Kurusu Saburo, "Nichi-Ran kaisho ni tsuite" [On the trade negotiations between Japan and the Netherlands], in Japan, Gaimusho, Tsusho-kyoku, *Genka no Waga Tsusho Mondai* [Present Japanese trade problems] (Tokyo: Nihon Kokusai Kyokai, 1936), pp. 137–42.

34 Abe, *ibid.*, pp. 262–67; Toyo Boseki Kabushiki Kaisha, *Hyakunen-shi*, pp. 224, 249; Toyo Menka Kabushiki Kaisha, *Tomen yonjunen-shi* [A forty-year history of the Toyo Cotton Trading Co.] (Osaka, 1960), p. 94.

35 Nihon Yushutsu Men-orimono Dogyo Kumiai Rengo-kai [The Federation of Trade Associations of Cotton Textiles Exporters of Japan], *Men-Orimono Kaigai Shijo Chosa Hokoku: Ranryo-Indo no Bu* [Reports on the overseas markets for cotton textiles: the Dutch East Indies] (May 1928).

36 Taiwan Ginko, *Taiwan Ginko Yonjunen-shi* [A forty-year history of the Bank of Taiwan] (Tokyo, 1939), pp. 27, 252–57.

37 Toyo Menka K.K., *Tomen yonjunen-shi*, p. 93; Nichimen Jitsugyo Kabushiki Kaisha, *Nichimen shichijunen-shi* [A seventy-year history of the Japan Cotton Trading Co.] (Osaka, 1962), pp. 131–32.

38 Toyo Menka K.K., *ibid.*, pp. 94–95, 121–22, 132.

39 G.N. Carey to J. Simon, Batavia, 6 January 1934, in Department of Overseas Trade to Foreign Office, 21 February 1934 (FO 410/95), enclosure 1.

40 J. van Gelderen, *The Recent Development of Economic Foreign Policy in the Netherlands East Indies* (London: Longmans, Green, 1939), p. 21.

41 "Memorandum respecting changes in import trading methods in Netherlands East Indies," 5 January 1934, in Department of Overseas Trade to Foreign Office, 21 February 1934 (FO 410/95). J.S. Furnival, *Netherlands India: A Study of Plural Economy* (Cambridge: Cambridge University Press, 1939), pp. 431–32.

42 "Batavia hosho katsuyaku no taiyo" [An outline of the business activities of Japanese merchants in Batavia], *Takumu jiho*, no. 43 (October 1934).

43 "Nichi-Ran kaisho ni tsuite" [On the Dutch-Japanese trade negotiations], *Minami Shina oyobi Nan'yo Joho*, no. 56 (February 1934).

44 Nan'yo Kyokai, *Ranryo-Indo no Keizai Josei* [The economic condition of the Dutch East Indies] (Tokyo, 1936), pp. 35 ff.

45 Asahi Shimbun, Keizai-bu (ed.), *Showa Zaikai-shi* [A history of Japanese business circles in the early Showa period] (Tokyo, 1936), p. 294. 46. For the trade negotiations between Japan and the Dutch East Indies, see Gaimusho (ed.),

Tsusho Joyaku, pp. 1051–59; "Nichi-Ran kaisho no shuyo keika" [A summary of the Dutch-Japanese Trade negotiations], *Minami Shina oyobi Nan'yo Joho*, no. 78 (January 1935); Nan'yo Kyokai, *op. cit.*, pp. 35–53; Kurusu, *op. cit.*

47 G.N. Carey to J. Simon, Batavia, 2 July 1934, in Department of Overseas Trade to Foreign Office, 8 August 1934 (FO 410/95).

49 Gaimusho (ed.), *Tsusho Joyaku*, p. 1058.

50 "Japanese cotton piece goods trade," *MR* (September 1936).

3

Shipping Rivalry between Japan and the Netherlands in the 1930s: A Contemporary Japanese View

KOKAZE HIDEMASA

Introduction

To a large extent, the international economic rivalry in which Japan became involved during the 1930s was linked to problems of maritime transport in the region. In the case of the escalating trade rivalry between Japan and the Dutch East Indies in particular, much weight was placed on maritime issues. A successful solution to these was, in fact, a major premise for the opening of negotiations to resolve trade rivalry in general. In fact, trade rivalry and maritime transport were really two aspects of the same problem.

The following analysis of Japan-Dutch maritime rivalry has two specific purposes: the clarification of the relationship between individual nation states and their shipping industries, and the search for a key to the resolution of trade rivalry. The actual analysis is preceded by an outline of the prevailing situation, since this provides the background to the problem.

The Great Depression which started in 1929 cast dark shadows on the world shipping industry. As can be seen in Table 1, despite a large drop in maritime trade, there was no corresponding decrease in total tonnage during the 1930s. As a result, many ships with a

Table 3.1 *Indices of world trade, shipping, and freight rates, 1922–1938*
(1913 = 100)

Year	Index of world seaborne trade	Index of shipping tonnage		Indices of freight rates*
		Total	Active	
1922	92	135	119	122.0
1923	94	139	126	109.7
1924	106	134	126	113.4
1925	114	136	128	102.2
1926	115	136	128	109.7
1927	127	139	133	109.6
1928	130	143	137	98.8
1929	135	145	141	96.8
1930	126	148	140	79.1
1931	112	150	130	79.6
1932	101	148	122	75.4
1933	103	145	123	72.7
1934	112	140	126	74.2
1935	118	136	130	74.4
1936	124	139	134	84.6
1937	141	141	140	128.3
1938	135	144	142	97.6

Source: S.G. Sturmey, *British Shipping and World Competition* (London: The Athlone Press, 1962), p. 65.
Note: * Figures from *The Economist*.

tonnage capacity of over 10 million, had to be pulled out of the operation. Moreover, freight rates dropped sharply, reaching their lowest levels in 1933. The rate of moored ships, the index by which the degree of stagnation in the shipping business is measured, went beyond the 10% mark in the period from 1931 to 1935, reaching 20% in 1932 and 1933. Despite the gravity of the worldwide situation, however, the ratio of moored ships in Japan was a mere 5.2% at its worst in 1932, and 0.5% at its best in 1935.[1] The actual number of Japanese commercial ships also increased at a remarkable rate. Japan's performance was therefore strong.

The reason behind this phenomenon was the strength of the Japanese shipping industry vis-à-vis international competition. The British Imperial Shipping Comittee pointed out four specific reasons for Japan's predominance: the fall in exchange rates, the low level of sailors' wages, the protective policy of the government, and the support of the *zaibatsu*.[2] Whether or not their conclusions were accurate, it was interpretations of the Japanese situation such as this which encouraged the emergence of protectionist tendencies. These tendencies were, of course, appearing in any case, as the worldwide depression caused many nations to adopt protectionist measures, including high tariff duties. As a part of their strategy to counteract stagnation in the shipping business, many nations therefore began to adopt policies to protect their shipping interests. In other words, the appearance of strong national subsidies to protect particular flag carriers meant that no country was observing the principles of free competition. Rather than being specifically Japanese, the issue now took on international proportions.

During the first half of the 1930s, in the aftermath of the Great Depression, various international conferences were held, as the removal of trade barriers and economic isolationism became a major interest for nations striving for a system of international coordination. Shipping was one of the major commercial issues at the International Economic Conference held in London under the auspices of the League of Nations in 1933. From the Japanese point of view, the following issues were crucial for the revitalization of their shipping industry:

(1) freedom of the seas, including discriminatory treatment by flag, the boycotting of foreign vessels, the exclusion of foreign fleets, and the closure of coastal trade

(2) subsidies

(3) the adjustment of over-tonnage.[3]

In particular, Japan emphasized the importance of developing mechanisms for preventing protectionist measures. If other governments insisted on promoting the use of their national flag carriers for carrying exports and citizens by restricting foreign shipping, this would escalate competition in shipping and ultimately lead to the downfall of the entire world shipping industry. Japan criticized protection-ism as "a malicious doctrine" which "runs counter to the spirit of international coordination."[4]

The emergence of protectionism affected all of Japan's ocean shipping. Japan continued to stress the freedom of the seas, while other foreign countries began deploying measures to protect their own flag carriers. The existence of protectionism on a national level meant that maritime rivalry could no longer be resolved through negotiations between the parties directly involved the individual shipping companies, as had been the practice up until the 1920s. The various states involved had to intervene in the form of diplomatic negotiations.

The rivalry between Japan and the Netherlands over the Dutch East Indies, and that between Japan and Britain over British India and Australia were typical cases where such intervention occurred. The former case, in particular, exhibits typical elements of maritime rivalry in this period, in that the the shipping companies themselves lacked the ability to resolve the conflict. In fact, the processes through which the rivalry arose and was finally resolved symbolize the problem of maritime rivalry during the 1930s.

The Origins of the Rivalry between Japan and the Netherlands

As can be seen in Table 2, trade between Japan and the Dutch East Indies developed with a surplus of imports over exports in Japan's favour during the 1920s. This surplus continued into the 1930s, when Japanese goods, mainly cotton fabrics, began to enter the colony in enormous quantities. The expansion of trade was accompanied by a rapid increase in the number of Japanese vessels bound for particular regions. In relative terms, Southeast Asia became an increasingly important area of activity for Japanese trampers during 1933 and 1934, which clearly reflects the steady expansion of Japanese trade into the region.

Table 3.2 *Movements in Japanese trade with the Dutch East Indies, 1922–1939*

(million yen)

Year	Export	Import
1922	47.4	71.8
1924	59.3	92.4
1926	74.8	103.1
1928	73.4	112.9
1930	66.0	60.0
1931	63.5	46.1
1932	100.3	40.4
1933	157.5	55.7
1934	158.5	63.5
1935	143.0	78.2
1936	139.5	113.5
1937	200.1	153.5
1938	104.0	88.2
1939	127.8	71.6

Source: Nihon Gaikoku Boeki Nenpyo [Statistical abstract of Japan's foreign trade], corresponding years.

The introduction of Japanese vessels into this region was characterized mainly by the establishment of routes between Southeast Asia and Japanese ports, with almost no development of local routes. Table 3 gives figures for shipping on the regular routes in the region and shows that Japanese vessels were almost equal to Dutch and British vessels in terms of numbers. However, there were

Table 3.3 *Shipping tonnages of regular services (end of 1938)*

Nationality	Between East Asia and the South Seas		In the South Seas		Total	
	gross ton	no. of vessels	gross ton	no. of vessels	gross ton	no. of vessels
Japan	450,598	84			450,598	84
Netherlands	137,632	25	338,863	147	476,495	172
U.K.	70,839	9	374,305	122	445,144	131
U.S.A.			41,254	29	41,254	29
France			9,657	6	9,657	6

Source: Nanyo Keizai Kondankai, "Dai-niji Oshu senso boppastu mae ni okeru Nichi-manshi-Nanpo oyobi Nanpo sogo kan teiki koro" [Regular shipping services between East Asia and the South Seas and in the South Seas region before World War II].

absolutely no Japanese vessels operating within the region, that is on the established local routes, where Dutch and British vessels reigned supreme. In other words, the Japanese vessels were concentrated on routes connecting the region to Japan and China. However, since Dutch vessels also operated on such routes, maritime competition between the two countries was inevitable.

There were two aspects to this maritime rivalry between Japan and the Netherlands. The first was the competition between the Japanese and Dutch vessels operating on the Japan-Java route and on the Java-China-Japan Line (hereafter JCJL). The second aspect arose from competition in the area of coastal shipping, more specifically the competition between Koninklijke Peketvaart Maatschappij (the Royal Packet Navigation Company, hereafter refered to as KPM) and Japanese vessels that resulted from the expansion of direct Japanese routes to ports in Dutch East Indies waters.

KPM was the Dutch East Indies mail carrier. At the time of its establishment it managed routes between the Dutch East Indies and Australia, the southern parts of China, Thailand and Rangoon, Hong Kong and Saigon, Batavia, East Africa and South Africa, and the ports of the Dutch East Indies and the ports of the South Pacific. JCJL was established in 1902 jointly by three companies, including KPM, for the purpose of developing a Java-China-Japan mail line. At the time of its establishment, it managed routes between the Dutch East Indies and Japan, Shanghai, and Dairen.[5]

In 1921 the JCJL and three Japanese companies (Nihon Yusen [NYK], Osaka Shosen [OSK] and Nanyo Yusen established the Japan-Java Conference to manage and operate the route between Japan and the Dutch East Indies. After a temporary lapse, the conference was reorganized in July 1922 through the mediation of OSK. This led to a period of stability that continued until March 1931,[6] when Ishihara Sangyo began operations on the route, and the conference collapsed.

Ishihara Sangyo originated as Nanyo Kogyo Koshi, a limited partnership established in Osaka in 1920 by Hiroichiro Ishihara, in order to develop the Medan Mine in the state of Batu Paht in the Kingdom of Johor on the Malay Peninsula as a source of iron ore for the Yawata Steelworks. With the sudden fall in the price of iron following World War I, the company purchased three vessels of 7,000 tons (dead weight) in 1924 in order to cut down on transport costs. The company went on to add the following to its fleet: two 7,000 ton vessels and two 8,000 ton vessels in 1929, six 9,000 ton vessels in 1930, and two vessels of 9,000 tons in 1932, when it had a total fleet of fifteen vessels, with a total tonnage of 120,000 tons. The company had developed into a major shipowner.[7]

Ishihara also took part in the effort to rebuild Nanyo Soko in the mid-1920s, and became chief advisor to the organization in 1930, thus preparing the way for the expansion of his business activities into the South Pacific region. Nanyo Soko had been established in 1920 as a joint venture between China and Japan, through the initiative of the Bank of Taiwan. The main office was in Taipei, and the company owned warehouses in Canton, Saigon, Singapore, Batavia, Cheribon, Semarang and Surabaja. Hopes were high that it would promote trade with the South region. However, business never flourished, even at the beginning, and the managing director finally approached Ishihara to entrust him with the task of rebuilding the company.[8] This could only be achieved with the full scale expansion of Japanese business into the South Pacific, as well as the support of a shipping company which operated a regular line in the region. However, the three Japanese companies belonging to the Japan-Java shipping conference refused to accept Ishihara's request for support.[9] Ishihara therefore decided to open a Java route by himself, in order to protect Nanyo Soko and expand his export trade into the South Pacific.

Ishihara realized that when his vessels set out for Malaya in order to bring iron ore back to Japan, they were carrying no cargo at all. He therefore began to tranport export goods. Japanese vessels had previously been inferior to foreign ships in terms of facilities and speed,[10] but Ishihara decided on eight comparatively high quality vessels of 7,000 tons. From March 1931, regular lines were operated three times a month, with calling at the ports of Yokohama, Nagoya, Osaka, Kobe, Moji, Wakamatsu, Makassar, Surabaja, Semarang, Cheribon, Batavia, Singapore, and Batu Pahat. Trampers called at the ports of Taketoyo, Uno, Kagashima, Dairen, Keelung, Manila, Tawau, Pasuruan, Probolinggo, Panarukan, Bnjuwangi, Cilacap, Tegal, and Pekalongan.[11]

In 1931 Ishihara, who was attempting to lower the fares by 20–25%, rejected an offer by the four shipping conference companies to join them and thus avoid competition. Fierce rivalry arose, with the shipping conference lowering its freight to Java by 25% in March 1931, and by another 25% in May. Within the short period of two months, freight rates had therefore been halved. The fall in rates spread to the Singapore-Hong Kong-Shanghai route as well, influencing another shipping conference, the Straights-China-Japan conference.[12] Japanese and Dutch businesses appeared to welcome this shipping competition, while the Dutch government initially took an impartial stance.

However, the competition began to affect all the companies involved adversely, and, in 1932, the Japanese government set out to act as a mediator. The intention was to solicit the participation of the JCJL after arbitrating with the Japanese carriers. On August 26, a basic agreement was realized covering the following four points: the number of vessels, shipping rates, rebates, and the possibility of a "pool" system.[13]

JCJL had been the most severely hit by the competition. The company's share of export freight had fallen rapidly, from 54.3% in 1930 to 35.3% in 1932. In September 1932, a new agreement on rates was drawn up between the JCJL and the four Japanese companies. But, despite the fact that the new rates became applicable from January of the following year, the JCJL share continued to drop, reaching a low of 30.3% in 1933 (Table 4). Even agreements on rates could not wipe out all the competition. It was therefore essential that the shipping conference be strengthened through the adoption of a powerful "pool" system.

Table 3.4 *Freight tonnage from Japan to the Dutch East Indies, 1929–1933*

(% in parentheses)

Year	Java-China-Japan Line		Nanyo Yusen		Osaka Shosen		Ishihara Sangyo		Total
	(%)		(%)		(%)		(%)		
1929	184,806	(53.6)	86,347	(25.0)	73,942	(21.4)			345,095
1930	167,694	(54.3)	84,491	(27.4)	56,616	(18.3)			308,801
1931	142,172	(50.0)	52,513	(18.5)	47,611	(16.8)	41,838	(14.7)	284,134
1932	142,909	(35.3)	71,045	(17.6)	72,883	(18.0)	117,554	(29.1)	404,391
1933	150,081	(30.3)	100,138	(20.2)	80,550	(16.3)	164,554	(33.2)	495,323

Source: "Statistics of quantity exported to Dutch East Indies," in Gaimusho kiroku, B 2.0.0. J/N2-1-4.

In July 1933, a new Japan-Java conference was created with agreement on the following points:

(1) operations per month: three vessels for Ishihara Sangyo; two for JCJL, Nanyo Yusen, and OSK; but no decision for NYK;

(2) the same freight rates for all companies with no rebate system;

(3) important issues to be decided by unanimous consent, and all others by a majority;

(4) a "pool" system to be organized.[14]

As far as outward vessels (from Japan) were concerned, the pool system for 1935 was set at 32% for Ishihara Sangyo, 31% for JCJL, 18.5% for both Nanyo Yusen and OSK, with the NYK share to be decided through consultation with all companies. This new framework seemed to provide the basis for a reconstructed conference. However, the Dutch government intervened in order to protect JCJL and introduced renewed instability.

Although the Dutch East Indies government did not prohibit foreign vessels from participating in coastal trade, cargoes carried by Japanese vessels to the Dutch East Indies coastal ports were originally reloaded onto KPM vessels at the Java Island. During the 1920s Japanese shipping companies were therefore reluctant to open direct routes to these coastal ports, since this might lead to direct confrontation with JCJL and KPM. Moreover, pressure might be exerted by the Dutch authorities.[15] However in November 1928, in accordance with the desires of the Osaka Chamber of Commerce to promote trade, OSK began a Japan-Calucutta route, calling at Belawan twice a month.[16]

The increase in Japanese exports to Southeast Asia in the 1930s encouraged Japanese businesses to stress the necessity for opening direct routes to the various regions of the Dutch East Indies. At that time the direct freight rate between Kobe and Padang was 54 yen per ton of sundries. The freight from Kobe to Batavia was only 10 yen, but the KPM freight between Batavia and Padang was 44 yen, including reloading charges. This high freight rate was one of the reasons preventing Japanese goods from penetrating into Sumatra.

In May 1932, therefore, Nanyo Yusen extended its Java line to Padang and increased its freight rate to 25 yen per ton. In May 1933, Palembang was added as a port of call. Consequently, in 1933, 57.5% of the 7,319 tons of Japanese goods landed in Padang and 52.8% of the 5,643 tons in Palembang were carried by Nanyo Yusen.[17] This was a great blow to KPM, particularly in view of its original monopoly.

KPM warned Nanyo Yusen to abandon its new extension. Then in May 1933, the JCJL opened a Padang Line in competition with Nanyo Yusen,[18] so that Japanese vessels were now competing on coastal routes as well. At this point, KPM began to appeal to the Dutch government to adopt a policy of expelling all foreign vessels from Dutch East Indies waters.

The Failure of the Primary Negotiations, 1934

The Dutch government attempted a political solution to the joint issues of the JCJL's share in the pool and competition on coastal shipping lines. The matters were treated as diplomatic problems in conjunction with trade conflicts at the negotiation round table between Japan and the Dutch East Indies.[19]

In January 1934, the Dutch East Indies government proposed a meeting between government representatives of the two nations. The Japanese government accordingly sent Shin'ichi Nagaoka, former minister to the Netherlands, to Batavia to start the consultations. The Japan-Java shipping conference, which had agreed to the formulation of a pool, now found its members arguing intensely over precisely this point. The conflict started with a disagreement over the share of the cement cargo to the Dutch East Indies. In April 1933, the four companies of the conference (excluding NYK) signed a contract with import houses in the Dutch East Indies to transport cement to them. The contract stated that the monthly share for the four companies would be an equal 25% each, to a maximum of 48,000 barrels.[20] However, the emergency import restrictions by the Dutch East Indies that had been issued to protect Dutch businesses meant that in October the Dutch East Indies government had to order JCJL to take only 50% of its usual load. The fact that the Dutch import houses supported this ordinance further complicated matters. The shipping conference was able temporarily to override the difficulty by continuing with "equal shares" for the October load.[21] However, since JCJL insisted that, although they respected the agreement of the conference, government orders were a completely different matter, the three Japanese companies made every attempt to expedite the organization of a pool system.

In 1934, against a background of increasing trade rivalry between Japan and the Netherlands, JCJL began to adopt a stronger stance. Claiming support from the Dutch East Indies government, it insisted on a 33.3% share, while the Japanese side proposed that the JCJL share should be 28%, an amount based on the 1933 figures.[22] The Japanese side discussed the matter with the Japanese government, seeing the issue as a preliminary skirmish in the overall trade negotiations which were to take place between Japan and the Dutch

East Indies later that year. As a result, a concessionary figure of 31% was proposed. The JCJL response in May, however, was not favourable:

> The share held by JCJL prior to the advent of the Ishihara Sangyo line, in 1929–30, was 44.5%. When Ishihara Sangyo joined the shipping conference under Japanese government support, JCJL made one great sacrifice and gave one fourth of its share. The company cannot therefore agree to calls for any further sacrifices if NYK begins operations on the route.[23]

The Japanese side repeated its proposal for a 31%/69% split, on the condition that NYK should not be allowed to start operations in the forseeable future. No agreement was reached.

In May, Shinzaburo Ishihara, the managing director of Ishihara Sangyo, wrote to JCJL stating that his company had never received any support from the Japanese government and that the pool issue should be discussed and resolved among the conference members themselves. He further criticised JCJL for attempting to treat what were basically shipping problems as an international issue involving Japan and the Netherlands, disregarding the fact that the shipping business was based on the principle of operating without national boundaries.[24]

The main elements of the reply from JCJL were as follows:

(1) JCJL would be satisfied with a pool share of 31%.

(2) Should NYK decide to operate on the Japan-Java route, the JCJL share would remain unchanged, and the Japanese companies would divide the remaining pool points among themselves.

(3) The period of the agreement should be three years.

(4) The share of NYK on the Sumatra line should not surpass 50%, and vessels of other companies should not be permitted to enter.[25]

The Japanese side made the following four points in response:

(1) They agreed to a JCJL pool share of 31%.

(2) Should NYK decide to operate, however, all four companies

including JCJL should surrender proportional amounts of their pool points.

(3) The period of the agreement should be one year.

(4) Since the conference was for the Japan-Java route only, the Sumatra route was an issue outside conference concerns and therefore could not be an item for negotiation.[26]

At this point, however, JCJL brought the correspondence to a standstill by stating that, "Since the resolution of maritime issues has been entrusted to government hands, we are not at liberty to coordinate ourselves with the Japanese side."[27] KPM took a similar stance, suggesting the clear presence of the Dutch East Indies government behind the two companies. During government negotiations, the Dutch stance was to discourage consultations between shipping companies unless there was a prior government-level agreement on regulating shipping.[28] In other words, the Dutch government and the shipping business came to the negotiating table as one entity.

Three points of conflict emerged between the two nations; they were clarified through the processes of government and conference negotiations.[29] The first point of conflict concerned the "freedom of the seas," in other words the freedom of all vessels to call at any open port. In the emergency import regulations of September 1933, the Dutch had, in effect, prohibited any further extension of direct shipping routes from Japan, in order to protect Dutch vessels on coastal routes. The Japanese side, on the other hand, stated that the spirit of the international convention of September 1923 should be respected by the right of any ship to call at any open port. In other words, while Japan stressed the freedom of the seas, the Netherlands stressed the need for regulation through government intervention.

The second point was the issue of national pool points, or, the national flag principle (*Kokkishugi*). JCJL stated that if NYK were to be given pool points, this should be done through a reallocation of the shares of Japanese companies, while the Dutch pool points remained unchanged. This meant that, as far as JCJL was concerned, the four Japanese companies were to be treated as a single unit. The Japanese side, however, wanted equal treatment for all participating companies, regardless of their country of origin, arguing that the idea of national pool points contradicted the basic principles of the shipping conference, which assured equal treatment to all participating companies. Neither side was prepared to compromise. The Japanese side was afraid that if they accepted the national flag principle here, it would be applied to Japanese vessels in other regions.[30]

The third point of conflict was the matter of government intervention in the shipping conference. The Dutch side demanded government guarantees that the operations of vessels outside the convention would be regulated so that the convention would not lose its effect. However, the Japanese side insisted that the shipping conference should be signed through consultation and agreement between the parties involved, and that it was not possible for governments to regulate vessels outside the conference. These conflicts all arose as a result of the disparity between the Japanese emphasis on principles and the Dutch stress on the need to protect their own vessels.[31]

In November 1934, fearing a possible collapse of the shipping conference, JCJL proposed a compromise set of terms as the preliminary for a fresh round of negotiations. However, the Japanese members refused to reconsider their position. In the same month, the Dutch East Indies government notified the Japanese government that they were ready to implement emergency measures to protect their own vessels. The Japanese government replied that it had no legal power to restrict the activities of Japanese firms. At last, in late November, the two countries agreed to hold a conference of the shipping companies concerned at Kobe.[32] The Japanese government expressed their willingness to restrict the activities of Japanese companies, but the four Japanese companies would not change their stance.[33]

In the trade negotiations, there was a clear conflict between the Japanese insistence that the Dutch side remove its discriminatory import restrictions and the Dutch position that they had the right to take protective measures against the fall of the yen, just as other countries did. Negotiations were suspended in late December with no agreement. As a result, the shipping issue, which was critical to the outcome of the entire trade negotiations process, was no longer an item for negotiation between governments, but was entirely in the hands of the private members of the shipping conference. The all important meeting was held in Kobe in February 1935. However, before any real negotiations began, the Dutch side insisted that only English be used, while the Japanese side, at the instigation of Ishihara, wanted both English and Japanese. The meeting therefore came to an abrupt halt before it had even begun properly.[34] The individual companies withdrew from the conference on 3 March. On the expiration of the freight agreemnt in June, the shipping conference finally ceased to exist.

The Success of the Second Round of Negotiations, 1935–1936

After the dissolution of the shipping conference, severe competition between vessels of the two countries broke out. The four Japanese companies organized their own shipping conference and established a joint head office in Kobe with branches in Tokyo, Yokohama, Nagoya, Osaka, Moji, Makassar, Surabaja, Semarang, Cheribon, and Batavia. From April, the four comapanies began joint operations and increased rebate rates.[35] Despite their efforts, the JCJL share increased rapidly from 30% to 80%. According to Hart, the Director of the Dutch East Indies Department of Economic Affairs, this was because of the good service given by Dutch vessels, as well as importers, and national sentiment.[36] However, in reality it was largely due to the protectionist measures adopted by the Dutch East Indies government, including restrictions on the loading of Japanese vessels based on an import quota system, and the strengthening of discriminatory measures.

For example, according to the Japanese Ministry of Foreign Affairs, the Dutch East Indies government had instituted unduly complicated procedures for the loading of lumber from Sungklirang on the island of Borneo, while a similarly obstructive attitude was being shown by the local authorities in Samarinda.[37] In both of these cases, the local authorities had asked the Japanese companies involved to use either KPM or JCJL, but their cargoes would be impossibly expensive.

Such problems aside, since the increasing rivalry between Japanese and Dutch shipping firms had brought freight rates down to as much as 30–40% below the formal figures, both sides were running into the red with each trip made.[38] Serious efforts were therefore made to stop the competition. The Japanese government, for its part, desired a speedy reopening of negotiations, since they were the precondition for trade negotiations. It took measures for the establishment of Nanyo Kaiun Kaisha—a union of the four Japanese lines—and the introduction of the Shipping Control Act.

In July 1935, under the leadership of the government, the four Japanese lines were integrated to form Nanyo Kaiun Kaisha with an initial capital of 8.5 million yen. The company had fourteen vessels, of which four (23,200 tons) came from Ishihara Sangyo, four (20,000 tons) from OSK, four (16,100 tons) from Nanyo Yusen, and two (14,100 tons) from NYK. Heiji Asano, the former director of the shipping department of the Ministry of Communications, became president of the new company, and the directors were all representatives sent by the original four companies. Nanyo Kaiun was a national joint organization comprising both public and private sectors, and received a government subsidy of 400,000 yen each year.[39]

Ishihara's participation in Nanyo Kaiun was based on the understanding that the new company was a demonstration to the Dutch East Indies government of Japan's uncompromising stance. However, Terai Hisanobu was appointed managing director of the company, although Ishihara was the largest share holder, because of the latter's antagonism towards the Netherlands.[40]

With the merger of the Japanese companies into Nanyo Kaiun Kaisha, there were now only two parties to the negotiations. The issue of the redistribution of pool points to NYK disappeared automatically, and the national flag issue was also resolved by the effective compromise of the Japanese side. The management of the new Japanese company wanted to reopen negotiations quickly and bring them to a successful conclusion, since this was the great precondition to broader trade negotiations between Japan and the Dutch East Indies. It therefore concentrated its energies on preliminary negotiations with JCJL.

Ishihara, however, was opposed to this policy. In December 1935, he resigned from his post as advisor to Nanyo Kaiun and established the Nanyo Koro Kabushiki Kaisha with four company vessels and two charters in order to enter the Japan-Java route as a non-participant in the conference.[41] The Japanese government warned that it was willing to force him to obey regulations and to stop his vessels, but Ishihara did not yield.[42]

In May 1936, the government submitted a "Shipping Control Bill" to the Imperial Diet. Article 3 of the bill allowed the government to recommend measures to prevent competition, if such competition jeopardized the sound development of the Japanese shipping industry. It further stipulated that the government could order shipping companies to reach agreement on operating their vessels, and that if necessary, it could restrict or even prohibit the operation of a line. Article 4, stipulated that if the government judged that rates and other conditions of line management went counter to the public interest, it could give the necessary orders to specific operators. It was tacitly admitted that this law was aimed at controlling Ishihara. The bill passed the Diet with a partial amendment, and was enforced from 1 August. This left Ishihara with no choice but to withdraw from Southeast Asia.[43] Thus the Japanese government had been forced to resort to legislative controls in order to prevent outsiders from entering the Japan-Java line.

Table 3.5 *A comparison of pool points* (%)

Ports	Exports		Imports	
	Nanyo Kaiun	JCJL	Nanyo Kaiun	JCJL
All ports in Java and Makassar	64.25	35.75	60.00	40.00
Padang, Palembang	50.00	50.00	50.00	50.00
Menado	50.00	50.00	50.00	50.00
Reloading onto KPM (Royal Packet Navigation Co.)	40.00	60.00	40.00	60.00

Source: "Nichi-Ranin kaiun kyotei" [Shipping agreements between Japan and the Dutch East Indies], in Gaimusho kiroku, B.2.0.0. J/N 2-2.

In May 1936, Terai arrived in Java to reopen the shipping conference negotiations. In June 1937, an official agreement was signed with JCJL, to be implemented from 1 July, which settled the market share issue and various other items.[44] The new share for Japanese vessels is shown in Table 5. The two sides also agreed on the urgent need to raise freight rates. The signing of the agreement on maritime issues was a preliminary step on the road to trade negotiations. In September 1936, the Netherlands suspended the exportation of gold, thus resolving all barriers to exchange. Trade negotiations started in October 1936, and a trade agreement between Japan and the Dutch East Indies was concluded in April 1937.

Conclusion

The shipping conflict between Japan and the Netherlands centered on the concept of the freedom of the seas. The main issues involved the national flag issue and the regulation of vessels outside the shipping conference. Japan initially took the position that maritime issues should be resolved, not through government intervention, but by the shipping conference concerned. However, after the collapse of the first round of negotiations, the Japanese side, under government initiative, took measures that amounted to a compromise with the Dutch view. By integrating the four shipping companies involved and establishing Nanyo Kaiun, they effectively accepted the national flag principle. The Shipping Control Act made it possible for the government to intervene in line management on the grounds of public interest. This represented a decisive step towards the use of government power to exclude vessels outside the shipping conference, namely those of Ishihara Sangyo, from the South Pacific route. These measures were taken because successful shipping negotiations were a prerequisite for general trade negotiations. By this compromise, Japan was able to bring both sets of negotiations to a successful conclusion, and thus avoid further trade and shipping friction.

However, the abandonment of the principle of the freedom of the seas was the direct cause of two problems that were later to occur on the South Pacific route. The first was that the barriers raised against the trampers led to a serious shortage of vessels during busy seasons. The second was that, since the coastal routes were all under the leadership of the Dutch East Indies, Japanese needs could not always be met. Inconveniences therefore arose in transporting goods between Japan and the Dutch East Indies. These problems were potential inhibiting factors for the penetration of Japanese business into the Dutch East Indies.

From a contemporary Japanese perspective, the international shipping rivalry between Japan and the Netherlands was a struggle against protectionism in which the Netherlands was willing to employ diplomatic pressure in order to reduce the fierce competition from Japanese vessels in Southeast Asian routes. In the context of increasing international economic rivalry, direct government intervention proved to be the only possible solution. Although the *de facto* abandonment of the principle of the freedom of the seas brought about a reduction in the rivalry, Japan became locked in a vicious circle. The diplomatic resolution of one economic problem only led to the birth of new difficulties. Diplomacy was not enough. However, it was the search for non-diplomatic solutions that was to lead Japan inexorably towards World War II.

Notes

1 Nakagawa Keiichiro, *Ryotaisenkan no Nihon Kaiungyo* [Japanese shipping in the interwar period] (Tokyo: Nihon Keizai Shinbunsha, 1980), p. 25.

2 Imperial Shipping Committee, *British Shipping in the Orient* (London, 1939).

3 Taibei Senpaku Teikyo Zaidan, *Kokusai Keizai Kaigi to Kaiun Mondai* [International economic conferences and shipping problems] (Nihon Kaiun Shukaijo, 1934), p. 5.

4 *Ibid.*, p. 24.

5 Nihon Yusen Kaisha, *Showa Shichi-nen Shimo-hanki Kaiun oyobi Keizai Chosa* [Shipping and economic surveys for the second half of 1932] (Tokyo, 1933).

6 Nihon Yusen Kaisha, *Wagasha Kaku Koro no Enkaku* [The development of the ocean services of N.Y.K.] (Tokyo, 1932), pp. 256–57.

7 Ishihara Sangyo Kaiun Kaisha, *Sogyo Niju-nen Shi* [A twenty-year history of Ishihara Sangyo Kaiun] (Tokyo, 1941), p. 24.

8 Ishihara Hiroichiro, *Sogyo Sanjugo-nen o Kaiko site* [Reminiscences of the 35-year history of Ishihara Sangyo] (Tokyo, 1956), p. 70.

9 *Osaka Mainichi Shinbun* [Osaka Daily News], 17 August 1931.

10 Gaimusho, "Nan-yo koro" [Shipping routes to the Southern region], in Gaimusho kiroku, F.1.6.0.7. vol. 4, pt. 2. This unpublished record is held in the Gaiko Shiryokan (Japanese Foreign Ministry Archives).

11 Ishihara Sangyo Kaiun Kaisha, *Sogyo Niju-nen Shi*, p. 30.

12 *Ibid.*, p. 225.

13 Nihon Yusen Kaisha, *Wagasha kaku koro no enkaku*, p. 258.

14 Ishihara Sangyo Kaiun Kaisha, *Sogyo Sanjugo-nen o Kaiko site* (manuscript), pp. 41–42.

15 Gaimusho, "Nan-yo Koro."

16 *Ibid.*

17 Gaimusho, "Nichi-ran tsusho joyaku kankei ikken: kaiun kankei" [File on the commercial treaties between Japan and the Netherlands: Shipping], in Gaimusho kiroku, B.2.0.0. J/N 2–1–4.

18 *Ibid.*

19 For the background to the negotiations, see Gaimusho (ed.), *Tsusho Joyaku to Tsusho Seisaku no Hensen* [An official history of the commercial treaties and trade policies of Japan] (Tokyo: Sekai Keizai Chosakai, 1951), pp. 1051–52.

20 Ishihara Sangyo Kaiun Kaisha, *Sogyo Sanjugo-nen o Kaiko site* (manuscript), p. 87.

21 *Ibid.*, p. 88.

22 Gaimusho, "Nichi-ran tsusho joyaku kankei ikken: kaiun kankei"; Ishihara Sangyo Kaiun Kaisha, *Sogyo Sanjugo-nen o Kaiko site* (manuscript), p. 89.

23 Ishihara Sangyo Kaiun Kaisha, *Sogyo Sanjugo-nen o Kaiko site* (manuscript), p. 89.

24　*Ibid.*, p. 93.

25　*Ibid.*, p. 94.

26　Gaimusho, "Nichi-ran tsusho joyaku kankei ikken: kaiun kankei."

27　*Ibid.*

28　*Ibid.*

29　*Ibid.*

30　*Ibid.*

31　*Ibid.*

32　Ishihara Sangyo Kaiun Kaisha, *Sogyo Sanjugo-nen o Kaiko site* (manuscript), p. 105; Gaimusho, "Nichi-ran tsusho joyaku kankei ikken: kaiun kankei."

33　Ishihara Sangyo Kaiun Kaisha, *ibid.*, p. 109.

34　Ishihara Hiroichiro, *Sogyo Sanjugo-nen o Kaiko site*, pp. 84–85.

35　Ishihara Sangyo Kaiun Kaisha, *Sogyo Sanjugo-nen o Kaiko site* (manuscript), pp. 123–25.

36　Gaimusho, "Nichi-ran tsusho joy aku kankei ikken: Showa ju-jugo-nen Nichi-ran kan kosyo kankei" [File on thecommercial treaties between Japan the the Netherlands: Trade negotiations, 1935–45], vol. 1, in Gaimusho kiroku, B.2.0.0. J/N 2–2; *Tokyo Asahi Shinbun*, 9 May 1935.

37　Gaimusho, "Nichi-ran tsusho joyaku kankei ikken: kaiun kankei."

38　*Kobe Yusin Nippo*, 2 May 1935.

39　Asahara Johei, *Nihon Kaiun Hatten-shi* [A history of the development of Japanese shipping] (Tokyo: Choryu-sha, 1978), p. 371.

40　*Ibid.*, p. 371.

41　*Ibid.*, p. 374.

42　*Osaka Mainichi Shinbun*, 21 December 1935.

43　Asahara, *Nihon Kaiun Hatten-shi*, p. 376.

44　Nihon Yusen Kaisha, *Terai Hisanobu* (Tokyo, 1965), pp. 142–45.

4

The Japanese Navy and the Development of Southward Expansion

SUMIO HATANO

I

In his memoirs, Vice-Admiral Toshitane Takada who was a member of Japanese Navy Ministry staff before the outbreak of the Pacific War states that there were two versions of the navy's *Nanshin-ron* (views on southward expansion). One argued for Japan's natural development into the South Seas as a maritime power; the other unrealistically prompted southward expansion for the sake of countering the army's *Hokushin-ron* (views on northward or continental expansion).[1]

The first view insisted that Japan's basic national policy after the Sino-Japanese War in 1894–95 should be based on maritime advancement rather than on continental expansion, and that military priority should be placed on the improvement of naval forces rather than on ground fighting forces. Such a view is evident in the thinking of Navy Minister (1898–1906) Gonbee Yamamoto who promoted a firm long-term national defense policy that placed priority on naval forces.[2] However, the dominance of such thinking in Japan's national defense and foreign policies did not last long. As a result of the Russo-Japanese War, Japan gained special rights in Manchuria and Korea, and established the foundation for continental development. Thereafter, until 1941, the Japanese national policy was based on continental development.

After the Russo-Japanese War, the army took the initiative to formulate a unified national defense policy which would establish a national defense line on the continent. As a result, the Imperial National Defense Policy was drafted among military and government leaders in 1907. However, Japan's national defense policies and strategies were not necessarily unified and integrated by this policy paper.[3] Yet, as the army increased its involvement in China, the navy was obliged to play an auxiliary role in national defense matters. For example, the now famous "Study of National Defense Issues" prepared and issued by six naval officers in 1913 still argued for placing priority on the improvement of naval forces. However, it took an affirmative view of the continental development policy, and promoted such development without the use of armed force. Consequently, how to control the army-led continental development policy which involved armed force became a problem for the navy.[4]

Takada also points out that the navy's *Nanshin-ron* was sometimes unrealistic, since it was trying to establish a naval power build-up within a limited military budget. One of the navy's motives was to contend with the army for an increased share of armaments and larger budget appropriations. For example, the radical and aggressive *Nanshin-ron* put forth by the navy's staff between 1934 and 1936 clearly was aimed at strengthening the navy's position for a naval build-up. At the same time, it was aimed at restraining the army's *Hokushin-ron* at a time when Japan could possibly break-away from the London Naval Treaty of 1930 and achieve a revision of the Imperial National Defense Policy.[5]

II

The basic tenant of Japan's international relations after the Russo-Japanese War shifted from Anglo-Russian confrontation to Anglo-German confrontation. Allied with Great Britain and Russia by the Anglo-Japanese Alliance of 1902 and the Russo-Japanese Pact of 1907, Japan increased her commitment to the encirclement of Germany.

With these international alliances in place, the First World War broke out, and Great Britain made a request that Japan destroy the German fleet in Chinese coastal waters. Great Britain would have preferred not to ask Japan to enter the war, since Australia, New Zealand, and the United States would react negatively. However, Great Britain could not help but seek Japanese assistance because of the shortage of British naval forces in the Far East. As a result, Great Britain asked Japan to enter the war on the condition that Japan would limit the scope of military operations to Chinese coastal waters. Japan did not agree to such limitations, but entered into the war after notifying each country that she had no territorial ambitions.

In the fall of 1914, the Japanese government took the position that the occupation in the German colonial territory of the South Seas Islands (most of Micronesia) was going to be temporary. Whether the occupation would become permanent or remain temporary would be decided after the peace conference. However, navy policy makers, such as Admiral Saneyuki Akiyama, the chief of the Naval Affairs Bureau, insisted on a permanent occupation policy and troubled the Japanese government by acknowledging the following two policies in regard to the German territory.[6]

First, the navy policy makers felt that permanent Japanese occupation of the South Seas Islands not only would remove the influence of Germany which was an obstacle to southward expansion, but also would have the strategic effect of cutting off American westward expansion into the Pacific. Secondly, they believed that "Although the South Seas Islands in themselves have minuscule value, they are extremely important as stepping stones and a base for southward development in the future." Many naval policy makers recognized the South Seas Islands as a stronghold for moving into Southeast Asian regions such as the Dutch East Indies.[7]

The possession of the South Seas Islands in 1914 enhanced Japanese interest in Southeast Asia. Full scale plans were devised to make Southeast Asia the next direction of expansion. Research and studies for Japanese emigration and business advancement into Southeast Asia were also started.

Throughout the 1920s, there were few navy policy makers who argued for military advancement into Southeast Asia using the South Seas Islands as a base.[8] Actually, as early as 1922, when the navy withdrew from the South Seas Islands leaving only one or two naval attachés and handed over the government to the South Seas Agency, the Cabinet secretly decided to prepare for building military facilities on the islands in response to requests from the navy. However, no active preparations took place until the mid-1930s. The navy satisfied its desire for a southward expansion by directly and indirectly supporting research on Japanese emigration and business advancement into Southeast Asia. The navy's view was in agreement with such a peaceful expansion policy.

Commander Kan'e Chudo, who became a radical supporter of southward expansion in the 1930s said that he had increased his interest in the economic value of Southeast Asia by reading literature on Southeast Asia published during the First World War and traveling in the South Seas Islands and Southeast Asian Islands after his graduation from Naval Military Academy (1916). Many naval officers who were considered radical advocates of a southward advance in 1930s such as Chudo, Captains Shingo Ishikawa, Yoshimasa Nakahara, and Tatehiko Konishi shared similar experiences. Some of their common views were that the South Seas Islands were rich in natural resources, but Western powers already controlled the area; the Japanese should advance into this region without delay to promote industrial development and trade; and that the navy should actively support this expansion through the development of new sea routes by providing information and financial support.[9]

They argued for an economic policy and peaceful southward expansion. However, one distinctive characteristic was an anti-Western sentiment, which maintained that the rich natural resources in Southeast Asia were beginning to be dominated by Western colonial powers. This anti-Western sentiment grew throughout the 1920s and led to action against the Washington Treaty System.

III

The navy's idea of southward expansion in the first half of the 1930s coincided with the view held by the anti-Washington group. This group, which included Ishikawa, Nakahara, and Chudo argued increasingly for expansion and opposed the West in the midst of a series of incidents including the Manchurian Incident, the founding of Manchukuo, and the withdrawal from the League of Nations. For example, in 1933, Admiral Nobumasa Suetsugu, who was the central figure in the group, wrote that the conflict between the powers who wanted to maintain the *status quo* (such as Great Britain and the United States) and the powers who wanted change (such as Japan) was just as inevitable as the principle of survival of the fittest in the "biological world." He argued that Japan should withdraw from both the Washington Naval Treaty and the London Naval Treaty and unilaterally expand naval forces.[10]

This group sympathized with the "Asian Monroe Doctrine" which held that Japan was responsible for maintaining peace and stability in Asia and did not allow the intervention of other countries. They did not unilaterally argue for southward expansion as the direction of Japanese expansion, since they tended to approve of *Hokushin-ron* promoted by the army as a policy essential for the survival of Japan.

In 1935, the army attempted to negotiate with the navy in order to consolidate the basic direction of Japan's national policy into the continental policy. In response to the army's initiative, the navy proposed that a gradual southward advance be carried out and that the navy be expanded in preparation for pressure from Great Britain, the United States, and the Netherlands. In this proposal for a national policy, the navy stated that the scope of a continental policy should be limited to building up Manchukuo and that a further northward advance should not take place. It was a policy of "simultaneous northward and southward expansion," maintaining the *status quo* in the north and advancing into the south.[11]

On the other hand, the army's proposal for a national policy was aimed at advancing deeply into the continent and "eliminating the threat of the Soviet Union in the Far East." Consequently, no compromise emerged from these negotiations between the army and the navy. The famous "Fundamentals of National Policy" adopted by military and government leaders in 1936 recorded both views on northward and southward expansion. Although the navy failed to direct the national policy towards "simultaneous northward and southward expansion," it was able to achieve the approval of "the plan for economic advancement particularly towards Southeast Asia through peaceful means" as a part of the national policy. This had great significance for the development of the southward expansion program.

In the summer of 1935 and continuing through 1936, the navy organized a Policy Study Committee for the South Seas Area. It consisted of twenty-two major staff members from the Navy Department and Navy General Staff, and launched the first systematic Southeast Asian study since the establishment of the navy. It emphasized the study of a specific expansion policy towards Southeast Asia, and proposed two measures. The first was to achieve emigration and economic advancement through fiscal and personnel aids from the Nanyo Kohatsu Kaisha (South Seas Development Company) and the Colonial Ministry rather than from the navy directly.[12] For instance, a report prepared by this committee proposed that the first step in dealing with Portuguese Timor was to have the South Seas Development Company freely exercise its ability to gain a foothold in Timor and lead the native population towards a pro-Japan sentiment. The second measure directed that Taiwan and the South Seas Islands should be utilized as transit bases for advancement into Southeast Asia.[13]

The committee made proposals such as the expansion of the research function of the colonial government in Taiwan and the South Seas Agency; the unification of the administrative organization of the colonial government in Taiwan and the South Seas

Agency; improvement of the transportation and communication facilities necessary for transit bases linking the Japanese mainland and Southeast Asia. Consequently, this study committee did not simply occupy itself with making policies which would argue for an expanded naval force, but it had the goal of forming practical policy guidelines for systematic southward expansion. These guidelines were characterized by "covert aid" as a means of advancement (through the South Seas Development Company) into the targeted area, Southeast Asia, particularly the Dutch East Indies, and the utilization of Taiwan and the South Seas Islands as transit bases. These guidelines were approved in the "Fundamentals of National Policy," and authority was placed behind them.

IV

There were three factors which prompted the formulation of the "Fundamentals of National Policy" based upon the above guidelines. First, the problem of fuel shortages for naval vessels became serious in the latter half of the 1920s, and the petroleum in the Dutch East Indies became a focus of attention. In 1932, at the navy's initiative, the cabinet adopted the Petroleum Industry Law, which mandated a petroleum reserve, the development of overseas petroleum wells, and development of an alternative fuel industry. As a result, the navy independently launched into the development of overseas petroleum wells and alternative fuels. The target area for developing overseas petroleum wells was the Dutch East Indies and the surrounding areas. Specific actions can be seen in the activities of the Kyowa Kogyo Kaisha (Kyowa Mining Company) which was established in June 1936 through the introduction of private capital in order to obtain overseas petroleum well rights.[14]

Kyowa Mining Company, whose establishment was planned and promoted by the navy, had a guarantee of monopolistic rights to research; any oil discovered would be sold to the navy. Additionally, a part of the budget of the Navy Department was approved for the financial stability of the company. The company drilled for oil at a dozen different sites by 1941, but only one well produced petroleum. In short, as the crisis of international isolation became more serious, the request for self-sufficiency in petroleum increased. This prompted the navy's southward expansion program to target the Dutch East Indies more specifically.[15]

Another factor was the enhancement of the status of Taiwan and the South Seas Islands. After the First World War, research and intelligence gathering activities on south China, Southeast Asia, and Australia increased in Taiwan. Chudo, who was stationed in Taiwan in the latter half of the 1920s, became aware of Taiwan's strong interest in Southeast Asia. As a result, he came to believe in Taiwan as "the stronghold of the southward advance," and, with Nakahara, stressed to the top echelon of the Navy the necessity of South Seas studies. This proposal was the origin of the study committee.[16]

One example of the increased role of Taiwan was a long pending issue which preceded the Sino-Japanese War of 1937—the issue of iron ore development in French Indochina. The Japanese Consulate General in Hanoi reported that "Taiwan, which is the advance stronghold of the empire's southward advancement policy, should naturally lead the project, and Taiwan Takushoku Kaisha (Formosa Development Company), which was established for this purpose, should carry out the enterprise." The navy accepted this view and actively supported the development of iron ore.[17]

Meanwhile, there was no progress in the building of military bases in the South Seas Islands, since it was an area where the building of military facilities was banned. However, there was steady economic development, and financial independence was even feasible after 1930. The navy increasingly emphasized the strategic value of the South Seas Islands as "advancement and defense bases for the Japanese mainland." However, the London Naval Treaty of 1930 had limited the possession of submarines and cruisers, and, as a result, the navy's strategic plan against the United States in the western Pacific Ocean suffered a serious blow. In order to correct this deficiency, the decision was made to build air bases in the South Seas Islands.[18]

The Japanese withdrawal from the League of Nations in 1933 did not remove the ban of building military bases in the South Seas Islands, but the secret building of air bases linking the islands began under the direction of the South Seas Development Company in 1934. In the same year, Captain Konishi, who was a prominent promoter of southward expansion, was appointed a naval attaché in the South Seas. Taking advantage of the situation, Konishi began to play a central role in the establishment in 1937 of the Research Institute for South Seas Economy. This research institute printed reports and papers concerning the Southeast Asian situation.[19]

The guidelines for southward expansion formulated between 1935 and 1936 relied on a peaceful and gradual southward advance through economic development and emigration. They also served to control and eliminate aggressive and impetuous views on southward expansion. Actually, the Pakhoi Incident in September, 1936 (a murder case in which a Japanese national was murdered in Pakhoi, Canton province, which was on the opposite shore of Hainan Island) was a turning point. The Navy General Staff, of which Captain Nakahara was a central figure, expounded aggressive views about the occupation of Hainan Island. This occupation would serve to "implant and establish imperial power" on Hainan Island to acquire the right to station forces, establish corporations, build military facilities, and open air routes. However, the top echelons of the Navy Department felt that the occupation of Hainan Island "would reveal the navy's aggressive southward advancement policy." They opposed the proposal and feared that it would arouse the leading powers such as Great Britain, the United States, and France. Thus, they did not adopt this proposal.[20]

Although the guidelines for a peaceful and gradual southward advance seemed to be useful, a new course would soon be needed for the following two reasons. First, anti-Japanese pressure from local authorities supported by Great Britain and the United States

had increased in the Dutch East Indies, and obstacles to the advancement of Japanese emigrants and corporations had been thrown up.
However, the most important factor was that the navy had
expanded its involvement in the operations in south China as the
army further expanded its role on the Chinese continent as the result
of the outbreak of the Sino-Japanese War in 1937 .

After the outbreak of the Sino-Japanese War, the navy took
charge of a naval blockade of the Chinese coast. It also occupied
major ports in south China such as Amoy and Canton. In February
1939, it finally occupied Hainan Island. The purpose of this series of
military interventions in South China was to stop and cut-off the
flow of aid sent by leading powers to the Chiang Kai-sek government. The initiatives concerning policy direction and economic
development in the occupied areas were very conscious of the southward expansion policy. In particular, the occupation of Hainan
Island had very significant meaning for the development of the
navy's policy, for Hainan Island is located at the mid point between
Taiwan and Southeast Asia. Thus, Taiwan-Hainan Islands came to be
considered a transit base for southward expansion.[21]

From the time immediately before the Sino-Japanese War until
1944, retired admirals served as the governors general in Taiwan. In
addition, in 1938, the Naval Military Office was established to aid
the governor general. The views of naval staff in the Naval Military
Office significantly influenced the policy of the colonial government
in Taiwan. In the fall of 1938 and continuing in the following year,
the colonial government in Taiwan promoted the establishment of a
policy to assume control of Hainan Island and the South Seas
Islands. In 1939, the Navy Department urged the adoption of the
"Colonial Government in the South Seas" proposal for annexing the
South Seas Agency.[22]

Iizawa Shoji, a civilian advocate of the southward expansion,
declared that the South Seas policy had entered a new phase with
the possession of Hainan Island.[23] He argued for building a military
facility on Hainan Island, and insisted that Japan should overpower

French Indochina and Singapore by deploying forces on Hainan Island. However, the Navy had no intention of going ahead with a military advancement into Southeast Asia using Hainan Island as a stronghold. Consequently, non military means were considered important. The significant point of policy on Hainan Island was not the building of military facilities, but the development of resources like iron ore and industries. Therefore, the navy actively supported these developments through the colonial government in Taiwan and the Formosa Development Company. The navy financially supported the development of iron ore in French Indochina through the Formosa Development Company.[24]

Establishment of trade relationships promoted by the South Seas Development Company and the Nippon Mining Company in Portuguese Timor—joint venture plans—and plans of joint development of iron ore mines were all carried out under the navy's financial and political support. Also Chudo, who was stationed in Amoi from 1939 to 1940, was engaged in developing a policy to make Chinese merchants residing in French Indochina and south China sympathetic to Japan. This was because strong cooperation with the Chinese merchants was considered important in carrying out a policy of southward expansion.[25]

During the period of the Sino-Japanese War, the navy's southward expansion policy considered the development of a route linking Taiwan, Hainan Island, and Southeast Asia. Its major goal was to expand special rights and penetrate into Southeast Asia from south China through gradual and non-military means.

The outbreak of the Second World War in Europe was an opportunity for Japan actively to advance southward because the war switched the attention of Western colonial powers to Europe. Captain Nakahara of the Japanese Navy wrote in his diary in January, 1940:

> Japan as a nation must be re-oriented as a sea power, concentrating her efforts on naval expansion. In this way, Japan can establish once and all the New Order in East Asia and really settle the China Incident. (To

attain this purpose, Japan should not hesitate even to fight Britain and the United States.)[26]

But such a radical switch in Japan's national policy, advocated by middle-grade officers, could hardly win the support of the more cautious naval leaders.

In fact, the navy's policy (as agreed upon in October 1939) was based on the premise that Japan must not become involved in the European war. Instead, it gave foremost priority to a speedy settlement of the China war, emphasizing that Japan's pressing "central aim" was to make third parties stop their assistance to the Chinese Nationalists. In this respect, the leaders of the navy did not differ much from those in the army and the Foreign Ministry. This policy of non-involvement in the European war was endorsed by all these ministers in late December. This decision prevailed over the dissenting view that "the South Seas regions must become a part of our Empire's self-sufficient economic sphere."[27]

In other words, the navy's southward expansion policy was to be undertaken since it supported the army's continental policy. The navy could disguise its true policy of a southward expansion since it appeared to be part of the attempt by the army to achieve an early settlement of the Sino-Japanese War. It was al so as a result of this process that the navy's expansion policy could no longer control and restrain the army's continental policy, since the navy's *Nanshin-ron* was now part of the army's *Hokushin-ron*.[28]

Notes

1   "Takada Toshitane sho sho kaisoroku" [Memoirs of Rear Admiral Toshitane Takada] deposited in the War History Department, Japanese Defense Agency (hereafter as WHD Archives).

2   Jun Tsunoda, *Manshu mondai to kokubo hoshin* [The Manchurian question and Japan's national defense policy] Hara shobo, 1967, p. 648.; Kaigunsho, ed., *Yamamoto Gonbei to kaigun* [Adm. Yamamoto Gonbei and the Japanese Navy] Hara shobo, 1968, pp. 131–33.

3   Tomoko Masuda, "Kaigun gunbi kakucho o meguru seiji katei, 1906–1914" [The political process of naval arms expansion, 1906–1914], in Kindai Nihon

Kenkyu kai, ed., *Kindai Nihon Kenkyu* [A study of modern Japan], vol. 4, Yamakawa shuppansha, 1982, pp. 411–33.

4 The lead author of the *Kokubo mondai no kenkyu* (A study of the national defense problem) was Rear Admiral Tetsutaro Sato, a naval strategist and exponent of Mahan's doctrine in Japan.

5 For details, see Sadao Asada, "Nihon kaigun to gunshuku: Tai-Bei seisaku o meguru seiji katei" [The Japanese navy and naval limitation: The political process with regard to policy toward the United States], in Chihiro Hosoya and Makoto Saito, eds., *Washington taisei to Nichi-Bei kankei* [The Washington system and Japan-U.S. relations], Tokyo daigku shuppankai, 1978, pp. 353–60.; Sumio Hatano, "Nihon kaigun to nan-shin" [The Japanese navy and the southward expansion policy], in Hajime Shimizu, ed., *Ryotaisen kan ki nihon to nan ajia kankei no shoso* [Some aspects of Japan-Southeast Asia relations in the interwar period], 1986, pp. 208–12.

6 Yoichi Hirama, "Kaigunshi teki ni mita nanshin no ichidanmen" [One aspect of the southward expansion policy of the Japanese navy], in *Seijikeizai Shigaku*, no. 250 (Feb. 1987), pp. 85–99.

7 "Taisho sen'eki senji shorui" [Wartime documents on the first World War], vol. 30, WHD Archives; also see, Masaaki Gabe, "Nihon no mikuronesia senryo to nanshin, 1" [Japanese occupation of Micronesia and southward expansion, part 1], in *Hogaku Kenkyu* (Keio University), vol. 55, no. 7 (July 1982), pp. 84–85.

8 Hajime Shimizu, "Taisho shoki ni okeru nanshin-ron no ichi kosatsu" [A study of "Nanshin-ron" in the early Taisho period], in *Ajia Kenkyu*, vol. 30, no. 1 (April 1983), pp. 1–53.; Tohru Yano, *Nihon no nan'yo shikan* [Japanese historical view of the South Seas], Chuo koron sha, 1979, pp. 123–24.

9 "Chudo Kan'e sho sho mendan kiroku" [Records of interview with Rear Adm. Kan'e Chudo], WHD Archives; Shinpachiro Goto, "Kaigun no nanshin ni tsuite" [On southward expansion of Japanese navy], supplement to *Senshi Sosho; Chugoku homen kaigun sakusen 2* [War history series; Naval operations in China, part 2], Asagumo Shimbunsha, 1971.

10 Hatano, "Nihon kaigun to nanshin," pp. 214–17.

11 Nihon kokusai seiji gakkai, ed., *Taiheiyo senso eno michi; bekakn, shiryo hen* [Road to the Pacific War; supplement, document] Asahi Shimbunsha, 1963, pp. 216–22; Shigeru Fukudome, "Hanko ni kisita teikoku kokubo hoshin" [The national defense policy came to naught], in *Himerareta showa shi* [Secret history of the Showa], 1957, 176–77.

12 For collected materials on the "Tai nanyo hosaku kenkyu iinkai" [The policy study committee on the South Seas], see Akira Doi et al., eds., *Showa shakai keizai shiryo shusei; Kaigunsho shiryo* [Collection of sources on the social and economic history of the Showa period; Documents of the Navy Ministry], vols. 1–2, Ochanomizu shobo, 1978–79.

13 *Ibid.*, vol. 1, pp. 261–62.

14 Irvin H. Anderson, Jr., *The Standard-Vacumm Oil Company and United States East Asian Policy, 1933–1941*, Princeton University Press, 1975, pp. 71–74.; Munehiro Miwa, "Jinzo sekiyu seizoukeikaku to sono zasetu" [The production plan of artificial petroleum and its setback], a master thesis for submission to the Tokyo Institute of Technology in 1984.

15 "Kyowa Kogyo kabushiki kaisha no enkaku to jigyo gaiyo" [Outline of business and history of the Kyowa Mining Company], in "Nakasuji Toichi shiryo" [Papers on Captain Toichi Nakasuji], WHD Archives.

16 "Chudo Kan'e shi mendan kiroku."

17 "Nanyo ni okeru teikoku no riken mondai zakken" [Miscellaneous documents on the problem of concessions in the South Seas], in Japanese Foreign Ministry Archives: E4–2–3–1/1.

18 Mark R. Peattie, *Nan'yo; The Rise and Fall of the Japanese in Micronesia 1885–1945*, University of Hawaii Press, 1988, pp. 230–50.

19 *Ibid.*, pp. 192–93.

20 Toshihiko Shimada, "Kawagoe Chogun kaidan no butaiura 1" [Behind the Kawagoe-Chang Chun conversation, part 1], in *Ajia Kenkyu*, vol. 10, no. 1 (April 1963), pp. 60–67.

21 Hatano, "Nihon kaigun to nanshin," pp. 224–26.

22 Jun Tsunoda, ed., *Gendaishi shiryo* [Documents on contemporary history], vol. 10, Misuzu shobo, 1963, pp. 451–63.; Kohki Ohta, "Kainanto ni okeru kaigun no sangyo kaihatsu" [Development of Hainan Island by the Japanese navy], in Seijikeizai shigaku, no. 199 (Dec. 1982), pp. 3–5.

23 Shoji Iizawa, *Nanshin seisaku no saininshiki* [Recognition of southward advance policy], Takayama shoin, 1939, p. 226.

24 "Yamamoto Yoshio sho sho gyoumu memo" [Memorandum of Rear Admiral Yoshio Yamamoto], WHD Archives.; Ohta, "Kainanto ni okeru kaigun no sangyo kaihatsu," pp. 2–5.

25 "Chudo Kan'e shi mendan kiroku."

26 Diary of Rear Adm. Yoshimasa Nakahara, 15 January 1940, WHD Archives.

27 The description of Japan's reaction to the outbreak of the war in Europe is based on the *Japanese Foreign Ministry Archives*; A1–1–0–30, "Shina jihen shori ni kansuru seisaku" [Policy relating to the settlement of the China incident], 3 vols.

28 For details on *Nanshin-ron* after the outbreak of the European war, see Sadao Asada and Sumio Hatao, "Japan's Decision to move South, 1939–41," in Robert Boyce and Esmonde M. Robertson, eds., *Paths to War; New Essays on the Origins of the Second World War*, Macmillan, 1989, pp. 385–407.

PART II

Responses to the Japanese Challenge

5

The British Merchant Community in Singapore and Japanese Commercial Expansion in the 1930s

IAN BROWN

The external expansion of Japanese economic power in the 1930s was felt in Singapore in two principal ways. The first was a very sharp increase from the early years of the decade in the import of Japanese manufactures, notably cotton and rayon textiles, but also *inter alia* galvanized iron sheets, cement, bicycles, matches, cast iron pipes, crockery. The second was a dramatic increase from the close of 1934 in the involvement of Japanese shipping in the carrying of crude rubber from Singapore to the Atlantic ports of the United States, crude rubber being Singapore's principal primary export in this period and the United States the principal consumer in the world crude rubber market. This essay seeks to examine the response of the British merchant community in Singapore to these primary elements in Japan's commercial expansion. It must be emphasized from the outset that the response was a complex one, and essentially for two reasons. First, there were important divisions of opinion within the community as to the reasons for Japan's recent dramatic commercial advance, broadly between those who focused on 'unfair' Japanese commercial practices (which would now have to be met by the imposition of discriminatory restrictions against Japanese trade) and those who pointed to the contemporary emergence of a powerfully competitive industrial Japan (whose commercial

practices and industrial organization western merchants and manufacturers would now do well to emulate). Second, and more important, there were major divisions of interest within the British
merchant community in Singapore, a reflection of the complex
diversity of trade and commerce carried on in the colony.

Singapore was built on its entrepôt trade, conducted within a
hinterland that extended north to Siam and south, west, and east
through the length of the Malayan archipelago.[1] That trade had two
major components important in the present context. On the one side
was the importation into Singapore, commonly in small consignments, of a range of primary produce cultivated and collected in the
hinterland: once in the colony it was sorted, graded and part-
processed before being shipped to the consuming markets of the
world. On the other side was the importation in large consignments
of a range of manufactures, principally from the industrial west but
increasingly from the industrializing east: in Singapore these were
most frequently broken down, repackaged into smaller consignments, and then shipped to the ports of the hinterland. These two
components of the entrepôt trade were closely complementary. The
existence of an unrivalled range of manufactures in the Singapore
market drew the produce trade into the port: in turn the produce
trade provided the network for the regional distribution of manufactures from the colony. Singapore's entrepôt role was underpinned
by two further considerations—the apparently unshakeable commitment of the colony's administration to free trade, trade free from
both impost and bureaucratic regulation; and the presence of a con-
centration of financial and commercial facilities clearly unmatched
in the region and indeed growing in experience and diversity as the
decades passed.

There were, inevitably, significant shifts in the structure and
direction of Singapore's trade over time. Here it might be noted that,
in the opening decades of the twentieth century, the produce trade
was dominated by just two commodities, tin and (increasingly)
rubber: furthermore it was a trade increasingly drawn from the

immediate hinterland of the Malay States. In other words, Singapore had become, to a significant degree, a Malayan port, specialized in the handling of the peninsula's commodity production. This development was reinforced by the rising importance of direct trade between the outlying ports of the region (including notably Batavia) and the major commodity markets and trading centres outside Southeast Asia. The structure of the British merchant community in Singapore reflected those changes.[2] From the first decade of the twentieth century, the principal firms there increasingly concentrated on the major primary exports, outstandingly rubber (and in this were commonly drawn into the management and administration of the rapidly expanding number of western rubber estates in the Malay States). In this way they reduced their interest in the marginal produce trade (for example the trade in copra, gambier, hides) and, of crucial importance in the present context, in the import of consumer manufactures, notably cotton textiles. The latter trade now appears to have become the principal commitment of a number of the smaller firms.

The diversified interests (and thus perceptions and responses) within the British merchant community in Singapore will be an important focus of this paper. But a warning is in order. It is difficult to tease from the historical record the full diversity of interest at work here, partly because no commercial records of sufficient detail and comprehensiveness appear to survive from the interwar period. But also the principal bodies of merchant opinion whose voices were heard and are recorded (the Singapore Chamber of Commerce, the British Association of Straits Merchants, and the Association of British Malaya) were, it was said, not representative of the full range of interests within the British merchant community in the colony in this period.

I

In February 1933, the governor of the Straits Settlements appointed a commission "to make a diligent and full inquiry into the trade of the Colony, the directions in which it has gained or lost, and the reasons for these gains or losses, and its future potentialities."[3] The commission had a strong merchant representation, for it included nominees of the Singapore Chamber of Commerce, the Singapore Chinese Chamber of Commerce, the Indian Merchants' Association, and commercial organizations in Penang and Malacca. As part of its extensive inquiry the commission undertook a comparatively brief, if detailed, examination of the recent sharp increase in the import of Japanese manufactures into the colony.[4] A number of the commission's witnesses were profoundly disturbed by that development, arguing that unless means were found to check Japan's expansion "a few years may see the elimination of the European import merchant and the Chinese and Indian distributors from the trade of Malaya."[5] But the commission, presumably reflecting the views of its prominent merchants, found this assertion excessively alarmist. And indeed it is clear that in these early years of the 1930s, many important commercial houses in Singapore (and certainly the dominant voices within the western merchant community) were not severely disturbed by Japan's advances in the import trade. From some perspectives, indeed, they could welcome it. A range of influences was at work here.

Central was the argument that if Singapore was to maintain its position as *the* distribution emporium in Southeast Asia for imported manufactures, then the composition by country of origin of the manufactures brought into the colony for re-export must simply reflect the preferences of the bazaars in Singapore's hinterland; and in the early 1930s, those preferences, particularly in the highly important cotton textile trade, were strongly for Japanese manufactures. It was the argument, in other words, that it was not Singapore's role to secure preferred markets for the manufacturers of the mother country, and specifically for the increasingly distressed cotton textile manufacturers of northwest England.[6] The practical working out of this argument could clearly be seen in the colony's textile trade in the early 1930s. For the best part of a century, the leading merchant firms in Singapore had placed their orders with Lancashire, then the dominant producer in this market; now they turned increasingly to Japan.[7]

To some observers, even those with no apparent commitment to Lancashire, this last development was seriously worrying. Drawing on the near-contemporary experience of leading Dutch importers in the Netherlands Indies, they argued that as the major Singapore houses came to deal increasingly in Japanese manufactures they became vulnerable to the establishment of competing Japanese import, distribution and retailing networks. Within a very short time, the latter would claim the trade in Japanese manufactures, leaving the European houses in a now contracting range of western imports where Japan was either unable to compete or found it not worth her while to do so. There was thus, in this view, a real prospect that the functions of importer and distributor in the colony would eventually pass into Japanese hands.[8] But prominent merchant opinion tended to play down that ominous prospect. As far as the immediate hinterland of the Malay States was concerned, the dominant control of distribution networks by Chinese and Indian dealers presented a formidable obstacle to Japanese encroachment; strong Japanese competition was clearly not to be felt across the full range of manufactures imported into and distributed from the colony. Most important, although Japanese manufactures had recently made dramatic advances in many lines (again the cotton textile trade was the outstanding example), for reasons internal to Japan that advance was certain to slow and possibly be partially reversed. Here it was argued that the considerable price advantage now enjoyed by Japanese manufactures in the Singapore market had been secured through a reduction in costs, improvements in efficiency, and, above all, the sharp depreciation of the yen from late 1931. The argument continued that the advantages gained by exchange depreciation could be only temporary, and that, in time, internal costs in Japan (particularly the production costs of those industries heavily dependent on imported raw materials) must surely rise, thus weakening Japan's international competitiveness.[9]

A final strand within merchant opinion was the recognition that the influx of notably cheap Japanese manufactures into the Southeast Asian market had conferred "an immense benefit" upon an Asian population whose money incomes had plummeted with the collapse in primary product prices.[10] The merchants' concern here was not purely an altruistic one, for clearly the buoyancy of real income in local markets served to sustain the trade (immediately in a wide range of manufactures, and then in primary commodities) which constituted their livelihood.

Despite the prominence of these more sanguine perceptions of Japan's dramatic advance in the import trade, the 1933 commission remained sufficiently concerned to give serious consideration to the ways in which it could be repulsed. Four measures were reviewed— an increase in the tariffs then in force in the Malay States and their extension to the Straits Settlements; the compulsory marking of all imports with the name of the country of origin; the introduction of quotas governing the import of articles in which Japan competed; and the levy of a depreciated exchange tax on all Japanese imports.[11] But each was dismissed as either ineffective, seriously damaging to Singapore's free port status (the foundation of her prosperity), or severely inimical to the interests of the poorer classes within the local population. In its conclusion, the commission could only step back from the issue.

> Japanese competition is not peculiar to the trade of the Colony. ... The world-wide seriousness of the problem is recognized, and its solution must be found on larger issues than that presented by its effect upon our local trade.[12]

But then added a warning.

> ... the conditions existing in the Straits Settlements are almost without parallel elsewhere in the Empire. Methods which might meet the situation in other territories could only be introduced here by abandoning the policy upon which Singapore was founded.[13]

On 7 May 1934 the British Government announced the imposition of quotas on the import of foreign cotton and rayon piece goods in most (but not all) British colonies.[14] The immediate initiative for this action was the breakdown of Anglo-Japanese commercial talks, begun the previous February, which had sought to construct market-sharing arrangements in these trades; its longer-term stimulus was pressure on London from a distressed Lancashire. The Straits Settlements was to be included in the quota colonies. And, with the other participating territories, the local administration was now instructed by London to introduce legislation that would give effect to the new imperial policy.

The Singapore Chamber of Commerce, the British Association of Straits Merchants, and the Association of British Malaya (the last two organizations were in London) declared their strong opposition to the imposition of textile quotas, principally on the ground that this "would inevitably damage, most seriously, the entrepôt trade of the colony."[15] In framing its legislation, the Singapore administration had in fact sought to safeguard that trade by excluding from the quotas textiles imported for the purpose of re-export and by providing for the establishment of re-export depots, both publically administered and privately licenced, in which imported textiles destined for the outports would be landed and held. But the body of merchant opinion argued that this last provision offered a far from adequate protection to the entrepôt trade. The fullest statement of this argument was contained in a memorandum prepared by the Singapore Chamber of Commerce and submitted to the Governor of the Straits Settlements towards the end of September 1934 (by which time the quotas were in place).[16]

The Chamber's memorandum was concerned only with the trade in Japanese textiles (naturally so as Japan was the focus of the new textile restrictions), although Japanese manufactures now in fact constituted the most important part of the textile re-export trade. Three principal points were made. It was noted that prior to the introduction of quotas, merchants trading in Japanese textiles had operated in a free market; they were free to dispose of the consignments they brought into the port either in the local (Malayan) market or in the extra-Malayan markets of the wider hinterland, or alternatively they could hold them in godowns [warehouses] to wait for more favourable market conditions. With the imposition of quotas on foreign textiles imported for local consumption, that freedom disappeared; crucially, consignments declared for re-export could not now be redirected to the local market as trading conditions changed. The effect of this restriction, the Singapore Chamber of Commerce argued, was to kill the speculative element in the textile trade—the merchants' practice of placing large orders in Japan in anticipation of market advance, with the knowledge that, on delivery in Singapore, consignments could be directed to wherever market advantage then lay. And it had been that speculative element which, to an important degree, had ensured that the port was richly supplied with textiles, had secured Singapore's position as the pre-eminent regional market in this trade. Second, the Singapore Chamber of Commerce argued, on the basis of extensive inquiries among the port's textile dealers, that the important re-export trade in split packages (that part of the trade in which imports in bulk were broken down into small packages for re-export) simply could not be conducted in the re-export depots. The trade took two forms. In one, Singapore dealers received large numbers of small but precisely-detailed orders from the outports, a few pieces each of several different textiles (to which other goods, for example general provisions or items of hardware, would frequently be added), all to be shipped in the same case. In the other, traders from the outports came into Singapore, selected their requirements piece-by-piece at the premises of one or more dealers, and then themselves took their consignments to the ship by which they were returning. These highly diversified, fragmented transactions could not be handled in the vast spaces of the government's re-export godowns. Finally, the Chamber argued that any scheme of trade regulation, however sympathetically administered, would inevitably involve traders and dealers in delays and uncertainties

as forms were completed and permits sought. This could only discourage trade, the more so as Singapore's merchant community had
long pursued its interests free from bureaucratic regulation. The
essential thrust of the Chamber's argument was that in the changed
conditions brought about by the introduction of quotas, the outports
in Singapore's wider hinterland would increasingly turn to other
markets to meet their textile requirements. The position of Singapore
as the pre-eminent regional textile market would be seriously threatened. But this was not all. To the extent that outport traders were less
frequently drawn to Singapore to secure textiles, they would less frequently bring into the port the primary produce cultivated and collected in the hinterland. The position of Singapore as the
pre-eminent regional centre for the sorting, grading, processing, and
shipment of primary commodities would be seriously damaged.

Merchant opposition drew on two further arguments. It was
pointed out that to restrict the import of cheap Japanese textiles for
local consumption would be to deny the poorer classes an important
defence against the economic distress threatened by collapsing primary commodity prices; and moreover, that the restriction was
being imposed simply to save Lancashire. Put crudely, "the Malay
peasant [and] the low paid Asiatic is to be taxed in the interests of
the Lancashire manufacturer."[17] Second, it was argued that Lancashire would, in fact, secure little or no advantage from the imposition of quotas. The harsh realities were that Lancashire textiles
had become seriously uncompetitive in Southeast Asia and that quotas would not restore their earlier market share. If

> customers cannot—or will not—now buy Lancashire products, they
> are not likely to be induced to do so by restricting or prohibiting the
> sale of similar, but much cheaper, foreign products. They will simply
> supply their needs elsewhere, or through other channels.[18]

And again:

> If Japanese producers cannot send their goods to purchasers through
> the Singapore market, they will find another avenue by which to reach
> them.... Lancashire will gain little or nothing.[19]

It was clearly unjust that the Malay peasant, the Chinese coolie, or, indeed, the Singapore trader should suffer in defence of a manifestly uncompetitive Lancashire manufacturer. It was senseless that they should suffer while Lancashire secured no advantage.

These arguments were forcefully put by Singapore merchants to the local administration, at meetings between the governor and representatives of the Singapore Chamber of Commerce on 11 May and 31 May and again when the government's textile quota legislation was brought before the Legislative Council on 11 June.[20] And they continued to be advanced after the quotas were in place—in the memorandum prepared by the Singapore Chamber of Commerce for submission to the governor in September 1934;[21] in letters from the Association of British Malaya and the British Association of Straits Merchants to the Colonial Office and to the Board of Trade;[22] and in meetings in London and Manchester between John Bagnall, the managing director of the Straits Trading Company (Singapore) and an unofficial member of the Straits Settlements Legislative Council, and the colonial secretary (Sir Philip Cunliffe-Lister) and prominent members of the Manchester Chamber of Commerce.[23] But they were never effectively answered. Indeed on occasions the official response was transparently weak.[24] In reality the fears of the Singapore merchant community were not of central interest to government; the imposition of textile quotas was an imperial policy, initiated by the metropolitan government in defence of metropolitan interests. As the governor of the Straits Settlements told the Legislative Council: "I would never sponsor this Bill as a piece of mere domestic legislation."[25] The quota legislation was pushed through the Straits' legislature in one sitting on 11 June 1934. All the unofficial members voted against, and the legislation was carried only on the administration's inbuilt majority.

As noted above, the Singapore Chamber of Commerce continued at least into September to inveigh against the "great and irreparable harm ... being inflicted upon the entrepôt trade of [the] port."[26] But by late 1934 or the beginning of 1935 its opposition had faded. A government report published in March 1935 was to comment that this later absence of public complaint should not be taken as an indication that "public opinion is necessarily favourable but [rather] that the community including all nationalities of importers has received the scheme with grace and loyalty."[27] However more than grace and loyalty appear to have lain behind the Chamber's later quiescence. Important here was the fact that the Chamber's declared opposition to textile quotas had never commanded the support of a significant minority of its members. At a special general meeting of the Singapore Chamber of Commerce on 1 June 1934, held specifically to consider the administration's recently-announced proposals, one member, L.A. Davies of Henry Waugh & Co., pointed out that those Singapore houses which had long specialized in the import of Lancashire piece goods, houses which in the preceding few years had seen their trade contract sharply in the face of Japanese expansion, would strongly welcome the protection now proposed.[28] He opposed the resolution before the meeting, that the local government be urged not to impose quota restrictions on the import of foreign textiles into Singapore. Davies' stand drew considerable support, for 9 members voted against the resolution (with 23 in favour). He therefore felt sufficiently secure to launch a powerful attack on the Chamber's officers:

> the firms represented on the committee are not vitally interested in the Manchester piece goods trade and ... are indifferent to the survival of that trade in the markets served by Singapore.... [The] shipping, carrying and associated interests are the first thought of this Chamber. Importers, who have so much at stake, deserve a little more consideration.[29]

The disaffection of importing interests then surfaced in the correspondence columns of the *Singapore Free Press* in late January 1935 when "Ten Members of the Singapore Chamber of Commerce" (led by L.A. Davies) testily declared that, when making representations to government, the Chamber's committee had studiously ignored the views of the minority whose interests as merchants did not coincide with their own.[30] And it was prominently aired at the annual

general meeting of the Chamber the following March.[31] As a result
of this division, serious consideration was given to the establishment
of a distinct importers' association in Singapore.[32] In these circumstances, clearly, the declared opposition of the Chamber of Commerce to the textile quotas lost some of its credibility.

But the principal reason for the weakening of the Chamber's
opposition was that, on the government's evidence, its fierce warning that textile quotas would inflict great and irreparable harm upon
the entrepôt trade of Singapore proved to be without foundation. It
had first to be acknowledged that the trade now regulated (the trade
in foreign cotton and rayon piece goods) in fact constituted only a
relatively minor part of Singapore's entrepôt trade.[33] More importantly, data prepared by the Registrar-General of Statistics clearly
indicated that in the first year of regulation (that is to the end of June
1935) the re-export trade in regulated textiles substantially maintained its immediate preregulation volume.[34] It is true that the second half of 1934 saw a fall in textile exports to the Netherlands
Indies as compared with the corresponding period of 1933. But, presumably, the important influence here was the imposition of restrictions on the import of Japanese textiles by the Dutch authorities
rather than unwillingness on the part of traders in the Netherlands
Indies outports to deal through Singapore's re-export depots, and,
crucially, that fall was more than off-set by an increase in exports to
Siam. There was no evidence that new direct channels of trade had
developed between the outports and the industrial economies, trade
that would exclude Singapore.[35]

In December 1937, some three and a half years after it had
imposed quotas on the import of foreign cotton and rayon piece
goods for local consumption, the Singapore administration extended
the restriction to made-up cotton and rayon manufactures.[36] The
administration had found that Japanese textile producers, facing
severe restriction on the import of piece goods, had expanded their
trade in made-up articles, and to such an extent that the effectiveness

of the action taken in mid-1934 to restore the position of British manufacturers in the Malayan textile market had been seriously weakened.[37] On this occasion the Singapore merchant community warmly approved the administration's initiative.[38] Indeed there was some surprise that the extension of the restriction to made-up manufactures had not been carried out earlier.

II

The discussion now turns to consider the dramatic increase from the close of 1934 in the involvement of Japanese shipping in the carrying of crude rubber from Singapore to the Atlantic ports of the United States. According to HM Trade Commissioner in Singapore, the entry of Japanese lines into this highly important trade was prompted by recent reversals they had suffered in the shipment of Philippine sugar to the American market.[39] It was signalled by an application in August 1934 from Mitsui Bussan Kaisha (MBK) and Kokusai Kisen Kaisha (KKK) for admittance to the Straits-United States Conference which at that time had seven members (six British lines and one American).[40] Most of the cargo carried from the Straits in Conference ships consisted of rubber. The Japanese request for admission was granted. Under American law they could not be refused.[41]

The Japanese organizations posed an immediate, severe threat to the existing British and American interests, for on entering the Conference they outbid their competitors when purchasing rubber in Singapore yet sold in New York at a lower price than any other dealer was able to accept.[42] Inevitably the trade fell increasingly into their hands. Having not previously operated on this route, in August–October 1934 MBK and KKK carried about 10 percent of the rubber shipped from the Straits to the United States; between November 1934 and April 1935 this had risen to 15 percent; to 25 percent in June–July 1935; to 34 percent in August–September.[43] In November–December 1935, some 15 months after having entered the Conference, the Japanese lines had secured almost 50 percent of rubber shipments to the United States. This remarkable Japanese advance threatened not only the British lines in the Conference but also the British merchant houses in the Straits which had long commanded the export trade in rubber. In August 1936 one British house stated that it did not expect to remain in that trade for more than a year.[44] Another firm gave itself two years.

There was a sharp contrast of opinions as to the reasons for the Japanese advance. On the one side were merchant allegations of Japanese malpractice—commonly that the Japanese lines operating from the Straits passed on to Japanese merchants engaged there in the purchase of rubber, part or all of the subsidy they were said to receive from their government.[45] The alternative view, advanced prominently by administration, held that the ability of the Japanese to purchase rubber in Singapore at above the local market price and to sell in New York below, derived from superior business organization—the integration of buying, dealing, insurance, shipping, banking, and distribution functions into a single structure, thereby opening major opportunities for greater commercial efficiency and the reduction of costs.[46] The conclusion to be drawn from this last argument—and it was drawn frequently—was that if the British exporting and shipping interests in Singapore were to repulse the Japanese advance in the rubber trade, they would have to emulate Japanese commercial practice and organizational structure.[47] There was a sharp irony here. Just two or three years earlier those dominant voices in the Singapore merchant community had been quick to contrast the archaic industrial practices and structures of Lancashire with the highly efficient methods and organization found in Japan's textile industry; now it was they who needed to follow the Japanese example. This was not the only irony. Two or three years earlier, prominent merchant opinion had argued that the interests of the Malay peasant and the low-paid Asiatic were being well served by the unrestricted influx of cheap Japanese textiles. Could it not now be argued that the interests of the Malay rubber smallholder were being served by the willingness of MBK and KKK to pay above the market price for their output?[48]

In September 1935 a deputation of the British and American lines in the Straits-United States Conference went to Japan to propose to MBK and KKK that their share in the rubber trade, then running at well over 30 percent, be limited to 14 percent.[49] The Japanese refused. Why should they agree? With the Japanese share rising close to 50 percent, negotiations were resumed in December 1935, but this time in Singapore. The British and American lines now proposed that the shipment of rubber from the Straits to the United States be divided between the members of the Conference by means of a quota, with the allocation of cargo being administered through a central booking office. Here was a further irony, for just a year earlier the dominant interests in the Singapore merchant community had sternly opposed the introduction of quotas (on the import of foreign textiles for local consumption) as constituting a damaging breach of the free trade tradition which for over a century had secured the colony's prosperity. The Japanese lines rejected this proposal out of hand and offered instead a voluntary restriction of 6,000 tons a month, equivalent to about 30 percent of the trade. Extended bargaining followed. In June 1936 the two parties were close to agreement: MBK and KKK would be limited to 5,500 tons a month or 26 percent of the trade, whichever was the greater.[50]

At this point the Straits rubber dealers intervened. They informed the Conference that they were not prepared to allow the Japanese lines to take more than 16 percent of the trade.[51] Their resistance arose from two related concerns. It was feared that to allow the Japanese lines such a large share in the carrying of rubber from the Straits to the United States as was close to being agreed would open the way for Japanese dealers in the Straits to secure a comparable dominant position in the local rubber trade. The structure of Japanese business, in which shipping and merchant functions were vertically integrated into a single organization, enabled local Japanese dealers to outbid their western competitors in Singapore's rubber market, either because integration secured important economies or because, allegedly, it permitted the inconspicuous transfer of a substantial proportion of freight receipts from shipping to merchant departments. Second, only approximately one half of the rubber produced in Malaya entered the free market. That was the rubber produced on smallholdings; the rubber produced on the European-owned estates was handled directly through the managing agencies. To allow MBK and KKK 26 percent of rubber shipments as the western lines were close to agreeing therefore implied that they would be handed at least half of the rubber actually offered for sale in the Straits.[52] The commanding position in this trade held until so recently by British houses would be signed away. The Japanese lines would not accept 16 percent (at an earlier point in the bargaining they had been offered 25 percent), and the negotiations again collapsed.[53]

On 17 June 1936 the British and American lines in the Straits-United States Conference cut their rate from US$12.75 to US$8.00 per ton of rubber.[54] This reduction was held until 31 March 1937 and involved the lines in heavy losses. The action was prompted by two considerations. In early June 1936, one of the principal British rubber dealers in the Straits, to protest against the settlement then being proposed with MBK and KKK, chartered a (non-British) vessel outside the Conference to ship some 4,000 tons of rubber to New York. The sharp reduction in the Conference rate thus served to protect those dealers who had remained loyal, indeed to prevent them too from breaking rank.[55] Second the reduction was designed to bring pressure to bear on the Japanese lines—to drive them finally into an agreement, perhaps, or to force them to retreat from the trade.

For the months in which the reduced rate was in force (June 1936–March 1937) the Japanese share in the shipment of rubber from the Straits to the United States was indeed much reduced. At the close of 1935 it had approached 50 percent; in this period it was about 20 percent.[56] But other influences were also at work (and indeed the Japanese were in retreat before the Conference rate was cut).[57] Important here was rising anti-Japanese prejudice in both the United States and the Straits. American dealers who earlier had been content to buy from MBK were in 1937 establishing direct contacts in Singapore.[58] In the Straits, Chinese rubber dealers boycotted the Japanese lines.[59] Indeed the Hin Giap Trading Company, who were the agents in Penang for MBK and who therefore had been responsible for the heavy shipments of rubber from Penang to the United States in Japanese vessels, were in 1937 boycotted by other Chinese firms in the port. When Hin Giap Trading tried to ship through the East Asiatic Company, that concern too fell victim to a Chinese boycott. The Japanese retreat from the Straits-United States rubber trade was also a reflection of sharply increasing demands for tonnage on other sectors. From April 1937 MBK and KKK withdrew vessels from the Straits for redeployment on Japan-United States routes; the outbreak of the Sino-Japanese war in July of that year caused a further withdrawal of tonnage.[60] Thus it was that in the closing months of 1937 (August–November), the Japanese share in the shipment of rubber from the Straits to the United States fell to just 11.4 percent, and this despite the fact that from 1 August the Conference rate had been raised to US$15.00 per ton of rubber.[61]

III

Reference was made earlier to the shifting principles espoused by the dominant merchant interests in Singapore in the face of Japan's commercial expansion. Having sternly opposed the restriction of Japanese textile imports in 1934, in part because it would damage the interests of the Malay peasantry, the following year they sought to restrict Japanese shipments of rubber, although that too would have hurt the Malay community (by denying smallholders higher prices for their production). But, as a concluding remark, reference must also be made to the shifting principles espoused by government. When the western shipping lines and rubber dealers in the Straits proposed that shipments to the United States be divided with

MBK and KKK by means of a quota, to be administered through a central booking office, they urged government intervention if those arrangements could not be secured by voluntary agreement with the Japanese.[62] But government would not intervene to impose this restriction. "[No] powers exist to enable the Government to stop any-one from buying or shipping rubber and I do not see how they could be created consistently with general Government policy," minuted a Colonial Office official in June 1936.[63] But "general policy" had not prevented the metropolitan administration, with domestic political pressure at its back, from intervening to limit severely the ability of the Malay peasant and the low-paid Asiatic to buy cheap Japanese textiles. In such ways does the defence of interest force men into self-contradiction.

NOTES

I wish to thank the participants in the workshop on "International Commercial Rivalry in Southeast Asia in the Interwar Period" held in Shimoda in April 1988 as well as Dr. Paul Kratoska of the National University of Singapore for their valuable comments on an earlier draft of this paper. I am also indebted to Mr. Roderick MacLean, as Executive Director of the Singapore International Chamber of Commerce, for allowing me to consult the Chamber's annual reports for the 1920s and 1930s, held in the Singapore offices; and to the Nuffield Foundation whose generous financial assistance enabled me to make a research visit to Singapore in 1987. I remain responsible for all errors of fact and interpretation.

1   The structure of Singapore's foreign trade in this period is extensively considered in Wong Lin Ken, "Singapore: Its Growth as an Entrepôt Port, 1819–1941," *Journal of Southeast Asian Studies*, IX, 1 (March 1978), pp. 50–84; Chiang Hai Ding, *A History of Straits Settlements Foreign Trade 1870–1915*, Singapore, National Museum, 1978; W.G. Huff, "The Economic Development of Singapore 1900–1939," Ph.D. diss., University of London, 1986.

2   Reference may be made here to J.H. Drabble and P.J. Drake, "The British Agency Houses in Malaysia: Survival in a Changing World," *Journal of Southeast Asian Studies*, XII, 2 (September 1981), pp. 297–328.

3   *Report of the Commission appointed by His Excellency the Governor of the Straits Settlements to enquire into and report on the Trade of the Colony, 1933–1934*, Singapore, Government Printing Office, 1934 [hereafter cited as *SSTC*].

4   *Ibid.*, vol. 1, pp. 55–70.

5   *Ibid.*, vol. 1, p. 63.

6 Addressing the annual general meeting of the Singapore Chamber of Commerce in April 1928, the Chairman noted that although the Chamber's officers were closely watching the increasing competition from Japan in the textile trade, "it was to Lancashire that they must look for the first move." *Singapore Chamber of Commerce Report for the Year 1927*, p. 45. [These annual reports are hereafter cited as *SCCR* followed by the year. They were published by the Singapore Chamber of Commerce, and each Report appeared in the year after that to which it referred.] As will be noted below, the anti-Lancashire sentiment of senior figures in the Chamber increased sharply as Japanese competition intensified in the early 1930s.

7 *SSTC*, vol. 1, p. 59.

8 *Ibid.*, vol. 1, pp. 60–61, 63.

9 *Ibid.*, vol. 1, p. 63; *SCCR 1933*, p. 26.

10 *SSTC*, vol. 1, p. 63.

11 *Ibid.*, vol. 1, pp. 61–63.

12 *Ibid.*, vol. 1, p. 63.

13 *Ibid.*, vol. 1, p. 63.

14 Hiroshi Shimizu, *Anglo-Japanese Trade Rivalry in the Middle East in the Inter-War Period*, London: Ithaca Press, 1986, pp. 46–49.

15 British Association of Straits Merchants to the Under Secretary of State for the Colonies, 8 June 1934. Public Record Office [hereafter PRO] CO323 1305/31838/4.

16 Committee of the Singapore Chamber of Commerce, "Memorandum regarding the effect of the Importation of Textiles (Quotas) Ordinance 1934 on the entrepôt trade of Singapore," 19 September 1934. PRO CO323 1306/31838/4.

17 Straits Settlements, *Proceedings of the Legislative Council*, 11 June 1934, p. B87. This quotation is the Acting Colonial Secretary's characterization of the merchants' argument.

18 Oliver Marks [Secretary, The Association of British Malaya] to the Under Secretary of State for the Colonies, 5 July 1934. PRO CO323 1305/31838/4.

19 *Ibid.*

20 *SCCR 1934*, p. 15; Straits Settlements, *Proceedings of the Legislative Council*, 11 June 1934.

21 Committee of the Singapore Chamber of Commerce, "Memorandum regarding the effect of the Importation of Textiles (Quotas) Ordinance 1934 on the entrepôt trade of Singapore," 19 September 1934. PRO CO323 1306/31838/4.

22 Oliver Marks [Secretary, The Association of British Malaya] to the Under Secretary of State for the Colonies, 14 August 1934; Edward Boustead and Co. [Hon. Secretaries, British Association of Straits Merchants] to the Permanent Secretary to the Board of Trade, 8 November 1934. PRO CO323 1306/31838/4.

23 R. Bond [President, Manchester Chamber of Commerce] to Sir Philip Cunliffe-Lister, 15 November 1934. PRO CO323 1306/31838/4.

24 In response to the argument that the effect of the imposition of quotas on the import of foreign textiles for local consumption would be to tax the poorer classes of Malaya in the interests of the Lancashire manufacturer, the Acting Colonial Secretary argued before the Legislative Council that: "as a result of conditions fostered under British administration, the Malay peasant [and] the low-paid Asiatic has been able in the past to increase very much his consumption of [textiles]... and it would seem that the demands of [these classes] have, up to as recently as 1929, been met very largely by the products of British manufacturers." He went on to note that, from 1929, there had been a considerable fall in the price of British textiles in the Malayan market (it was left to a later speaker to point out that the price of Japanese textiles had fallen far further) before concluding: "it is not unreasonable to expect permanent residents within the limits of the British Empire to make a certain proportion of their purchases from the products of Empire manufacture, particularly at the present time when we seem to have reason to believe that there are signs of returning prosperity." Straits Settlements, *Proceedings of the Legislative Council*, 11 June 1934, p. B87.

25 Straits Settlements, *Proceedings of the Legislative Council*, 11 June 1934, p. B94.

26 Committee of the Singapore Chamber of Commerce, "Memorandum regarding the effect of the Importation of Textiles (Quotas) Ordinance 1934 on the entrepôt trade of Singapore," 19 September 1934. PRO CO323 1306/31838/4. The Chamber offered anecdotal evidence in support of its view, noting, for example, that "one of the oldest and largest Chinese firms in High Street—Messrs. Hon Hing & Co.—are opening up in Medan [East Sumatra] as their customers in that district are beginning to avoid Singapore."

27 J.I. Miller, *Report on the Working and Effects of Quotas on Cotton and Artificial Silk Piece Goods in Malaya and Sarawak during the period 7th May to 31st December, 1934*, Singapore, Government Printing Office, 1935, para. 38. PRO CO852 19/1.

28 *SCCR 1934*, pp. 18–19.

29 *Ibid.*, p. 18.

30 *Singapore Free Press*, 28 January 1935.

31 *SCCR 1934*, pp. 33–35.

32 HM Trade Commissioner, Singapore to the Comptroller General, Department of Overseas Trade [London], 4 April 1935. PRO CO852 19/1.

33 *Singapore Free Press*, 28 January 1935.

34 J.I. Miller, "Report on the Working and Effects of Quotas on Cotton and Artificial Silk Piece Goods in Malaya and Sarawak during the period 1 January to 30 June 1935," 29 August 1935; J.I. Miller, *Report on the Working and Effects of Quotas on Cotton and Artificial Silk Piece Goods in Malaya and Sarawak during the period 7th May to 31st December, 1934*, Singapore, Government Printing Office, 1935, para. 33–34. PRO CO852 19/1.

35 This is an appropriate point to note briefly the impact of the quota scheme on the position of United Kingdom textiles in the Malayan market, for after import of textiles from the United Kingdom into Malaya (that is import for both local consumption and re-export) rose substantially (in terms of volume) in the three years which followed restriction (1935–37), but then fell back. But even in the peak year of 1937, United Kingdom imports were still less than 70 percent of the average for the period between 1927 and 1929; and whereas in the period from 1927 to 1929, textile imports from the United Kingdom had accounted for 46 percent of the total, in 1937 they had fallen to 31 percent. Textile imports from Japan from 1935 to 1937 were virtually half that of 1933; but they still stood at double the volume imported from Japan from 1927 to 1929. It should also be noted that over the period from 1933 to 1937 the gross import of textiles from India into Malaya rose (in terms of volume) by over 750 percent. A. Gilmour, *Annual Report on the Administration of the Quota System Regulating the Importation of Cotton and Artificial Silk into Malaya and Sarawak during the period 1 January to 31 December 1938*, Singapore, Government Printing Office, 1939, p. 6. PRO CO852 224/3.

36 *Straits Times*, 4 December 1937.

37 Minute by C.G. Eastwood, 24 December 1936, on Shenton Thomas [Governor of the Straits Settlements] to W.G. Ormsby Gore [Secretary of State for the Colonies], 21 November 1936. PRO CO852 53/4.

38 R.B. Willmot [HM Trade Commissioner, Singapore] to the Comptroller-General, Department of Overseas Trade [London], 10 December 1937. PRO CO852 109/10.

39 Précis of report submitted by R.B. Willmot [Singapore], T.L. Relton, 5 March 1936. PRO CO852 58/3.

40 *British Shipping in the Orient. Thirty-Eighth Report of the Imperial Shipping Committee*, London, HMSO, 1939 [hereafter cited as *BSO*], para. 282, 284–85.

41 Memorandum [prepared by the British lines], 11 August 1936. PRO CO852 58/3.

42 *BSO*, para. 288.

43 *Ibid.*, para. 286.

44 Memorandum [prepared by the British lines], 11 August 1936. PRO CO852 58/3.

45 Walter Fletcher [Director of Hecht, Levis and Kahn, London rubber dealers and merchants] to the Editor of *The Times*, 19 June 1936. Copy sent to the Colonial Office and now held in PRO CO852 58/3.

46 Minute by G.E.J. Gent, 24 June 1936, on Walter Fletcher to the Editor of *The Times*, 19 June 1936. PRO CO852 58/3.

47 "Report on the Position of British Shipping," 28 July 1937. PRO CO852 117/6. [This report was prepared by an informal committee in Singapore, comprising the Financial Secretary, the Chairman of the Singapore Harbour Board, the Registrar-General of Statistics, and Sir John Bagnall. It was

prepared for submission to the Imperial Shipping Committee in London.] *Straits Times*, 22 July 1936.

48 Minute by G.L.M. Clauson, 22 June 1936, on Walter Fletcher to the Editor of *The Times*, 19 June 1936. PRO CO852 58/3.

49 Memorandum [prepared by the British lines], 11 August 1936. PRO CO852 58/3.

50 *Ibid.*

51 *BSO*, para. 288.

52 *Ibid.*, para. 284; Memorandum [prepared by the British lines], 11 August 1936. PRO CO852 58/3.

53 *BSO*, para. 289.

54 *Ibid.*, para. 289–90.

55 Memorandum [prepared by the British lines], 11 August 1936; Walter Fletcher to Sir John Maffey [Colonial Office], 27 November 1936. PRO CO852 58/3.

56 *BSO*, para. 289.

57 In the six months February–July 1936, the Japanese share had already fallen back to about 30 percent. *BSO*, para. 289.

58 "Report on the Position of British Shipping," 28 July 1937. PRO CO852 117/6.

59 R.B. Willmot [HM Trade Commissioner, Singapore] to M.W. Donald [Empire Division, Department of Overseas Trade, London], 26 October 1937. PRO CO852 117/4.

60 *BSO*, para. 290; R.B. Willmot to M.W. Donald, 26 October 1937. PRO CO852 117/4.

61 *BSO*, para. 290.

62 Memorandum [prepared by the British lines], 11 August 1936. PRO CO852 58/3.

63 Minute by G.L.M. Clauson, 22 June 1936, on Walter Fletcher to the Editor of *The Times*, 19 June 1936. PRO CO852 58/3. Two further arguments were advanced by government: that the Japanese penetration of the rubber trade had served the interests of Malayan producers [Minute by G.L.M. Clauson, 22 June 1936]; that rather than seeking government protection against the Japanese, British shipping lines and dealers in the Straits should seek to emulate the efficient practices of their newly-arrived competitors [G.L.M. Clauson to Shenton Thomas, 30 October 1936. PRO CO852 58/3]. The principles which underlay these arguments had clearly not been applied when the metropolitan administration had taken action to protect Lancashire in the Malayan textile market.

6

Japanese Import Penetration and Dutch Response: Some Aspects of Economic Policy Making in Colonial Indonesia

ANNE BOOTH

Introduction

In 1901, when Queen Wilhemina made her famous speech from the throne concerning the declining welfare of the indigenous population of Java, the structure of the Indonesian economy was, in most respects, typical of a tropical colony.[1] This was particularly true of the foreign trade sector. Exports were dominated by a small number of primary products, of which sugar, coffee, tobacco and tin were the most important; more than 80 per cent of all exports were produced by large estates. There was a substantial imbalance between exports and imports, with much of the export surplus being used to finance remittances abroad on both current and capital account. Although the Netherlands was a small trading nation, Dutch imports accounted for about one third of all imports into Indonesia; the Netherlands and Great Britain together provided almost half of all imports. Dutch-owned trading houses dominated the colony's export and import trade and the financial sector; Dutch and British interests also controlled most of the large estates and mining companies, including the new but rapidly developing petroleum industry.

Almost three decades later, in 1929, the share of the Netherlands and Britain in Indonesian imports had fallen considerably; at the same time there had been a marked increase in imports from two other major industrial powers: Germany and the U.S.A. (Table 1). This change reflected both the growing importance of capital goods in Indonesian imports, and also the growth in per capita incomes of all races in the colony which in turn had led to increasing demand for the kinds of consumer durables which only the major industrial powers could produce. But, by the 1920s another country had also greatly increased its share of Indonesian imports, so that in 1929 it accounted for about the same percentage as Germany, Great Britain, and the U.S.A. That country was Japan. As the first Asian country to industrialise, Japan was still technologically backward compared with the industrial giants of West Europe and North America. But it could manufacture cheaply a range of consumer goods such as cotton cloth, household utensils, and bicycles which appealed to that part of the indigenous population in countries such as Indonesia who were sufficiently affluent to be able to afford a few goods and services beyond what was necessary for bare existence. An important reason for the growth of demand for these types of imports was

Table 6.1 *Percentage distribution of Indonesian imports by country of origin, 1900–1939*

Year	Netherlands	United Kingdom	Germany	U.S.A.	Japan	Other[a]
1900	35.5	12.7	1.6	1.5	0.2	48.5
1915	28.8	20.5	1.1	3.9	3.4	42.3
1920	26.0	18.5	3.4	15.9	12.0	24.2
1929	19.3	10.6	10.5	11.8	10.4	37.4
1934	13.0	8.1	7.3	6.1	31.9	33.6
1939	20.8	7.0	8.6	13.3	17.8	32.5

[a] Includes imports from Singapore and Penang.

Source: Mededeelingenvan het Centraal Kantoor voor de Statistiek, 161, Handelsstatistiek NEI 1874–1937; Indisch Verslag, 1940, p. 339.

that the first three decades of the century had witnessed the rapid emergence of a new type of export producer, the indigenous small-holder. By 1929 over one third of all agricultural exports was being produced by smallholders, compared with only ten per cent in 1898.[2]

Over the five years from 1929 to 1934, the origin and composition of Indonesian imports underwent a further dramatic change. While the nominal value of imports contracted to about one quarter of its 1929 size, the share of Japanese imports in the total leapt to over 30 per cent. This was higher than the share of the Netherlands, Germany, and Great Britain combined (Table 1). At the same time the value of Japanese imports from Indonesia contracted, mainly because of the development of the sugar industry on Formosa, so that the balance of trade which had run in Indonesia's favour up to 1928, turned sharply in Japan's favour over the next five years.[3] The growth of Japanese exports to Indonesia in these years was much more rapid than the growth of her exports to Asia taken as a whole, so that, by 1933, exports to Indonesia comprised 17 per cent of all exports to Asian countries (excluding the colonies of Korea and Formosa) and 8.5 per cent of total Japanese exports. (The corresponding percentages in 1928 had been 8.8 per cent and 3.7 per cent.) In absolute terms, the value of exports to Indonesia was higher than to any other Asian country except British India and China by the early 1930s. Furthermore the official figures almost certainly underestimated the importance of Indonesia as a final destination because a substantial share of Japanese exports to the Straits Settlements almost certainly found their way to Sumatra and Kalimantan.

Although traditionally the Netherlands had always prided itself on its free trade principles, both at home and in its colonies, the magnitude of the changes in Indonesia's trading relationships was such that a response from the Dutch colonial authorities was inevitable. To many in Indonesia, the growth in Japanese exports was viewed as part of a longer term political strategy to undermine the authority of the European colonial powers in Southeast Asia; even such a balanced observer as van Gelderen spoke of an urgent need for "economic defence against monopoly and semi-political penetration."[4] Beginning in 1934, the Dutch colonial authorities began to implement a series of policies which together represented an apparently remarkable break with previous economic management; in fact by 1939 an American observer was writing of "six years of economic planning in Netherlands India."[5] This planning, instigated and implemented by a group of administrators in the Ministry of Economic Affairs under the leadership of Hart and van Mook, took the form of substantial government intervention in, and regulation of, markets for exports, imports, and domestic production in both the agricultural and industrial sectors. According to Barber, from being a "stronghold of free trade and free capitalist enterprise," the economic system of colonial Indonesia underwent progressive modification through the 1930s "in the direction of closer, more detailed and far more studied government control." Furthermore this reaction was in large measure a reaction to the threat posed by growing Japanese economic influence:

> The Dutch have feared the political consequences of Japanese economic penetration and the entire Japanese question in Netherlands India is thus tinged with political considerations. Political considerations weighed heavily in determining the free trade and open door policy of pre-crisis years, since the Netherlands government was well aware that stronger powers, if denied access to the raw materials of the East Indies, might easily be disposed to challenge Dutch control. If free trade, however, enables the Japanese to achieve economic dominance and political influence in the islands, the traditional policy was useless, or worse. Hence a change was indicated, just as when a century ago the Dutch decided that free trade in that day meant the promotion of British goods and influence at the expense of Dutch interests and would have none of it.[6]

While it is not the purpose of this article to dispute the fact that the perception of the "Japanese problem" on the part of the Dutch colonial authorities was heavily overlaid by political and strategic concerns, we will argue that, in fact, there were quite straightforward economic explanations for the rapid growth in Japanese exports to Indonesia in the 1920s and early 1930s. These explanations are to be sought not only, or even primarily, in the trade policies pursued by the Japanese government in these years, but also in the fiscal, monetary, and exchange rate policies of the Dutch colonial authorities. Given these policies, the growth of imports from Japan would probably have occurred anyway, even if Japan had harboured no longer run military and strategic ambitions in Southeast Asia. Indeed a parallel can be drawn between the 1930s and the 1970s, which witnessed an even more pronounced growth in Japanese economic influence in Indonesia. Again this growth in economic penetration had simple economic explanations in terms of the structure and resource endowments of the two economies, although in some quarters of the Indonesian government, suspicions were aroused that once again economic and commercial expansion had deeper significance in terms of Japanese geo-political ambitions in the Western Pacific.

The second purpose of this article will be to argue that the regulatory measures introduced by the Dutch authorities in the latter part of the 1930s should be seen not simply as anti-Japanese policies introduced by an increasingly paranoid colonial government, but rather as part of a completely new economic strategy adopted in reaction to the experience of the 1930s, of which Japanese economic penetration was just one component. We will argue that by the mid-1930s, it was clear to planners in the Ministry of Economic Affairs that if Indonesia were to progress economically and socially, and if living standards were to improve, it would have to diversify its economy and strengthen its industrial base. The policies which they endeavoured to implement over the last few years of Dutch colonial rule in the archipelago were, in fact, radical by the standards of the day. They foreshadowed those subsequently pursued by successive postindependence governments, not just in Indonesia, but in other parts of the developing world. Indeed if there had been no Pacific War, if these policies could have been followed systematically over a longer period of time, and if the transition to independence had taken place in a more orderly and less violent way, Indonesia today could have become a very different country. These are heroic

counter-factual assumptions, but they do force us to view late colonial economic policy making in Indonesia in a new light. But in
order to do that, we must begin with a brief survey of colonial economic development and the role of the Dutch in Indonesia in the
decades before the 1930s.

Growth in the Colonial Economy and the Impact of Foreign Investment

The last century of Dutch colonial rule in Indonesia witnessed a
remarkable transformation of the economy. Not only did the volume
of production of traditional foodcrop and export staples grow, but
new export staples emerged, often with dramatic speed, in response
to new markets in the industrialising countries of Europe and North
America. Although comprehensive national income data have been
compiled only for the interwar years, sufficient evidence on growth
of output is available since the middle of the nineteenth century to
allow at least a rough estimate to be made of gross value of production for a number of years between 1850 and 1937. That it grew in
real terms seems indisputable. Table 2 shows production of major
agricultural and mineral commodities at a number of points in time
between 1850 and 1937, valued at 1937 prices. Over the almost nine
decades from 1850 to 1937, growth averaged three per cent per
annum, although there were considerable fluctuations, with average
annual growth rates being rather lower in the last 15 years of the
nineteenth century and in the 1930s. As population growth was
below two per cent per annum, real output per capita was thus
growing at around one per cent per annum for much of the last century of Dutch rule.

It would thus appear that, around the middle of the nineteenth
century, Indonesia entered what one economic historian has termed
"the phase of intensive growth," characterised by increasing per
capita output. [7] Certainly there were some fluctuations in output
thereafter, but the emergence of many new staples, most notably

Table 6.2 *Gross value of production of rice and export commodities, 1850–1937*

Production value (1937 prices)[a]		Annual average growth rate	
(million guilders)			
1850[b]	92.41		
1885[c]	256.87	1850–1885	3.0
1900[d]	361.57	1885–1900	2.3
1913[e]	537.12	1900–1913	3.1
1920[f]	639.53	1913–1920	2.5
1925[f]	872.50	1920–1925	6.5
1930[f]	1064.63	1925–1930	4.1
1937[f]	2142.32	1930–1937	2.2
		1850–1937	3.0

[a] Rural Java rice price; Java ports wholesale price index for export commodities excepting quinine, palm oil, and palm kernels where unit export values were used, and petroleum where U.S.A. wholesale prices were used.

[b] Rice, coffee, sugar, tobacco, tea.

[c] Rice, coffee, sugar, tobacco, tea, quinine, tin, gold.

[d] Rice, coffee, sugar, tobacco, tea, quinine, tin, gold, copra, petroleum, coal.

[e] Rice, coffee, sugar, tobacco, tea, quinine, tin, gold, copra, petroleum, coal, rubber.

[f] Rice, coffee, sugar, tobacco, tea, quinine, tin, gold, copra, petroleum, coal, rubber, palm oil, palm kernels.

Sources: Mededeelingen van het Centraal Kantoor voor de Statistiek 167, De Economische Ontwikkeling van Nederlandsch-Indie; Indisch Verslag 1940.

Mededeelingen van het Centraal Kantoor voor de Statistiek 146, Prijzen Indexcijfers en Wisselkoersen op Java 1913–37.

rubber and petroleum, more than compensated for the changing fortunes of traditional staples such as sugar and coffee. And in addition to the commodities used to compute the gross value of output shown in Table 2, there was also a considerable expansion in industrial output, culminating in the rapid growth of the factory sector in the late 1930s. The growth of agricultural, mining, and industrial output in turn stimulated growth in other sectors, such as wholesale and retail trade, construction, transport, and banking. Although we do not have the data before 1920 to compile complete GDP figures, it is probable that GDP growth was even faster than the growth in output shown in Table 2.

How important was foreign capital in this growth and diversification of the colonial economy? During the period of the *cultuurs-telsel*, from 1830 to 1870, foreign capital played almost no role in the rapid growth which took place in export production. As Van Niel has pointed out, "European capital, the only capital available at the time, had had varied experiences with colonial agrarian enterprises, and was not attracted to investment in Java because of the high risks."[8] Faced with these obstacles to the private cultivation of export crops, and "desperate for profit from the colony," the Dutch king was persuaded by Van den Bosch to try a quite different mechanism for increasing export crop production. This involved the imposition by government of obligations to grow crops on individual villages.[9] The extraordinary success of the scheme in its first decade in increasing both volume and value of exports can be attributed to several factors: international market conditions were propitious, and the System was successful, at least in the short run, in breaking the labour bottleneck through the brutal but effective method of coercion.[10] However, as the export economy expanded, the government found processing crops, especially sugar, difficult to organise, and increasingly made use of local contractors. These contractors (usually, although not always, Dutch) in turn were able to expand their businesses by ploughing back profits, although the decline in prices in the 1840s meant that some enterprises collapsed, and the government ran up substantial losses on its sugar account.[11]

The practice of financing the expansion of export businesses from operating surpluses was gradually modified in the 1850s and 1860s as the financial sector began to develop and banks and trading houses increased their "consignment credits" to exports. This system was intended to advance short term credit to cover current costs of production; it was however also used to finance investment. The crash finally came in 1884 when sugar prices halved in a matter of months; many export businesses were unable to pay back their loans and the colonial banking system was in a state of crisis from which it had to be rescued by an Amsterdam banking consortium. Modifications in lending practices followed, but the debacle served to strengthen the reluctance of the European financiers to lend to colonial exporters, and they continued to take only a "meagre interest in the extension of risk-bearing capital to enterprises of tropical produce."[12] Although private capital imports did accelerate after 1890, and in the second decade of the twentieth century averaged over one hundred million guilders per annum, they seldom exceeded ten per cent of commodity export earnings (Table 3). Furthermore, only in one decade, the 1890s, did private capital inflows more than offset net additions to private balances abroad.

While some of this foreign capital went into agricultural estates, especially those producing crops such as rubber and high quality cigar tobacco for which the world market was growing rapidly, a considerable amount went into oil and other mining developments, and also into transport and industry. As would be expected, Dutch

Table 6.3 *Trends in the capital account of the balance of payments, 1831–1939*
(annual averages: millions of guilders)

	Current account surplus/deficit	Net additions to private balances abroad	Private capital imports[a]	Balancing items[ab]
1831–1840	-1.6	2.5	-2.5	-1.6
1841–1850	9.2	7.0	0	2.2
1851–1860	12.8	7.8	-1.0	6.0
1861–1870	20.1	23.1	-3.2	0.2
1871–1880	23.2	20.1	-3.5	6.6
1881–1890	10.9	30.3	-20.1	0.7
1891–1900	-3.8	23.9	-27.6	-0.1
1901–1910	21.3	51.3	-42.5	12.5
1911–1920	100.0	206.6	-104.3	-2.2
1921–1930	53.3	136.0	-56.2	-26.5
1931–1940	22.6	39.4	-7.1	-9.7

[a] Negative sign denotes inward flow of capital.

[b] Includes imports and exports of monetary gold and silver, changes in official gold and silver reserves, changes in floating debt of the government, issues of government bonds, purchases of securities abroad, and remittances of life insurance premiums and pension funds.

Source: Korthals Altes (1987), Table 1.

investment dominated; according to Creutzberg more than 2.2 billion from an estimated 2.6 billion guilders of private foreign investment was in Dutch hands in 1922, with much of the rest belonging to British interests.[13] In spite of the so-called "open door" policy to foreign trade and investment, Dutch enterprises were clearly advantaged in what was by far the largest overseas possession of the Netherlands.[14] An important point to note about foreign investment in colonial Indonesia was that much of it was direct, rather than portfolio. Svedberg has shown that, at least up to the first world war, over 90 per cent of foreign private investment in Indonesia was direct. In fact, according to his figures, Indonesia accounted for over two thirds of all the direct foreign investment in Southeast Asia in 1914.[15]

However direct private investment by Dutch, British, and other corporations in the Indonesian economy was by no means the only form of foreign investment in the late colonial economy. As Callis pointed out, "No one can appreciate the extent to which the Indies had recourse to foreign capital without taking into account the large sums poured into the country by way of government loans."[16] His figures showed that "rentier investments," which were mainly government bonds, made up more than one third of total foreign investment in the colonial economy. Government borrowing abroad to finance the budget deficit in fact began in the late nineteenth century, when expenditures exceeded revenues mainly because of the costs of the Achinese War. But with the inauguration of the Ethical Policy after 1900, the composition of government expenditure underwent considerable change. A Dutch historian has recently commented that "development was the prime mandate of the Ethical Policy";[17] this mandate was reflected in the growth of specialist services charged with implementing irrigation expansion, agricultural extension, rural credit, indigenous education, public health, and land settlement outside Java. Between 1900 and 1920, real government expenditures grew at over three per cent per annum, and, by 1921, government spending amounted to over 20 per cent of national income as calculated by Polak.[18] Close to half this amount was devoted to public works and the provision of "development services." But revenues failed to keep up, and, during the second decade of the century, the size of the budget deficit averaged almost 80 billion guilders per annum.

Almost all this deficit was funded through foreign borrowing, and it seems clear that such borrowing permitted the colonial government to accelerate the pace of public sector capital formation compared with what could have been achieved solely from domestic resources. But the cost was a rapidly growing foreign public debt. In the early 1920s, the public debt amounted to almost one quarter of national income, which was certainly high by the standards of the day, and almost all of it ultimately constituted foreign liabilities . With the advent of a more conservative Governor-General in 1921, the situation changed rapidly. Public expenditures fell steeply relative to national income, and the cuts were most severe in development expenditures. Government share of total expenditure on fixed assets, which had been almost 25 per cent in 1921 fell to little more than ten per cent by 1930.[19] By 1929 both total public debt outstanding, and debt service charges had fallen relative to national income. But the early 1930s witnessed another sharp increase in the budget deficit as tax revenues fell faster than expenditure. By 1933, the budget deficit was almost eight per cent of national income, and the accumulated public debt 75 per cent of GDP.[20] By this time government expenditure on capital works had fallen to virtually nothing, and almost the entire budget was devoted to recurrent expenditures of which wages and salaries were by far the largest part.[21]

The Colonial Drain and the Balance of Payments

The evidence that, at least in the interwar years, much of the borrowing on government account went to finance recurrent rather than capital expenditure, together with the continuing evidence that private capital remittances exceeded private capital imports would suggest that the colonial economy derived very little net benefit from either direct foreign investment or foreign borrowing. Indeed critics of Dutch colonial policies have pointed to the very large export surpluses as evidence that much of the wealth produced in Indonesia was remitted abroad, either in the form of company profits to overseas shareholders, or in the form of individual remittances made by well-paid employees in both the public and the private sector. Certainly the magnitude of the "colonial drain" from Indonesia through the balance of payments in the last century of Dutch rule is well recognised. Golay has shown that the ratio of commodity imports to exports never rose above 65 per cent before 1870; for most of the nineteenth and early twentieth centuries, the Indonesian ratio was the lowest in Southeast Asia.[22] Hanson examines the data for 34 developing countries in the latter half of the nineteenth century and reaches the conclusion that only four "fit the pattern of experiencing export surpluses amounting to 25 per cent or more of total exports."[23] These four were Indonesia, Brazil, Thailand, and British India. Until 1870, much of the commodity export surplus financed the colonial contribution to the Netherlands budget and net additions to private balances held abroad. Thereafter, in spite of increases in invisible imports and inward flows in non-monetary gold and silver, much of the enormous export surplus financed private remittances on both current and capital account.

The issue of "unrequited export surpluses" or "colonial drain" was an intensely emotional one in many Asian colonies in the late nineteenth and early twentieth century, and was frequently used by participants in the struggle for independence as an illustration of colonial exploitation. But recent scholars have tended to cast doubt on its importance. In the Indian case it has been argued that, in fact, a considerable part of the commodity export surplus (almost half according to Hanson's data) went on financing imports of precious metals. [24] In fact Hanson suggests that this may also have been true in Indonesia. But the figures on net imports of non-monetary gold and silver presented by Korthals Altes suggest that they played only a minor role in offsetting the balance in commodity trade and were substantially smaller than outward remittances on current account.[25] The question thus remains of the extent to which the commodity trade surplus (which, as we have seen was extremely large by international standards) can be seen as evidence of "exploitation,"either in the sense that it was used to finance unrequited transfers to the home government or outward remittances on private account which were higher than would have been justified by the normal workings of the market. There can be little doubt that the very large unrequited transfers abroad on government account during the years of the *cultuurstelsel* were exploitative in that the domestic economy received virtually nothing back in return. But to what extent did the high level of outward remittances on private account represent simply a "fair return" to the foreign factors of production (capital and skilled labour) invested in the Indonesian economy in ever increasing amounts through the late nineteenth and early twentieth centuries? Certainly many colonial economists thought that this was how they should be regarded. Boeke argued as follows:

> ... colonial capital, whether organised as a private enterprise or as a government activity, serves, works, fertilises, produces; and even if the results of its productive achievements are in part intended for export abroad, all that is left over for, or given to, the native community is pure gain for it. Without western leadership, without help and cooperation from western capital, the "colonial" country would not have developed as it has.[26]

An argument along these lines obviously begs some important questions. Could not some part of the capital and labour imported from abroad have been supplied from domestic sources at lower cost? To what extent were the Western enterprises really essential to the growth of the export sector? Did not the rapid growth of the smallholder export sector after 1900 prove that local producers were just as adept at meeting the challenge of growing world markets, and that indeed they were more efficient in the sense that they used production technologies more appropriate to domestic factor endowments? Were the large profits accruing to Western enterprises in

Indonesia, which were mainly remitted abroad, largely due to government protection against competition from these more efficient domestic producers? It was argued in the case of the rubber sector, for example, that domestic smallholders were just as efficient as foreign ones, who only maintained their dominant position in the interwar period because of government assistance through the allocation of export quotas.[27] In these circumstances, at least part of the returns accruing to the foreign shareholders of the estate companies must be seen as oligopoly profits, rather than as a competitive return to "the enormous risks involved in colonial investment."[28] This is not to say that the colonial economy received no benefits at all from the foreign investment and foreign borrowing which took place, or (more extreme still) that the foreign investment was positively damaging, and the economy would have been better off without it. But it seems indisputable that, had more even-handed policies been pursued by the colonial government to both foreign and indigenous producers, the growth of the domestic economy might have been more rapid.

On the other hand, there is little doubt that the income derived from Indonesia was extremely important to the Netherlands. Economic historians have stressed the importance in the Dutch budget of the government to government remittances in the decades from 1830 to 1870. In his study of industrial retardation in the Netherlands in the 1830s and 1840s, Griffiths argued that "the colonial surplus was to prove the crucial variable in the delicate equation of government solvency."[29] The government remittances ceased in the 1870s, but private remittances on both current and capital account grew rapidly and accounted for a growing share of national income. Using data based on estimates of net profits earned by the corporate sector, Polak has estimated the share of total Indonesian national income accruing to non-residents from 1921 to 1939.[30] This was as high as ten per cent of total national income in the mid-1920s, although it fell rapidly thereafter and became negative in the early 1930s, reflecting the net losses made by the corporate sector. Of course not all these remittances were made to the Netherlands, but given the overwhelming importance of Dutch interests in the colonial economy, it must be assumed that the Netherlands took the greater part. According to the estimates of Derksen and Tinbergen, first published in a confidential memorandum during the second world war, income from Indonesia amounted to 15 per cent of total Dutch national income in the decade from 1925 to 1934. This estimate included income received from company profits, dividends, rents, pensions, and trade in colonial goods and services; in addition, an attempt was made to take into account the "secondary" or multiplier effects of this income.[31] The obvious implication of this calculation was that, if the Netherlands lost control of the colonial economy, there would be a substantial drop in Dutch national income.

Macroeconomic Adjustment in the Interwar Years

For the two interwar decades, the last of Dutch rule in Indonesia, we have a more complete quantitative picture of trends in output and income than for any previous part of the colonial period. Of particular value is Polak's national income study, which calculated income accruing to each of the major ethnic groups in Java and the Outer Islands, as well as government export income and income accruing to non-residents.[32] In real terms, European and foreign Asiatic incomes grew much more rapidly than Indonesian incomes during the 1920s; although the non-indigenous populations were also growing faster, per capita income growth of both the Europeans and the Chinese, particularly the former, was more rapid (Table 4). Throughout the 1920s, the share of total income accruing to non-residents fluctuated between six and ten per cent, while that of Europeans and foreign Asiatics was steadily growing and accounted for 23 per cent in 1930, at which time they constituted under three per cent of the population. But, in spite of the fact that incomes accruing to indigenous Indonesians were growing more slowly than those accruing to other races, the growth of per capita income of indigenous Indonesians between 1921 and 1928 was still quite rapid by Asian

Table 6.4 *Growth in real incomes by ethnic group, 1921–1939*

	Annual average growth[a] in			Population
	Incomes			
Indonesian population	1921–28	1929–34	1935–39	1920–30
Java	2.8	0.6	4.8	1.7
Outer Islands	4.3	-0.3	5.3	2.8
Total	3.3	0.3	4.9	2.0
European	8.6	-5.3	7.2	2.2
Foreign Asians	10.2	-0.8	6.2	4.4

[a] Calculated by fitting an exponential function to the data.
Source: Polak (1943), Table 16.4.

standards. Of the countries for which national income estimates exist, only Burma grew more rapidly in per capita terms in the 1920s (Table 5).

The 1920s was a period of rapid growth in export volume in Indonesia; in fact the annual average growth of over eight per cent was higher than that achieved in any period since the 1830s.[33] It was also higher than that achieved in many other Asian countries in the interwar years; only the Philippines experienced a similar growth in export volume, while that in countries such as Thailand and British India was much slower.[34] But previous periods of rapid export growth, such as the 1830s and the decade leading up to the first world war, were also periods of rising export prices. In the 1920s by contrast, export prices were falling more rapidly than import prices; however the rise in export volume together with the fall in import prices meant that the purchasing power of exports in terms of imports (the income terms of trade) continued to grow (Figure 1). The rapid growth in volume of exports up to 1930 was due mainly to the emergence of two important new commodities, rubber and oil. Oil production more than doubled during the decade, while rubber production trebled; by 1930 these two commodities accounted for 30 per cent of total export earnings, even before the collapse of the

Table 6.5 *Index of growth of real per capita incomes in selected Asian countries,*
1916–1939

(1938 = 100)

Year	Japan[a]	Indonesia[b]	Philippines[c]	India[d]	Burma[e]
1916	60.3	84.8		100.3	112.1
1918	68.4	86.5	107.2	87.5	
1921	71.1	91.1		96.7	96.6
1926	71.1	101.5		104	110.3
1927	73.8	106.3		104	
1928	76.1	109.1	104.7	103.5	
1929	74.8	108.7		107	
1930	75.0	107.3		105	
1931	74.2	100.6		102.8	122.4
1932	75.7	96.3		102	
1933	81.1	93.2		100.7	
1934	86.8	90.5		101.2	
1935	90.7	91.4		99.7	
1936	92.4	95.2		101.7	113.8
1937	95.3	101.7		101	
1938	100	100	100	100	100
1939	106.4	98.3		101.3	
Annual Average Rates of Growth					
1921–39	2.3	0.1	-0.3	0.3	0.2
1921–28	1.0	2.8	-0.2	1.0	2.4

[a] GNE per capita 1934–36 prices.
[b] GDP per capita 1983 prices.
[c] Gross value added per capita 1939 prices.
[d] National income per capita 1938–39 prices.
[e] NDP per capita 1901–2 prices.

Sources: K. Ohkawa and M. Shinohara, *Patterns of Japanese Economic Development: A Quan-titative Appraisal* (New Haven: Yale University Press, 1979), Table A3; Pierre van der Eng "The Real Domestic Product of Indonesia, 1880–1989," *Explorations in Economic History*, vol. 29, 1992, pp. 343–73; Richard W. Hooley, "Long Term Economic Growth of the Philip-pine Economy, 1902–61," *Philippine Economic Journal*, vol. VII (1), pp. 1–24; S. Sivasubra-moniam, *National Income of India, 1900–1 to 1946–7*, Ph.D. diss., Delhi School of Economics, 1965; Aye Hlaing, *An Economic and Statistical Analysis of Economic Development of Burma under British Rule*, Ph.D. diss., University of London, 1965.

sugar industry. The importance of export production in the economy at this time can best be appreciated by the ratio of commodity export earnings to national income; it peaked at 35 per cent in the mid-1920s,

Figure 6.1 *Income terms of trade, 1913–1939*

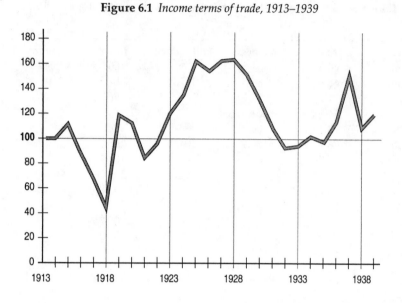

fell slowly until the early 1930s, and then rose once more, reaching almost 35 per cent again in the late 1930s.

The growth of real incomes in the 1920s was reflected in a rapid growth in imports in real terms (Table 6), particularly in the years from 1923 to 1929. Over these years well over 25 per cent of all commodity imports comprised textiles and textile products, most of which were bought by indigenous Indonesians. Although the real value of textile imports grew less rapidly than total imports in the 1920s, the increase was nevertheless substantial, reflecting the growth in indigenous purchasing power. Japan supplied an increasing proportion of these imports through the 1920s, especially cotton cloth.

The most immediate impact of the world depression was on export volume and export prices. Export volume growth was in fact still positive through the decade of the 1930s, although very low compared with the 1920s, but export prices contracted from 1930.

Table 6.6 *Growth in real value of Indonesian imports, 1913–1939*
(1933 = 100)

	All Imports[a]	Textile Products[b]	Imports fromJapan[b]
1913	100	100	100
1920	87	89	572
1925	105	208	640
1926	118	185	656
1927	124	174	765
1928	142	172	805
1929	158	172	987
1930	135	160	925
1931	114	117	1169
1932	92	88	1315
1933	91	77	1894
1934	85	77	1783
1935	83	74	1638
1936	84	76	1462
1937	110	97	1898
1938	111	94	1129
1939	108	92	1365

[a] Nominal value of imports deflated by the general imports component of the Wholesale Price Index.
[b] Nominal value of imports deflated by the textile imports component of the Wholesale Price Index.
Sources: As for Tables 1 and 2.

According to Polak's series on real income by region and ethnic group, total income accruing to all ethnic groups except indigenous Javanese fell, with the most severe downturn in real incomes experienced by the Europeans on the one hand and the Indonesian population outside Java on the other (Table 4). To a large extent, this simply reflected the greater involvement of these two groups in the export economy. Incomes of the indigenous population in Java continued to rise, although at a rate below that of population growth, indicating a general decline in living standards, at least until 1935. The fall in real incomes was reflected in a fall in the real value of imports, although this was far more pronounced for imports as a whole than for textile and clothing imports. Imports from Japan almost doubled in real terms between 1929 and 1933 (Table 6).

Perhaps the most striking feature of the Indonesian economy in the early 1930s was the magnitude of the deflation experienced, especially in rural areas. While the Sauerbeck index of United Kingdom wholesale prices fell by only 2.2 per cent per annum between 1930 and 1935, and the Bombay Labour Secretariat cost of living index fell by 5.6 per cent per annum, the Batavia cost of living index fell by 10.9 per cent, and the index of prices of rural foodstuffs by

Table 6.7 *Movements in prices in selected countries, 1921–1939*
(1913 = 100)

Year	Java[a]	Java[b]	India[c]	Japan[d]	Nether-lands[e]	U.K.[f]	U.S.A.[g]
1921	238	216	173	200	202	182	140
1925	160	165	155	202	179	160	148
1926	159	174	155	179	168	148	143
1927	157	158	154	170	168	143	137
1928	154	148	147	171	169	141	139
1929	153	157	149	166	168	135	137
1930	150	152	137	137	161	114	124
1931	134	102	110	116	151	98	105
1932	112	76	109	122	141	94	93
1933	99	62	102	136	139	93	94
1934	90	61	97	134	140	97	107
1935	87	64	101	140	136	99	115
1936	84	60	102	149	132	105	116
1937	90	68	107	183	137	120	124
1938	92	70	n.a.	207	n.a.	107	113
1939	94	66	n.a.	227	n.a.	112	111

[a] Batavia Retail Price Index.

[b] Rural Java Cost of Food Index.

[c] Bombay Labour Office Cost of Living Index (Base: July 1914).

[d] Tokyo Wholesale Price Index.

[e] Amsterdam Cost of Living Index (Base: 1911–13).

[f] Sauerbeck Index of UK Wholesale Prices.

[g] Wholesale Price Index, USA.

Sources: *Statistical Pocketbook of Indonesia, 1941*, pp. 116–26; *Mededeelingen van het Centraal Kantoor voor de Statistiek 146, Prijzen Indexcijfers en Wisselkoersen op Java 1913–37; Japan Statistical Yearbook*, 1949, Table 361, *Statistical Abstracts of the U.S.A.*, 1942, p. 372.

15.9 per cent per annum (Table 7). The Tokyo Wholesale Price Index by contrast was relatively stable. The adherence of both the Netherlands and the Indies governments to the gold standard until 1936 is the reason usually given for the magnitude of the deflation, although it does not explain why prices fell further and faster in Indonesia than in the Netherlands.[35] Kindleberger argues that "the Dutch and the Swiss clung to gold at the old parity as an act of faith"; of the gold block as a whole he comments: "If recent history would not permit depreciation and pride forebade exchange control (except in the case of Italy), the remaining remedy was deflation."[36] The Dutch colonies had no choice but to follow suit, in spite of the dissenting voices raised by some economists, such as Verrijn Stuart. He stressed the effect of the deflation on the real burden of debt servicing for both government and private enterprise, and, indeed, the ratio of government debt service charges to export earnings in Indonesia had risen to 20 per cent by 1933.[37]

But in spite of the magnitude of the deflation in Indonesia, the guilder underwent a considerable real appreciation against the currency of the colony's major trading partners, particularly Japan (Table 8). By 1934 the real value of the yen in terms of guilders was little more than half what it had been in 1928. Clearly this was a crucial factor in the continuing real growth of Japanese imports after 1930, and particularly after 1932, when Japan abandoned the gold standard and devalued.[38] Another important explanation for the success of Japanese imports in Indonesian markets was, paradoxically, their inferior quality. In a period of declining real incomes, we would expect considerable substitution of lower quality for higher quality goods; such substitution would be most pronounced for basic wage goods such as textiles. As van Gelderen conceded, "Japanese goods were exceedingly cheap, often, but not always, bad, but cheap, and therefore within the reach of the masses with their limited income."[39] It was clearly in the interests of the large estate companies to support a policy of importing cheap wage goods from Japan as they were desperate to prevent further erosion of their

Table 6.8 *Nominal and real rates of exchange[a] of the guilder against other currencies, 1913–1939*

Year	Pound		Dollar		Yen	
	Nominal	Real	Nominal	Real	Nominal	Real
1913	12.1	12.1	2.5	2.5	1.2	1.2
1921	11.7	9.0	3.1	1.8	1.5	1.3
1925	12.0	12.0	2.5	2.0	1.0	1.3
1926	12.1	11.3	2.5	2.2	1.2	1.3
1927	12.1	11.1	2.5	2.2	1.2	1.3
1928	12.1	11.1	2.5	2.2	1.2	1.3
1929	12.1	10.7	2.5	2.2	1.2	1.3
1930	12.1	9.2	2.5	2.1	1.2	1.1
1931	11.3	8.3	2.5	2.0	1.2	1.1
1932	8.8	7.4	2.5	2.1	0.7	0.8
1933	8.3	7.8	2.0	2.0	0.5	0.7
1934	7.5	8.0	1.5	1.8	0.4	0.7
1935	7.3	8.2	1.5	2.0	0.4	0.7
1936	7.8	9.7	1.6	2.2	0.5	0.8
1937	9.0	9.7	1.8	2.5	0.5	1.1
1938	8.9	12.0	1.8	2.2	0.5	1.2
1939	8.3	10.4	1.9	2.2	0.5	1.2

[a] Number of NEI guilders which could be obtained for one unit of the currency shown. The "real" rate of exchange is the nominal rate corrected for the relative rates of inflation in the two countries. The Indonesian rate of inflation was proxied by the Batavia Cost of Living Index. For Japan, U.K., and U.S.A. the price indexes given in Table 7 were used.
Sources: As for Table 7.

international competitiveness. Prevented by their home government from devaluing in step with major competitors such as British Malaya, their only means of surviving in the harsh international climate of the early 1930s was to reduce domestic production costs. A continuing supply of cheap imported wage goods was thus essential if wage goods were to be held down.

Although most Asian countries experienced some real appreciation relative to the yen in these years, the magnitude of the Indonesian appreciation seems to have been unusual. This no doubt helps to explain why the Japanese penetration of Indonesian markets was so successful even relative to other parts of Asia in the early 1930s.

This point can be illustrated by a comparison of the real appreciation (relative to the yen) of the NEI guilder with that of the Indian rupee (the common currency of the entire sub-continent including Burma) in the years between 1928 and 1936 (Table 9). Both the guilder and the rupee rose in value relative to the yen after 1932 (when Japan left the gold standard), but the appreciation was considerably greater in the Indonesian case.

Table 6.9 *Real appreciation of the Indone-sian guilder and British Indian rupee against the Japanese yen, 1928–1936*

	Rupees per yen	NEI guilders per yen
1928	1.6	1.3
1929	1.5	1.3
1930	1.4	1.1
1931	1.6	1.1
1932	1.3	0.8
1933	1.1	0.7
1934	1.1	0.7
1935	1.1	0.7
1936	1.2	0.8

Sources: As for Table 7.

Economic Recovery: 1935–39

After 1935, there was a quite rapid resurgence in the Indonesian economy, and incomes of all groups grew rapidly. In per capita terms, incomes accruing to ethnic Indonesians grew by three per cent per annum; although we do not have reliable estimates for European and Chinese populations after 1930, it would appear that their per capita incomes rapidly returned to pre-1929 levels (Table 4). To what was the recovery due? The decision to leave gold and devalue, finally taken by the Netherlands in 1936, certainly boosted export volume in Indonesia, especially for smallholders. But this improvement was largely offset by continuing low export prices, so that in 1939 the index of the income terms of trade (the purchasing

power of exports in terms of imports) was still well below its 1929
level. A more remarkable aspect of the recovery in the latter part of
the 1930s than the improvement in the export sector was the growth
in production for the home market of both foodcrops and industrial
goods. Output of the six main food staples in Java grew by three per
cent per annum between 1935 and 1940, compared with only 1.5 per
cent per annum in the previous five years. Industrial output growth
was even more spectacular. Using the data on wages and purchases
of domestic materials provided by Polak and other evidence from
Sitsen, Van Oorschot has estimated the real value of output in large,
small, and cottage industry for the years 1928–39.[40] The results show
a very rapid growth in real output in the large factory sector between
1935 and 1939 and a slower, although still impressive growth in the
small-scale sector (Table 10). Overall, output growth was almost 10

Table 6.10 *Real value of industrial output, 1928–1939*
(millions guilders, 1913 prices)

	Value of output[a]			
	Factory sector[b]	Small industry[b]	Household sector[b]	Total
1928	43	81	168	292
1929	54	89	183	326
1930	55	100	180	335
1931	49	100	134	283
1932	59	122	125	306
1933	67	138	111	316
1934	74	152	122	348
1935	76	172	137	385
1936	119	178	130	427
1937	148	180	133	461
1938	181	203	141	525
1939	212	212	127	551
Annual average growth rate				
	15.3	9.6	-2.5	5.9

[a] Nominal output value estimated from the wage data given in Polak (1943), Table 8.2, and deflated by Batavia Retail Price Index.
[b] For explanation of definitions see Polak (1943), p. 47.
Sources: van Oorschot (1956), p. 93.

per cent per annum in the years from 1935 to 1939. By 1939, according to Polak's national income figures by sector of origin, the manufacturing sector accounted for over 17 per cent of total incomes accruing to indigenous Indonesians. For the country as a whole, Polak estimated that manufacturing accounted for 14.9 per cent of Indonesian income, where the sector was defined to exclude the processing of both agricultural and mineral products for export.[41] Van Oorschot has broken down this percentage further into the three components of manufacturing industry which the colonial officials used for statistical purposes: large-scale factory industry, either using mechanised techniques or employing more than 50 workers (4.5 per cent); small-scale industries using manual techniques and employing fewer than 50 workers (5.9 per cent); and cottage industry carried on within households (4.4 per cent).[42]

In spite of the fact that much of the manufacturing sector growth occurred in the large-scale factory sector, while the household sector stagnated, the growth in manufacturing employment in the 1930s was substantial; indeed Van Oorschot has argued that almost half the estimated increment in the labour force in Indonesia in the 1930s was absorbed in factory and small-scale manufacturing, and that employment in these two sectors accounted for about 12.5 per cent of the labour force in 1940.[43] Given that the Population Census scheduled for 1940 was never held, it is not possible to check the accuracy of this assertion, but there is little reason to doubt that the percentage of the labour force in all sectors of manufacturing, including household enterprises, increased from the 10.4 per cent recorded in the 1930 Census.[44] A disproportionate share of this increase probably took place in Java.

What accounted for the remarkable growth in both industrial output and employment in the latter part of the 1930s? The reasons lie in the changes in government policy towards industrial development which occurred as a result of the impact of the depression on the foreign-owned and foreign-dominated sectors of the colonial economy. Although the encouragement of nonagricultural employment had been part of the Ethical Policy since its inception, little had been done before the early 1930s to encourage the development of manufacturing industry by way of direct government assistance. In 1931, the colonial government began to regulate production of the major export industries, and once the precedent of government intervention had been established, controls spread to imports. Import restrictions were seen as particularly necessary because of the growth of Japanese imports, especially of textiles which were both displacing European imports and making impossible any increase in domestic production. As Barber (1939, p. 198) pointed out, all the various arguments which were used to justify the adoption of quantitative restrictions on imports were at bottom concerned with the so-called Japanese threat. [45]

But the import restrictions and other powers to regulate domestic industry also achieved another aim—that of encouraging large multinational companies, many of them from the U.S.A., to establish branches in Indonesia. During the 1930s, companies such as General Motors, Goodyear, National Carbon, Unilever, and Bata all established plants; in addition, breweries, paper mills, canneries, and several large weaving and spinning mills were established by both Dutch and other interests. The importance of these investments can be seen in the balance of payments data presented by Polak; after 1930 new long term investments exceeded outward remittances of profits and dividends by increasing amounts until 1934.[46] It was this influx of foreign capital and technology into the factory sector which was responsible for the very rapid growth rates recorded by Van Oorschot. Some, such as the weaving mills were given import protection, while others were granted exemption from duties on imported inputs. All factories were legally bound to a licensing system which gave government officials discretion to regulate capacity, and in some cases to fix prices. This system survived into the postindependence period and still forms the basis of the system of industrial licensing in contemporary Indonesia.[47]

How did a colonial government hitherto committed to the pursuit of laissez faire policies justify such extensive government involvement in so many sectors of the economy? Boeke (1953, ch. 20) quoted at length from a speech of the then director of the Department of Economic Affairs in 1937 in which he stressed the exceptional nature of the events of the 1930s which had necessitated the growth of government intervention, not just in the Indies, but, indeed, in many other economies as well. However, as Boeke noted, when the director spoke of the future role of government in the development of the colonial economy,

> One gets the impression that not very much of the later Government's interference with the economic life of the Indies was left out in what the speaker had in mind for the future. On the contrary, as a system it was to be supplemented: as he saw it, the Government would have to concern itself not only with the execution of plans derived from private initiative, it would have to take the lead as representative of the common weal.[48]

One can explain this attitude by pointing out that the interventionist policies pursued in the 1930s had led to greatly enhanced power and prestige for the colonial civil servants in the ministries most involved in their implementation, primarily the Department of Economic Affairs, which had come to function very much as a planning body by the end of the decade. Not surprisingly, the senior officials in the department saw the second half of the 1930s as a "turning point" in colonial economic policies, and expressed confidence in the bright industrial future facing Indonesia. Sitsen, who as director of the Department of Economic Affair's industrial division, was hardly an unbiased observer, felt that, by 1940,

> it is clear that the people, formerly satisfied with a minimum of goods which they produced and bought only when absolutely necessary, gradually demanded more and were therefore willing to exert themselves more, although their requirements were still modest. A new spirit has been born and its influence has become perceptible.[49]

Sitsen stressed that in an economy where over 60 per cent of the population was still dependent on agriculture for the bulk of their incomes, the purchasing power of the agricultural sector would be a vital determinant of the pace of industrial growth.[50] He also argued that export markets could be important for some consumer products, although most of the industrial enterprises established in the 1930s were producing import substitutes rather than exportables. Farm incomes were in turn influenced by the agricultural terms of trade, and Sitsen argued that these would have to improve over their interwar performance if the industrial sector's growth was to accelerate. It is clear then, that many of the issues and problems which came to dominate development policy debates in the postwar period in Indonesia and elsewhere had been anticipated by the administrators of the Department of Economic Affairs in the 1930s. This is hardly surprising as any group of policymakers intent on promoting the rapid industrialisation of an agricultural economy have to be concerned with such questions as home and foreign demand, intersectoral terms of trade, and appropriate levels and forms of government assistance. These issues have continued to preoccupy the minds of policymakers in independent Indonesia down to the present day.

It was certainly not the intention of those who formulated policies in Indonesia in the latter part of the 1930s that the economy should become more closed and less reliant on foreign trade, or that the volume of foreign investment in the colony should be reduced. On the contrary, the attraction of new foreign investment was given high priority. The establishment in Indonesia of several large overseas firms in the 1930s meant that, by 1940, the total value of foreign private investment in Indonesia had grown to 3.6 billion guilders, compared with only 2.6 billion guilders in 1922.[51] About half this increase came from Dutch sources and the rest from other countries, especially the U.S.A. The primary aim of the policies pursued after 1934 was to make the Indonesian economy more diversified and thus less vulnerable to external shocks. Certainly the rapid growth of Japanese imports into the colony after 1929 was one reason for the policy changes which occurred, but these changes can hardly be viewed simply as a crude attempt to exclude Japan altogether from the Indonesian economy. Although there was some decline in the real value of Japanese imports into Indonesia after 1933, they had returned to 1933 levels by 1937. Had Japan decided to continue a policy of "peaceful" as distinct from "military" expansionsim in Southeast Asia in the 1940s, it is highly probable that her role in the Indonesian economy as a supplier of imports, and perhaps of capital as well, would have continued to grow. But history decreed otherwise. Whereas it was the sanguine expectation of the Dutch policy-makers that they would be able to continue their experiment in colonial economic development over many years, and perhaps over decades, their plans were brought to an abrupt end by Japanese military force in 1942.

Notes

1   In this essay, the term "Indonesia" will be used to designate the geographical area encompassed by the modern state of Indonesia, regardless of the period referred to.

2   Creutzberg, *Changing Economy in Indonesia, Vol. 1, Indonesia's Export Crops, 1816–1940* (The Hague: M. Nijhoff, 1975).

3   Indonesia's overall balance of trade was positive over these years. Commodity exports exceeded imports by about one third.

4   J. van Gelderen, *The Recent Development of Economic Foreign Policy in the Netherlands East Indies* (London: Longmans Green, 1939).

5   Alvin Barber, "Six Years of Economic Planning in Netherlands India," *Far Eastern Survey* vol VIII (17), pp. 195–203.

6   *Ibid.*, p. 202.

7   Lloyd G. Reynolds, *Economic Growth in the Third World, 1850–1980* (New Haven: Yale University Press, 1985), p. 8.

8   R. van Niel, "The Legacy of the Cultivation System for Subsequent Econoic Development" in Anne Booth, W.J. O'Malley, and Anna Weidemann, eds., *Indonesian Economic History in the Dutch Colonial Era* (New Haven: Yale Southeast Asia Studies Monograph series, No. 35, 1990).

9   R. van Niel, "The Effect of Export Cultivation in Nineteenth Century Java," *Modern Asian Studies* vol. 15 (1), p. 40.

10 Between 1827 and 1840, commodity exports grew in volume terms at over eleven per cent per annum, but from 1840 to 1870, growth slowed to under

two per cent per annum. See Bart van Ark, "The Volume and Price of Indonesian Exports, 1823 to 1940: The Long-Term Trend and its Measurement," *Bulletin of Indonesian Economic Studies* vol. 24 (3), December, pp. 87–120.

11 P. Creutzberg, *Changing Economy in Indonesia vol. 3 Expenditure on Fixed Assets* (The Hague: M. Nijhoff, 1977), p. 17.

12 *Ibid.*, p. 28.

13 *Ibid.*, p. 25.

14 Svedberg has shown that the share of Dutch companies in total foreign direct investment in Indonesia in 1938 was over eight times as high as the Dutch share in all countries outside Europe and North America. See P. Svedburg "Colonial Enforcement of Direct Foreign Investment," vol. 49, 1981, Table 1.

15 See P. Svedburg "The Portfolio-Direct Composition of Private Foreign Investment in 1914 Revisited," *Economic Journal* vol. 88, p. 770.

16 Helmut G. Callis, *Foreign Capital in Southeast Asia* (New York: Institute of Pacific Relations, 1943), p. 35.

17 J. Van Doorn, *The Engineers and the Colonial System: Technocratic Tendencies in the Dutch East Indies* (Rotterdam: Comparative Asian Studies Programme, 1982), Erasmus University.

18 J.J. Polak, *The National Income of the Netherlands Indies 1921–39*(New York: Institute of Pacific Relations, 1943). Reprinted in P. Creutzberg, ed., *Changing Economy in Indonesia, Volume 5 National Income* (The Hague, M. Nijhoff, 1980). It should be noted that a new set of GDP estimates for the interwar years produced by van der Eng are higher than those of Polak, so that the ratio of government expenditure to GDP would be lower. See Pierre van der Eng, "The Real Domestic Product of Indonesia, 1880–1989," *Explorations in Economic History* vol. 29, pp. 343–73.

19 Creutzberg, *Changing Economy, vol. 3*, Table 1.

20 See Anne Booth, "The Evolution of Fiscal Policy and the Role of Government in the Colonial Economy," in Anne Booth, W.J. O'Malley, and Anna Weidemann, eds., *Indonesian Economic History.*

21 P. Creutzberg, *Changing Economy in Indonesia, vol. 2, Public Finance 1816–1939* (The Hague: M. Nijhoff, 1976).

22 Frank Golay, "Southeast Asia: The 'Colonial Drain' Revisited" in C.D. Cowan and O.W. Wolters,eds., *Southeast Asian History and Historiography* (Ithaca: Cornell University Press).

23 John R. Hanson, *Trade in Transition: Exports from the Third World* (New York: Academic Press, 1980), pp. 124–27.

24 *Ibid.*, pp. 127–28.

25 W.L. Korthals Altes, *Changing Economy in Indonesia, vol. 7, Balance of Payments 1822–1939* (The Hague: M. Nijhoff, 1987), Table 1.

26 Jan Boeke, *Economics and Economic Policy of Dual Societies as Exemplified by Indonesia* (Haarlem: Tjeenk Willink, 1953), p. 203.

27 The classic study on this issue remains P.T. Bauer, *The Rubber Industry: A Study in Monopoly and Competition* (London: Longmans Green, 1948). It should be stressed that in spite of the preferential treatment accorded the estates their share of total production of several key export crops declined in the interwar years. By the late 1930s smallholders were producing almost half the total rubber output and an even higher proportion of coffee output.

28 J. Boeke, *Economics and Economic Policy*, p. 203.

29 Richard T. Griffiths, *Industrial Retardation in the Netherlands, 1830–1850* (The Hague: M. Nijhoff, 1979), pp. 47ff.

30 J.J. Polak, *National Income*, Table 15.1.

31 J.B.D. Derksen and J. Tinbergen, "Berekeningen over de Economische Betekenis van Nederlandsch-Indie voor Nederland," as reprinted in C. Fasseur, ed., *Geld en Geweten*, (The Hague: M. Nijhoff, 1980).

32 J.J. Polak, *National Income*, Tables 15.1 and 15.2.

33 These growth rates are calculated from the volume indexes calculated by Van Ark, "The Volume and Price of Indonesian Exports."

34 Anne Booth "Foreign Trade and Domestic Development," in Anne Booth et al., *Indonesian Economic History*.

35 Angus Maddison, Growth, *Crises and Interdependence 1928–38 and 1973–83*, (Paris: OECD Development Centre, 1985), p. 45.

36 Charles P. Kindleberger, *The World in Depression 1929–39*, (Harmondsworth: Penguin Books, 1973), p. 246.

37 G.M. Verrijn Stuart, "The Netherlands During the Recent Depression" in A.D. Gayer, ed., *The Lessons of Monetary Experience: Essays in Honour of Irving Fisher* (New York: Farrer and Rinehart, 1937), p. 248.

38 For a discussion of Japanese economic policymaking in the 1930s, see Kindleberger, *The World in Depression*, especially pp. 162–64, and Kozo Yamamura, "Then Came the Great Depression: Japan's Interwar Years," in Herman van der Wee, ed., *The Great Depression Revisited* (The Hague: M. Nijhoff, 1972). Yamamura gives a detailed account of the decision to leave the Gold Standard.

39 J. van Gelderen, *Recent Development*, p. 20.

40 H.J. Van Oorschot, *De Ontwikkeling van de Nijverheid in Indonesie* (The Hague: Van Hoeve, 1956) p. 93. Van Oorschot draws on data given in Polak, *National Income*, Table 8.2 and Peter H.W. Sitsen, "Industrial Development of the Netherlands Indies," *Bulletin 2*, (New York: Netherlands and Netherlands Indies Council of the Institute of Pacific Relations, 1943), Table XV.

41 Polak, *National Income*, Table 15.4.

42 Van Oorschot, *De Ontwikkeling*, p. 97.

43 *Ibid.*, p. 86.

44 Polak, *National Income*, p. 96.

45 Barber, "Six Years of Economic Planning," p. 198.

46 Polak, *National Income*, Annex 2.

47 Further details of these measures are given in G.M. Van Eeghen, "The Beginnings of Industrialization in Netherlands India," *Far Eastern Survey*, vol. VI (12), June 1937, pp. 129–33 and Ingrid Palmer, "The Indonesian Cotton Textile Industry During Inflation, 1950–65: A Case Study of an Industry in an Underdeveloped Country," Ph.D. diss., Australian National University, 1968. A discussion of the licensing system is given in Boeke, *Economics and Economic Policy*, chapter XXIII. See also the paper by S. Sugiyama in this volume, and H.W. Dick, "Japan's Economic Expansion in the Netherlands Indies between the First and Second World Wars," *Journal of Southeast Asian Studies*, vol 20 (2), (September 1989).

48 Boeke, *Economics and Economic Policy*, p. 234.

49 Sitsen, *Industrial Development*, p. 3.

50 *Ibid.*, p. 54.

51 Creutzberg, *Changing Economy, vol. 3*, p. 25.

7

Japanese-American Trade Rivalry in the Philippines, 1919–1941

MILAGROS C. GUERRERO

American trade and commerce in the Philippines in the years before World War II (1909–1941) were protected by tariff laws that ensured the United States a hefty share of Philippine foreign trade. The passage of the Payne-Aldrich Act by the American Congress in 1909 and the Simmons-Underwood Tariff Act in 1913 established preferential tariff arrangements between the United States and her colony. By means of these laws, American exports entered the Philippines duty-free. Philippine export products like sugar, tobacco, and hemp entered the American market free of duty within certain quota limits from 1909 until 1913. The tariff act of 1913 abolished these quota limitations and established complete free trade between the United States and the Philippines. As a result, American share in the foreign trade of the Philippines increased from 30 per cent in 1899 to 50 per cent in 1919 to 80 per cent at the outbreak of the war in 1941.[1]

On the other hand, while the United Kingdom and Japan had no preferential tariff arrangements with the Philippines, both maintained their positions as the second and third most important trading partners respectively of the Philippines from 1919 to 1921. In 1921, Japan outstripped the United Kingdom to become the second most important trading partner of the Philippines.

During the first thirteen years of the American regime, Japan enjoyed a favourable trade balance in her commerce with the

Philippines, with the margin widening by 1911 when Japan sold the Philippines P4,949,210 worth of goods and imported products worth P744,916 only.[2] The Philippines was unable to wrest any favourable balance of trade from Japan since then. While the United States enjoyed preferential tariff treatment with the Philippines, Japan loomed increasingly on the horizon as the major trading partner of the latter. Even so, until World War I, Japan ranked only as a poor seventh, eighth, or ninth trading partner of the Philippines. In so far as the volume and value of trade were concerned, she trailed behind the United Kingdom, France, Germany, Spain, China, and the Netherlands.

World War I, however, effected major changes in the foreign trade of the Philippines. Although the United States remained the Philippines' most important trading partner, there was a marked tendency on her part to withdraw from the Asian trade and to concentrate all her energy on the war in Europe. Thus, until the re-entry of the United States into the Pacific carrying trade, the Philippines relied more and more on Japan for her basic imports. While the share of the United States in the total imports of the Philippines amounted to four times that of Japan, the latter ranked second on the list of major exporters to the Philippines, with the United Kingdom pushed down to fifth place. In exports from the Philippines, the United Kingdom followed the United States with Japan a dangerous third pressing upon British trade.[3] Imports from Japan consistently remained second to the United States, a position worth noting considering the latter's economic predominance and America's protected market in the colony. Governor-General Theodore Roosevelt, Jr., noted that the United States had been able to obtain a favourable balance of trade with the Philippines because of its preferential tariff laws. On the other hand, without such protection, Japan's favourable balance of trade with the Philippines rose from less than P2 million in 1917 to more than P17 million in 1930.[4]

The Philippines also relied increasingly upon Japanese shipping. Because Japan had developed her merchant marine to a degree comparable with those of the United Kingdom and the United States, she controlled the Pacific carrying trade. In 1903, there were only 9 Japanese vessels engaged in trade in the Philippines as compared to 37 American and 133 British ships. By 1918, there were already 375 Japanese ships operating in the Philippines, providing stiff competition to 257 American and 290 British vessels. Moreover, the cargo transported by incoming Japanese ships was of American and European origin. The United States and Great Britain, however, were ahead of Japan in regard to the value of merchandise carried in their respective ships.[5]

In 1939 the British vessels ranked first, the Japanese vessels came second, and the American ships occupied third place in the foreign carrying trade of the Philippines. Great Britain, with small imports from, and even smaller exports to, the Philippines controlled much of the carrying trade for the country. While the United States had consistently purchased 80 per cent of Philippine export commodities, American ships carried only 7 per cent of Philippine outward-bound freight.[6]

The extent and character of Japan's participation in Philippine foreign trade can be shown more concretely by a direct comparison of the Philippines' import commodities with export crops. In quantitative terms, Japan procured much less of Philippine products than is often supposed. When compared with the United states, Japan was already a major consumer of Philippine export commodities before World War II. During the period from 1926 to 1932, Japan secured her second place position (after the United States) as a heavy user of Philippine unmanufactured abaca. But, in 1932, Japan ranked first as the greatest consumer of abaca, with the United States trailing behind.[7] Japan was also the biggest importer of Philippine lumber, driving to exasperation American lumber interests who feared that they would lose the field to their Asian rival. Japan was also a major importer of Philippine coconut, oil, base metals, sugar, and tobacco.[8] A study of the custom schedule for any month during the above period will show that more than two-thirds of her imports were raw materials rather than manufactured goods is shown by the fact that unmanufactured abaca, raw iron ore, base metals, and unsawn lumber from the Philippines entered Japan duty-free.

On the other hand, Japan sold to the Philippines finished products or semi-processed consumer goods. As Japanese industry matured, a great part of the exports shipped to the Philippines advanced steadily in degree of fabrication and sophistication. Japan found the Philippines a ready market for her cotton, silk, and rayon textile yarns, fabrics, and finished articles as well as iron and steel—products in which the Japanese ranked next to American exporters. The Philippines bought Japanese electrical and non-electrical machinery as well as paper and its manufactures (also rating second to American products). Although cotton products were the main items shipped to the Philippines, the main bulk of Japanese exports included a thousand other items ranging from paper balloons, needles, pins, and matches to heavy machinery and tractors. Japan even led the United States in exporting to the Philippines potatoes, onions, garlic, and other vegetables in which the latter was not self-sufficient.

Notwithstanding the tariff duties on Japanese goods and the United States preferential tariff arrangement with the Philippines, Japan displaced the United States in many ways as the leading supplier of the country—a situation made possible by Japan's proximity to the Philippines, the low cost of labour in Japan, and cheaper freightage and shipping. The following examples may illustrate this point. In 1928, the United States's share (by quantity) of Philippine imports of fish and fish products was 96.01 per cent, while that of Japan was a mere .002 per cent. In 1935, however, American sales dropped to 44.73 per cent as against Japan's increase to 50 per cent.[9] This change occasioned a concerted complaint against Japanese "dumping" from vested interests in fish and fish products in the Pacific Coast states. Likewise, in 1935, Japan secured the bulk of the trade in fresh and canned vegetable and, although a non-dairy country, offered competition to the United States in the sale of milk and milk products. Japan also offered stiff competition to the United States because she manufactured the types of industrial machinery required by the Philippines. Thus, the mining boom of 1938 led to a massive importation of mining machinery from Japan at a quantity much larger than American sales to the Philippines.[10]

Japanese exporters continued to make encroachments into the Philippine market, causing great losses among their American competitors. Nowhere was this more strongly felt than among American textile exporters. Indeed the Philippine textile market became the main arena of Japanese-American commercial rivalry in the years before the two world wars. Largely because of the far more numerous data on the Philippine textile market and Japanese-American rivalry from local and American sources than any other commodity, we are able to present an interesting case study.

Japanese-American Rivalry in the Philippine Textile Market: A Case Study

Textiles, particularly cotton, was the most important commodity of the Philippine import trade. In 1909, when the first tariff law in the Philippines was passed (the Payne-Aldrich Act), imports of cotton cloth were valued at P14 million, of which the United States got 12 per cent while Europe was the principal supplier. Since that year, however, when free trade relations took effect between the United States and her colony, the United States became the Philippines' major supplier. The Japanese began to wrest this dominance in 1929, 1930, and 1931.[11] In a brief letter sent to Francis L. Parker, Chief of the bureau of Insular Affairs, the Textile Export Association of the United States contended that the United States was losing its business in the Philippines to "a very alarming extent" because the tariff law did not adequately protect American products against Japanese goods. While the association acknowledged that the depressed state of American commerce in 1929 might have been responsible for the drop in total American exports of all textiles to the Philippines, it expressed grave concern over the fact that Japan was able to increase its business while the United States lost nearly half of its textile trade in its own colony. Indeed, in 1929, the United States exported to the Philippines cotton textiles worth P24,290,945 while Japan sold to the Philippines goods worth P5,885,703. In 1930, however, the United States shipped only P11,985,559 worth of cotton goods while Japan increased her exports to the Philippines, worth P6,241,657.[12]

In May 1932, the American share of the market was 83 per cent while that of Japan was only 8 per cent. But, in November 1932, Japanese sales of cotton goods rose to 56 per cent while American sales shrank to 32 per cent. Undoubtedly the lifting of the Chinese boycott of Japanese goods throughout Asia contributed to this increase in Japanese sales, but the decline in American sales was blamed by American exporters on high American production costs under the New Recovery program of the Roosevelt administration.[13] In 1934, the Japanese gained a 190 per cent increase in its textile exports to the Philippines while the United States lost 43 per cent. This situation was blamed on ineffective tariff protection of American goods in the Philippine market. According to an article by the Associated Press on 17 February 1934, the United States maintained control of Philippine foreign trade only because of the free trade relations between the Philippines and the United States.[14]

The sentiments of A.G. Kempt, General Manager of Neuss, Hesslein, Inc., a huge textile manufacturing firm, expressed the anxiety with which the textile interests in the United States viewed Japanese strength in the Philippine textile market. Kempt warned that unless some drastic action were taken, American goods would be confronted with the "definite and positive destiny of complete exclusion" from the Philippines. He attributed Japan's increased ability to undersell the United States in this market to the great difference in labour costs, the use of inferior and lower grades of cotton, the markedly lower protection given American goods under the Tariff Act of 1901 (adopted by later tariff laws), and the provisions for a higher wage scale and shorter working hours in the United States National Recovery Act.

Kempt charged the Japanese with copying American styles and designs in textile production, which enabled them to "steal" the American market. The Filipino consumer, attracted by the low prices of Japanese goods, would naturally buy a garment or fabric of the same design and style as those manufactured in the United States.

The existing tariff schedule, "antiquated" and "absolute inadequate," could not protect American exports to the Philippines. Kempt noted that, while the Japanese government was prompt in protecting its industries against foreign competition and would act quickly when the occasion warranted, the American government had been so "cumbersome and befogged that it could not stir itself to action."[15] The tariff schedule adopted in 1901 gave only of the ad valorem protection it had given American textiles twenty-five years earlier.[16]

Senator Ernest W. Gibson, who was appointed by the United States Congress on 16 June 1934 to head a special committee to investigate conditions in the Philippines, expressed concern that, while the United States was preparing to move out of her colony, Japan was, in fact, moving in. In the senator's view, the following factors (which should deserve America's special attention) seemed to buttress this conclusion: Japan's "Asiatic Monroe Doctrine"—the placing of Japanese traders in many parts of the Philippines (who were knowledgeable in the language and customs of the people); the establishment of a Japanese colony of 15,000 on Davao; the acquisition and control by many Japanese business corporations of large tracts of land; the subsidizing of college professors in their studies in Japan; and the implementation of a propaganda program designed to attract the Filipinos to Japanese culture.[17]

Senator Gibson noted in his report in 1935 that the increase in Japan's trade with the Philippines was accompanied by a commensurate decrease in the colony's trade with the United States. This was particularly evident in Philippine imports of cotton goods.[18]

On the other hand, the Bureau of Foreign and Domestic Commerce, United States Department of Commerce, submitted a "strictly confidential" memorandum which indicates that the United States was gravely concerned with the implications of the Philippine Independence Act upon the future of reciprocal trade relations between the Philippines and the United States. Evidence of this drive was the one conducted by the Philippine Sugar Association among the sugar centrals, urging them to purchase their tools, machinery, and supplies from the United States; to ship their sugar to the United States in American bottoms; and to place all their insurance in American companies. The Bureau also recognized that Filipinos were alive to the question of developing the country industrially and economically "in order to lessen the [Philippines'] practical dependence upon the American market." Indeed, there were plans on the part of the insular government to send trade commissioners, upon the establishment of the Commonwealth Government, to Japan or China. Perhaps to influence this trend, the Bureau proposed that, in the 1935 Philippine budget, provisions be made for the training of a diplomatic and consular corps, as much as possible, under American tutelage.[19]

While Filipino leaders and intellectuals were not apprehensive about any Japanese plan for taking over, they were nevertheless concerned over Japan's "peaceful penetration" of the Philippines. The fisheries throughout the archipelago were virtually controlled by the Japanese, often with the connivance of local Filipino officials. Even the government's plan to cultivate large areas of fertile land in Mindanao to rubber and cotton envisioned Japan as the most important market for these products. The Japanese had made great progress in the country's retail trade: not content with large gains obtained in the cities, they had steadily pushed for participation in markets of the countryside. With their superior business acumen and organization as well as their readily available capital, they were expected to play a dominant role in the future economic life of the Philippines.[20]

Indeed, the Chinese offered the only effective opposition to increased Japanese influence in retail trade, and any Filipino competition would, for a long time to come, be quite ineffectual. But, in consolidating their commercial position in the Philippines, the Japanese had succeeded to make inroads into Chinese control of the country's retail trade. The Chinese refusal to trade in cheap Japanese goods—part of an Asia-wide boycott of Japanese products—boomeranged in the Philippines. During 1934 and 1935, the Japanese opened more retail stores stocked with imports from Japan. Some of the larger and older Japanese bazaars also managed a fleet of trucks which brought "Made in Japan" goods to the countryside and sold door-to-door. These Japanese truck merchants succeeded in under-selling Filipino traders and Chinese merchants by 15 to 30 per cent. In Manila, while the Chinese outnumbered all other foreigners four-to-one (there were 29,991 Chinese against 2,374 Japanese and 1,972 Americans), they found themselves powerless against a small group of determined and efficient Japanese who could sell the goods the Filipinos wanted at prices they could afford.[21] Like the Chinese, the Japanese were knowledgeable in the languages and customs of the Filipinos. Thus, it was expected that, upon the independence of the Philippines, the Chinese and the Japanese would continue their struggle for domestic trade supremacy and that, with decreased tariff protection for American goods, the Japanese would be in a position to dominate the import market with the thousand and one articles that the Filipinos needed to buy.[22]

Only one political leader seems to have offered a workable solution to the perceived problem of Japanese "peaceful penetration." Manuel L. Roxas, Under-Secretary of Agriculture and Commerce (later first president of the postwar Philippine Republic), proposed in July 1934 that the Commonwealth Government, which would be inaugurated in the following year, should undertake serious economic planning and immediately establish various industries that would help reduce the economic dependency of the Philippines. Among the Philippine imports, Roxas singled out textiles, particularly cotton goods, because these constituted the country's single biggest item of importation. Roxas noted that the Filipinos had been clothed by American, European, and Japanese cotton mills at the

price of P45,000,000 annually. Roxas estimated that five cotton factories would be adequate to supply the country's need for cotton
goods. He was optimistic that the Philippines could grow all the cotton it needed, particularly if its cultivation were rotated with sugar
cane production.[23]

Discussions in the Philippine Legislature began in mid-1934
over tariff protection for American textiles and other products. In
addition to mounting concern over increased Japanese business in
the Philippines, discussions in the Legislature about a new tariff
law protective of American goods were also a response to the agitation of American textile importers in the Philippines and textile
manufacturers in the United States. The Japanese Embassy in Washington expressed its grave concern over this development. In a conversation with Stanley K. Hornbeck (Chief of the Division of Far
Eastern Affairs at the United States State Department), the Japanese
chargé, I. Fujii, expressed the Japanese government's apprehension
that the proposed measure was intended to cut the flow of Japanese
exports to the Philippines, and that it hoped that the United States
would prevent the approval of any tariff measure coming from the
Filipino law-making body. His instruction was "to request that the
American Government advise the Philippine Government against
making a tariff which would have the effect of interfering with
Japanese-Philippine trade."[24]

In Washington, D.C., the Resident Commissioner of the Philippines, Francisco A. Delgado, offered an alternative to tariff protection which he felt would be detrimental to the Filipinos. Import
quotas could be adopted for a period of years, with the United States
getting the "lion's share" and the remainder divided equitably
among other countries in accordance with their position as exporters
to the Philippines. Delgado assured the United States Congress that
this plan would be satisfactory with all of the trading partners of
the Philippines, for "no foreign nation would justly begrudge the
preferential treatment given the United States."[25]

American textile importers in the Philippines, however, considered the Delgado proposal inadequate for protecting American textiles from the "inroads" of Japanese goods. They preferred a much higher tariff against Japanese goods, but admitted that if a new tariff law could not be passed, then a quota system would be better than nothing at all.[26]

The Japanese Consul-General protested these attempts to limit Philippine importation of non-American textiles, but this was ignored by the Philippine Legislature. But soon after this protest was made, the Philippine Legislature was surprised to receive a message from Washington requesting that discussion of any proposed tariff legislation be postponed until the following year.[27] Speaking before the House of Representatives, Resident Commissioner Pedro Guevara indicated that the Philippine Legislature had indeed wanted to amend the tariff law to protect America's textile trade but that "for some reason beyond its control," it had failed to amend the tariff law. Congressman Hamilton Fish, interpellating, asked if it was not a fact that the State Department objected to the proposed legislation; Guevara retorted that Fish's query was "a very embarrassing question."[28]

The Bureau of Insular Affairs, the main agency responsible for colonial administration, did not favour any tariff legislation that would eventually raise the price of cotton and other textiles, as this would be detrimental to the interests of the Filipino people. Any action by the Philippine government, said Creed F. Cox, Chief of the Bureau, must be taken on their own initiative and without suggestion or prompting from the States. In Manila, Governor Frank Murphy held the opposite view. On 9 July 1935, in his message to the Philippine Legislature, he indicated that he favoured adjustment of the import duties on textiles and believed this would be in the interests of the Filipinos. The governor's remarks prompted a formal request from the Japanese for an explanation. Because the State Department had not initiated them, it was quite embarrassed and uncertain about how to respond to the Japanese request.[29]

Perhaps unaware of the pressure on the Phlippine Legislature, Senator Millard F. Tydings, co-author of the Philippine Independence Act, expressed dismay at the failure of the body to prepare a tariff law favourable to the Americans. He wrote his good friend, George H. Fairchild (who was a leading businessman in Manila) that he was contemplating the proposal of a bill in the United States Congress that would make complete independence an accomplished fact by the fall of 1940, six years earlier than that provided by the Tydings-McDuffie law. He was "driven" to this position, he said, because of the Philippine Legislature "sits idly by while Japanese trade drives out American trade." American trade was losing "hundreds of thousands of Filipino well-wishers while the Japanese retailers are occupying positions, it seems to us, with a more submissive demeanor extended to them than is extended to our native Americans in the islands."[30]

In a conversation between Assistant Secretary of State Francis V. Sayre and Japanese ambassador Hiroshi Saito on 11 April 1935, the former admitted that, indeed, the State Department had discouraged the Philippine Legislature from imposing a heavy duty on cotton textile imports from Japan. Sayre expressed the belief that "unless some remedial action" were taken by Japan, political pressure from the United States congressmen might become "unmanageable."[31] The response of the Japanese Foreign Office was that it would be "difficult" for the Japanese government to control such exports to the Philippines.[32] Even so, the United States government invited Japan to enter discussions about the regulation of Japanese exports of cotton textiles to the Philippines. Japan accepted the invitation and indicated that Japan would enter into an arrangement limiting its exports on the condition that its proposals be accepted by the United States. Japan specified that (1) there would be no increase in tariff for the duration of the arrangement; (2) that there should be no division into different categories of textiles of the total annual allotment; and (3) that the total Japanese allotment might be used at their discretion without division of the allotment into semi-annual, quarterly or monthly allotments.[33]

An interdepartmental committee on the Philippines (composed of representatives from the Commerce, War and State Departments) was created for the purpose of negotiating with the Japanese. It proposed the following terms of a voluntary arrangement limiting Japanese textile exports to the Philippines:

1. the arrangement should be made for a period of two years, with the proviso that it might be reconsidered and revised at the end of one year;

2. a definite quantitative limitation on imports fixed at 40,000,000 square meters;

3. a definite limitation on each type of cloth exported based on average exports for 1933 and 1934; (the types of cloth involved were bleached, unbleached, dyed, and printed cloths);

4. a maximum limitation on imports during any quarter of 15,000,000 square meters and during any one half year of 25,000,000 square meters;

5. a maximum limitation on quarterly exports of each type of cloth;

6. that the Japanese government should exercise its influence to prevent the demoralization of the price structure in the Philippine cotton textile market;

7. the limitation should become effective on 1 May 1935, since conversations begun in April and May and excessive shipments prior to limitation might nullify the beneficial effects of the arrangement; and

8. if tariff rates in the Philippines should be raised, it would be understood that the arrangement could be reconsidered or terminated.[34]

Ambassador Saito expressed the view of cotton goods manufacturers that, since they had purchased a large quantity of cotton from
the United States, if their sales of cotton textiles to the Philippines
and the United States were reduced, they would not have sufficient
credits to purchase American cotton. Saito added that it would be
very difficult to persuade the Japanese manufacturers that they
should voluntarily restrict exports of their products to American territory. Sayre countered that it was not the intention of the United
States to deprive Japan of a fair share of the Philippine market. However, the sharp increase of Japanese textile exports to the Philippines,
along with the wide margin between the price of American and
Japanese textiles tended to "demoralize" the price structure of the
Philippine textile market. Sayre warned that, although the United
States did not have any authority over the tariff policy of its colony,
some arrangement between Japan and the United States along the
lines proposed above might avert the passage of a tariff policy in
the Philippine Legislature that would be disadvantageous to Japanese textiles. [35]

In subsequent discussions, the State Department acquiesced the
assertiveness of the Japanese. Toyoji Inouye and Otoshiro Kuroda,
commercial secretary and attaché respectively of the Japanese
Embassy indicated that a definite guarantee that the Philippine government would not enact a tariff law against Japanese cotton textiles would be their *sine qua non* to voluntary restrictions of their
exports. The American proposals would not only put Japanese commerce in the Philippine in a cage, but would also handcuff it. Kuroda
added that the voluntary restriction would place Japan, at the end of
two years, "entirely at the mercy of the United States."[36]

Negotiations between the United States and Japan on their
respective share of the Philippine textile market continued for
almost seven months. Two prospective policies were discussed in
Washington; the imposition of tariff protection and the application of
a quota system. While the United States was inclined to favour the
former for the protection of its textile exports to the Philippines, this

was eventually discarded since it was counter to Secretary of State Cordell Hull's policy of reciprocity and low tariff. Both parties eventually agreed that the application of a quota system was the only feasible solution. The sticking point, however, was the upper limit of such a quota. The United States insisted on 40,000,000 square meters, which was based on the average of American textile exports for 1933 and 1934; Japan insisted on the maximum limit of 56,000,000 square meters which was based on Japanese exports to the Philippines in 1934. Indeed, Japan's cotton weavers and exporters, at a joint conference on 17 July 1935 of the Japan Cotton Spinners' Association and the Export Cotton Yarn and Textile Dealers' association, made a "spontaneous" decision to restrict exports to the Philippines.[37]

With this decision, the United States finally obtained an agreement with Japan providing for a voluntary restriction by Japanese exporters of cotton goods to the Philippines. The agreement was perhaps the best possible way out of the problem. Sixty-five members of the United States Congress, no doubt responding to pressure from American textile manufacturing interests, had already petitioned the Philippine Legislature to increase the tariff or to impose quota limitations on Japanese textile imports into the Philippines. Despite this vigorous agitation, however, the State Department was not inclined to put pressure upon the Philippine government to institute tariff barriers against Japanese cotton goods. In a conversation between Sayre and the Japanese ambassador, Sayre assured the ambassador that the American government did not contemplate the implementation of a Philippine tariff against Japanese cotton piece goods. He added, however, that the Japanese-American agreement should not be interpreted as binding on the Philippine government.[38]

To allay fears in the Philippines that the United States government had taken the initiative of determining tariff policy, Sayre assured the High Commissioner that the State Department had made no commitment to restrain the Philippine government from legislating any tariff increases against Japanese goods if it were inclined to do so. Sayre had made it clear to the Japanese that it was

the right of the colonial government to institute a new tariff policy if
it felt that such a policy were desirable in the interests of the Filipino people.[39]

Senate President Manuel L. Quezon's reaction to the negotiations in Washington was not without political colour. In a speech
before the Philippine Senate, Quezon said that he was in favour of
providing American textiles adequate protection. But, in light of
America's eventual withdrawal and recent independence legislation, it would be unwise to contemplate such a protectionist measure
since the entire trade relations with the United States itself were in a
'state of indefiniteness and flux.' He noted that the Philippine Legislature hesitated to take action on the proposed tariff because the
United States Congress was itself pursuing protectionist, and, therefore, unfair measures against Philippine products. He was referring
to limitations to free trade embodied in the Tydings-McDuffie Law
and, in particular, to the approval by the United States Congress of
the Jones-Costigan Act, which provided an excise tax on Philippine
coconut oil. An increase in the tariff on Japanese textiles would have
reduced the purchasing power of the Filipinos, as the increased
excise tax had done on coconut oil. The issue of whether or not the
textile market would be governed by either a tariff measure or a
quota system, in Quezon's view, would best be left to the trade conference that President Roosevelt promised he would convene in 1938
"to correct the imperfections and inequalities of the Tydings-
McDuffie Law."[40]

On 11 October 1935, the Japanese Ambassador informed Sayre
that the newly established Association of Japanese Exporters of Cotton Piece Goods to the Philippine Islands would voluntarily limit
exports of Japanese cotton goods for a period of two years beginning
1 August 1935. He assured Sayre that Japanese exports of these
materials would not exceed 45,000,000 square meters annually.[41]

In accordance with the "Gentlemen's Agreement" finally
reached on 11 October, both parties agreed that the maximum
amount that might be exported by Japan during any quota year

should not exceed 45 million square meters. If exports reached 49.5 million square meters during the first year, the maximum in the second year should not go beyond 40.5 million square meters. Both parties also agreed that the maximum quota for the half-year intervals would not exceed 26 million square meters.

The Japanese government also agreed that customs statistics of the Philippines would be used as the index of imports. Since customs statistics were based on the country of origin of the product, regardless of whether such goods were imported directly or through some other country, Japanese products, for example, were credited to Japan. The Japanese ambassador had no objection to this calculation. The Japanese government promised to do its best to prevent shipments to the Philippines of cotton piece goods produced by the Japanese mills in China and to prevent the transshipment of Japanese piece goods at Hong Kong and other points to the Philippines, but it requested that this point be excluded from the agreement.[42]

No sooner had the agreement been implemented than the American textile interests in the Philippines complained that the Japanese were evading their obligations by transshipping cotton goods from Hong Kong. The Mitsui Company, for example, was singled out for this particular violation. Its manager explained that importations of Japanese cotton goods had been contracted for export from the Crown colony to the Philippines months before the agreement was signed.[43]

However, available Philippine customs reports on cotton and rayon piece goods show that the Japanese-American textile agreement had been unsuccessful. The American cotton goods trade continued to lose its position in the Philippine market. Not only had the Japanese failed to abide by the agreement, but it appears that they also diverted the trade to cheap rayon in substitution of cotton and to cheap cotton cloths of Chinese and European manufacturers.[44] The most serious difficulty encountered by American textile interests was the appearance in the Philippine market of great quantities of Japanese textiles transshipped from Hong Kong. Thus, while direct imports from Japan in the first year of the agreement amounted to only 44.0 million square meters—well under the quota—the addition of cotton goods via Hong Kong brought the total to 52.7 million square meters. This was 3.2 million square meters in excess of the maximum quota permitted in any one year. Since shipments through Hong Kong had previously been negligible, their sudden appearance gave rise to suspicions that the quota agreement was being sabotaged. The rise of cotton imports from Hong Kong and China was significant, for it was generally believed that Hong Kong-based cotton goods had their ultimate origin in China where the Japanese owned 23,480 looms (as against 25,596 looms owned by the Chinese).[45]

The American-owned *Manila Daily Bulletin* noted that the fallacy of "agreement regulation" had been seen in advance. Only the "shrewd pressure of advantage and the direct voice of interest" could obtain results favouring American textiles. "It is high time now to press, in the United States," the newspaper advocated, for the abrogation of this "foolish agreement" and the "substitution for it of protection which will really protect."[46] American textile exporters to the Philippines, on the other hand, had criticized the Gentlemen's Agreement since its implementation, and had blamed the State Department for having sponsored it. The Philippine Legislature would have raised cotton textile duties to satisfy American interests if the State Department had not "intervened" by suggesting the Agreement as a substitute.[47]

In an effort to stabilize conditions in the Philippine cotton textile market, the High Commissioner's office suggested that Philippine import duties on all textile schedules from Japan and other countries be revised upward. The United States, on the other hand, passed two separate resolutions urging the Philippine Legislature to protect American cotton products by legislating against Japanese textile exports.[48]

However, because of the lack of a more inclusive law and more enforceable understanding than the textile agreement, the United

States and Japan agreed to a second twelve-month extension of the agreement covering the period from August 1938 to 31 July 1939. The extension provided for a limitation to 45,000,000 million square meters of Japanese cotton exports to the Philippines from whatever source.[49] The agreement was extended twice after July 1939 for a period of one year each.[50]

As a result of the enforcement of the agreement, the price of Japanese cotton goods increased and the United States position as a dominant source of Philippine cotton textile requirements recovered definitely. This resulted to a certain extent, in the indirect taxation of Philippine consumers for the direct benefit of American cotton producers.[51]

The case of the Japanese-American rivalry over the Philippine cotton goods market is a striking illustration of the advantages of a favoured market for American commerce. However, late in the 1930s, it was expected that the United States would also encounter the same problem with Japan with regard to other export items. Instead, the Tydings-McDuffie Law which provided for independence ten years after the establishment of a Commonwealth government in 1935, provided for the gradual imposition of a graduating tariff schedule on the products of the United States and paved the way for a revision of the Philippine tariff on Japanese goods.[52] The imposition of duties on American products would permit Japanese manufacturers to compete on an equal basis and would surely enable others to enter the market. The proposed reduction of American shipments to the Philippines by the Tydings-McDuffie Law and the expected decline in the export trade of the country would naturally result in the reduction of the country's purchasing power. The increased cost of American goods and the reduced purchasing power of the Filipinos would make them more price-conscious, with the result that they would buy in the cheapest and nearest available market. That market would be Japan.

Notes*

1 U.S., Technical Committee to the President, *American- Philippine Trade Relations* (Washington, 1940), p. 40.

2 Philippines, Bureau of Customs, *Annual Report*, 1911 (Manila, 1912), p. 26.

3 In 1918, Japanese trade with the Philippines amounted to P42,144,920 of which P26,208,111 were imports and P15,938,809 were exports. Great Britain's total trade with the Philippines amounted to P44,492,210 with exports (P39,963,396) exceeding imports (P5,528,814). The United States, on the other hand, had a total trade with the Philippines amounting to P295,943,058, with exports valued at P117,649,222 and imports valued at P178,293,837. See Philippines, Bureau of Customs, *Annual Report, 1918* (Manila, 1919), pp. 11–13.

4 Theodore Roosevelt, Jr. to F. LeJ. Parker [BIA Chief], confidential memorandum, October 1932, NARS, RG 350, BIA No. 6144, Incl. 171–1/2.

5 Philippines, Bureau of Census and Statistics, *Census of the Philippines, 1918,* Vol. 4: *Economic Census* (Manila, 1921), Part 2, p. 669.

6 E. Razon, *Shipping Competition in the Pacific*, published by the Philippine Council, Institute of Pacific Relations (Manila, July 1939), p. 2.

7 Philippines, Bureau of Customs, *Annual Report, 1932* (Manila, 1932), p. 5.

8 Japan manufactured plywood and veneer out of unsawn lumber from the Philippines. The bulk of the finished products was later sent to the United States and sold back to the Philippines. See Milagros C. Guerrero, *A Survey of Japanese Trade and Investments in the Philippines, with Special Reference to Philippine American Reactions, 1900–1941* (Quezon City, 1966), pp. 87–96.

9 U.S. Congress, Senate, Committee on Territories and Insular Affairs, *Complete Independence of the Philippine Islands*, Hearings on Senate Bill 1028, 16 February–15 March 1939 (Washington, 19339), pp. 223–24.

10 *Ibid.* See also Carl H. Boehringer, "Increasing variety of Japanese goods imported into the Philippine Islands," 15 October 1934, Special Circular no. 317, Department of Commerce, Division of Regional Information, Far Eastern Series no. 147, NARS, BIA no. 6144, Incl. 189-A.

11 The above data were provided by Speaker Jose Yulo to the Policy Committee of the Joint Preparatory Committee on Philippine Affairs, in "Confidential Minutes," 8 June 1937 in Joint Preparatory Committee on Philippine Affairs, Vol 2: Minutes and Memoranda of the Subcommittees, NARS, RG 59, No. 155.

12 Textile Export Association of the United States to Francis L. Parker, 30 March 1931, NARS, RG350, BIA No. C-1089, with Incl. 131.

13 "Japan Gaining Filipino Trade," Associated Press article cited in U.S., 73d Cong., 2d Sess., *Congressional Record* (9 April 1934), p. 6210.

14 *Ibid.* Textile interests in the United States ignored the causes of price disarrangement brought about by policy changes in the American economy.

While Japanese mills were so organized to help labour costs at a ridiculously low level, American mills were forced to increase their labour costs because of provisions in the National Recovery Act calling for such increases. In addition, American prices were high in comparison with those of Japan because of changes in the exchange rate in the Philippines, Japan, and the United States.

The devaluation of the dollar, plus cotton crop control, increased the price of cotton from 5 to 12 US cents per pound in the 1930s. This increase in the price of cotton, in addition to labour cost increases mentioned above, raised the price of cotton goods from 30 to 40 per cent. Because the peso was tied up with the dollar, no benefit was gained in the purchasing power of the peso in the American market. On the other hand, the yen was also devalued. In 1934, instead of the yen being worth a peso, it was about P.60 or a gain in the purchasing power of the peso in the Japanese market of about 40 per cent. The increase in the American prices of from 30 per cent to 40 per cent, plus the gain in the purchasing power of the peso as against the yen of about 40 per cent, was much more than the tariff protection afforded American goods in the Philippines. See "Cotton Piece Goods, Philippine Market Won by Japan," *American Chamber of Commerce Journal*, Vol. 14, No. 12 (December 1934), p. 97. See also U.S., Tariff Commission, *Recent Developments in the Foreign Trade of Japan, particularly in Relation to the Trade of the United States* (Washington, 1936), p. 25–*et passim*.

15 A.G. Kempt to Frank Murphy (Governor of the Philippines), private and confidential report, 23 February 1934, NARS, RG 350, BIA No. C-1094, with Incl. 119.

16 "Must we permit this?" *The Philippines Herald* (12 January 1935), NARS, RG350, BIA No. C-1094, Incl. 122.

17 U.S., 74th Cong., 1st Sess., Senate Document No. 57, Pt. 2: Investigations of Conditions in the Philippines (Being the Report of Senator W. Gibson as a member of the Senate Special Committee appointed 16 June 1934), (Washington, 1935), p. 7 in NARS, RG 350, BIA No. 22639, with Incl. 119.

18 *Ibid.*

19 C. K. Moser. Recent Developments Relating to the Philippine Islands, "Strictly Confidential," 31 August 1934, NARS, RG 350, BIA No. C-21, Incl. 238-1/2. Moser was Chief of the Far Eastern Section, Bureau of Foreign and Domestic Commerce, U.S. Department of Commerce.

20 Charles Burnett, Memorandum for the U.S. Secretary of War, "Some Observations on Present Conditions in the Philippines," 1 February 1935 in NARS, BIA, RG 350, Charles Burnett, "P" File.

21 [U.S., War Department, Military Intelligence Section], "Japanese Economic Penetration of the Philippines," mimeographed, 27 February 1935, NARS, RG 350, BIA No. 6144, Incl. 194. See also Carl H. Boehringer, "Increasing Variety of Japanese Goods Imported into the Philippine Islands, 15 October 1934," Special Circular No. 317, Department of Commerce, Division of

Regional Information, Far Eastern Series No. 147, NARS, BIA No. 6144, Incl. 189-A.

22 Burnett, "Some Observations."

23 "Dr. Roxas Urges Insular Aid for New Industries," *The Tribune* (28 July 1934) in NARS, RG 350, BIA No. 3262, Incl. 12.

24 Stanley K. Hornbeck, Memorandum of a conversation with the Japanese Chargé, 24 August 1934 in *U.S. Foreign Relations, 1934* (Washington, 1935), pp. 814–15.

25 Congressman J.W. Martin, Jr. to Secretary of State Cordell Hull, 7 February 1935, NARS, RG 350, BIA No. C-1094, with Incl. 119.

26 "Quota Plan Inadequate," *The Philippines Herald* (26 January 1935), in NARS, RG 350, BIA No. C-1094, Incl. 122. "Textile Policy Revealed," *The Philippines Herald* (10 July 1935), BIA News Summary No. 34-1935, NARS, RG 350, BIA No. C-1094, Incl. 122.

27 "Strangling United States Trade," *Washington Herald* (17 January 1935).

28 U. S., 73d Cong., 2d Sess., *Congressional Record* (House), 21 January 1935, p. 715.

29 Creed F. Cox, Memorandum on Cotton Textile Trade in the Philippine Islands, 11 July 1935, NARS, RG 150, BIA No. C-1094, After Incl. 135 and [Comments] on Legislation on Cotton Textiles, n.d., BIA No. C-1094, Incl. 137.

30 Millard E. Tydings to George H. Fairchild, 16 May 1935, NARS, Legislative Reference Section, Sen. 74-A, F23, 141.

31 U. S., *Foreign Relations, 1935* (Washington, 1936), Vol. 3, p. 952.

32 Memorandum of conversation between Eugene H. Dooman (Division of Far Eastern Affairs, State Department) and Mr. Fujii (Counselor of the Japanese Embassy), 25 April 1935, *ibid.*, p. 958.

33 Memorandum of conversation between Dooman and Fujii, 30 April 1935, *ibid.*, p. 960.

34 Memorandum of suggested terms of a voluntary arrangement limiting Japanese exports of cotton piece goods to the Philippines, 7 May 1935, *ibid.*, pp. 960–62.

35 Eugene H. Dooman, Memorandum of 23 May 1935, *ibid.*, pp. 963–65.

36 Dooman, Memorandum of 25 May and 15 June 1935, *ibid.*, pp. 966–71.

37 "Washington, Tokyo Ignores the Philippines," *The Philippines Herald* (30 July 1935), in BIA News Summary in NARS, RG 350, BIA No. C-1094, Incl. 122.

38 Francis V. Sayre to Frank Murphy, 13 October 1935; Memorandum of conversation between Sayre and the Japanese Ambassador, 11 October 1935 (Imports into the Philippine Islands of Japanese Cotton Textiles); Alvin H. Hansen, Memorandum to the Japanese Committee, 12 July 1935, NARS, RG 350, BIA No. C-1094, with Inc. 131.

39 Sayre to Murphy, 29 October 1935, *U.S. Foreign Relations, 1935* (Washington, 1936), Vol. 3, pp. 1013–16.

40 "Textiles must wait," *The Tribune* (19 July 1935), in NARS, RG 350, BIA No. C-1094, with Incl. 131.

41 D. C. McDonald (Acting BIA Chief) to Frank Murphy, Radiogram No. 576, 12 October 1935, NARS, RG 107, No. 1330.

42 Memorandum of Agreement, 11 October 1935 in *U.S. Foreign Relations, 1935* (Washington, 1936), Vol. 3, pp. 1007–8; Sayre to Murphy, [29 October 1935], NARS, RG 350, BIA No. C-1094, with Incl. 131.

43 Murphy to Secretary of War, Radiogram No. 526, 29 October 1935, NARS, RG 350, BIA No. C-1094, with Incl. 131. Sayre to Inter-Departmental Committee, Extract from BIA Radiogram No. 620 to the Governor-General, 30 October 1935, NARS, RG 350, BIA No. C-1094, with Incl. 131.

44 Paul V. McNutt, [Confidential] Letter to Franklin D. Roosevelt, 21 July 1937, *Quezon Papers*.

45 Miriam S. Farley, "First Year of Philippine Textile Agreement," *Far Eastern Survey*. Vol. 5, No. 21 (21 October 1936), p. 228.

46 Quoted in "Opinion," *Commonwealth Advocate* (June, 2d half 1936), p. 27.

47 Eugene H. Dooman, et al. to Stanley K. Hornbeck, [Confidential report concerning the Philippine Cotton Textile Agreement with Japan], 13 August 1935, NARS, RG 350, BIA No. C-1094, with Incl. 131.

48 McNutt, [Confidential] Letter to Franklin D. Roosevelt.

49 U.S. High Commissioner to the Philippines, *Annual Report*, January 1938–June 1939 (Washington, 1940), p. 334.

50 "Se extiende para otro año el convenio sobre los tejidos de algodon," *La Vanguardia* (16 July 1940), in Quezon Papers, Newsclippings.

51 U.S., Department of State, "Voluntary Limitation of Shipments of Japanese Cotton," in U.S., Joint Preparatory Committee on Philippine Affairs, *A Report of May 10, 1938* (Washington, 1939), p. 98.

52 U.S., Tariff Commission, *United States-Philippine Trade with Special Reference to the Philippine Independence and Other Recent Legislation* (Washington, 1937), Vol. 1, p. 141.

*Abbreviations
BIA—Bureau of Insular Affairs
NARS—U.S. National Archives
RG—Record Group

8

Nationalism and Pro-Japanese Activities in Thailand

Benjamin A. Batson

Southeast Asia in the interwar period consisted almost entirely of British, Dutch, French, American, and (to a very minor degree) Portuguese colonial possessions; of the Western imperialist powers, only the Americans in the Philippines had given any serious indication that their continued political control would be anything less than "indefinite." The one exception to this colonial mosaic, of course, was "independent" Siam (Thailand). But even in the case of Siam, the degree of real sovereignty has often been questioned and such labels as "semi-colonial" applied. Proponents of this view could cite a range of evidence. Siam was still subject to the system of "unequal treaties," by which, in the mid-nineteenth century, the Western powers had forced the Thai leadership to concede wide-ranging political and economic privileges, entailing severe restrictions on Thai sovereignty. Only in the 1920s were serious and sustained efforts at treaty revision undertaken and, while these efforts were ultimately successful, not until the late 1930s was the final dismantling of the system of treaty privileges accomplished. There had also been substantial territorial concessions to France and Britain. Furthermore, an extensive network of "foreign advisers" extended foreign, especially Western, influence through virtually every ministry of the Thai government. It was argued that, in many cases, "advice" in fact bordered on "control." And in the economic sphere, the commercialized sector of Siam's economy had been integrated into the world capitalist market system. Siam's external trade (and indeed many sectors of its internal commerce, including banking) was dominated by "foreign" interests—Chinese, Western (of whom the British were by far the most important), and, in the last decade before the outbreak of the Pacific War, Japanese as well. The June 1932 coup which overthrew the British-oriented absolute monarchy brought to power a regime bent on asserting more aggressively "nationalistic" policies, both in the political and economic spheres. But progress in reducing foreign influencing was often slow and uneven and, in the short run at least, the decline of traditional foreign interests—Chinese and Western—was replaced by a new external influence—Japanese.

If Siam in the late nineteenth and early twentieth centuries may be classified as "semi-colonial," the Thai leadership nevertheless succeeded in maintaining its country's independence in the formal, legalistic sense. This fact was to have profound consequences. It meant that, in most cases, top level decision making remained in Thai hands, whether in choosing economic priorities (*e.g.* favouring railway construction at the expense of irrigation and agricultural development) or political options, such as Siam's entry into World War I on the side of the Allies. And of particular relevance, Siam's unique status as an independent Southeast Asian state meant that both the form that nationalism took in Siam and the nature of Thai-Japanese relations in the first decades of the twentieth century would be markedly different from the nationalist movements and the relationships with Japan that developed in the colonial areas of Southeast Asia.

Thai Nationalism

Perhaps no term has been used more frequently in modern historical and political analysis than "nationalism," yet its meaning remains elusive. It can, it seems, appear in any area of the world in almost any group, be politically "rightist" or "leftist," be progressive or reactionary. In the words of one scholar, looking particularly at European evidence,

> As a conceptual tool, it often strikes the historian or political thinker as impossibly fuzzy: threatening to merge into patriotism or national consciousness at one end and fascism and anti-individualism at the other ...[1]

Thai "nationalism" would seem particularly difficult to categorize. Most other modern Asian nationalisms and all other modern Southeast Asian nationalist movements have had as their central motivation and goal the throwing off of foreign rule and the establishment of national independence, a focus which—at least in a legalistic sense—was absent in the Thai case. It has been suggested that, in the twentieth century, European nationalism on the whole has been a bad thing and Asian nationalism a good thing. To put it another way, nationalism of dominant groups within an established political entity tends to be expansive and dangerous, while nationalism seeking to establish a political expression of a felt national identity is justified and positive. In these terms, it may seem that modern Thai (and perhaps also Japanese) nationalism is, in a sense, more like that of Europe, and that, in both cases, the rise of nationalist impulses within the dominant groups of established political entities has led to the pursuit of some questionable goals.

The usual pattern of Southeast Asian nationalist movements can arguably be described as "nationalism-from-below," directed against the (colonial) state, mass-based if not mass-led (indeed the leaders were generally relatively privileged members of the "counter-elite," *e.g.* Rizal, Ho Chi Minh, Sukarno, etc.), and often politically leftist. Thai nationalism, in contrast, came predominantly "from above," sponsored by the state and its leaders, most notably the monarchy in the years prior to 1932 and the military in much of the period since. As such, it has tended to be traditionalist, conservative, and hierarchical—characteristics reflected in the literature's frequent use of such labels as "official nationalism,"[2] "elite national-ism,"[3] or *"sakdina* nationalism."[4]

This unique—in the Southeast Asian context—form taken by Thai nationalism prior to the Pacific War was, as suggested above, in considerable part due to Siam's non-colonial status and the conse-quent lack of an independence movement as a focus for nationalist sentiments. Similarly, Siam's success in maintaining at least a for-mal state of independence meant that Thai foreign relations in the late nineteenth and early twentieth centuries were quite different from those of the colonial areas of Southeast Asia.

The new international environment of the nineteenth century, and most importantly the imposition of a series of treaties and a new economic order, opened Siam to a flood of foreign influences—polit-ical, economic, and intellectual. The impact of the West, from nar-rower aspects of technology to organizational techniques and a wide range of "isms," was most apparent and has been most intensively studied. In Siam as elsewhere in Southeast Asia, however, a consid-erable part of this "Western" influence came not directly from West but through the intermediary of eastern neighbours, eit through imitation and second-hand borrowing or, in some c forcible imposition. By far the most important Asian influence ι and "model" for, the Thai elite (whether supporters or critics (existing order) during the late colonial era was the experience or Japan. Japan's special significance for Siam derived not just from Japan's unique apparent success in adopting the methods of the West to turn back the Western challenge, but also from the perceived affinities between the two countries. These included an early history of intense, if not always cordial, intercourse and a sharing of pur-ported Asian cultural values and particularly (albeit in different forms) the Buddhist religion. In more recent times, both had had similar treaty systems forced upon them by the Western powers and, to some degree, by the same Western agents.[5] Nevertheless, (and this is arguably the most important similarity of all) both had managed to maintain their existence as sovereign states through the zenith of

Western imperialist expansion. The result was that, by the end of the nineteenth century, they were the only two independent states in the East, with the exception of the somewhat ambiguous case of China.

Early Thai-Japanese Relations

Thai-Japanese relations dated back at least to the fifteenth and sixteenth centuries. For a time in the seventeenth century they had been of considerable importance, particularly to Siam, primarily because of substantial trade between the two countries carried on in part through intermediaries like the Dutch East India Company, and because of the activities of Japanese in Siam. These Japanese included merchants, Christians fleeing persecution at home, and assorted mercenaries and adventurers. By far the best known individual in this early period of intensive contact was Yamada Nagamasa, leader of the Japanese community in the 1620s. The firm historical data on Yamada is limited; nonetheless, beginning with a semi-fictional account written in 1707, the Yamada legend was repeatedly expounded and elaborated, and he came to be seen in Japan (and somewhat against the weight of the admittedly scanty historical evidence) as an early exemplar of friendly Thai-Japanese relations.[6] In the late nineteenth century, the name of Yamada, which, if it had ever been widely known had long since been forgotten, was reintroduced in Siam. The Yamada story was nourished and propagated by those of both countries who wished to promote a "restoration" of close Thai-Japanese relations. This campaign reached its peak in the years leading up to the Pacific War and the formal realization of a Thai-Japanese alliance.

In the first decades of the seventeenth century, Yamada and other Japanese warriors had played a significant role in dynastic disputes in Siam, that led to various complications and ultimately to an anti-Japanese reaction by the Thai court. These events, coupled with Tokugawa disapproval of an "irregular" succession to the Thai throne and the promulgation in the 1630s of the seclusion edicts closing Japan to foreign intercourse, led to a virtual suspension of relations which was to last for more than two centuries. Nevertheless, the break was not total; some trade continued, and a small Japanese community struggled on in Ayutthaya. However virtually cut off from any new Japanese immigration, it inevitably mixed with and was gradually absorbed into the local population. Only after the "opening" of both countries brought about by Western initiatives in the mid-nineteenth century would the direct contacts of the seventeenth century be restored.

Despite the long suspension of relations, Thai historical memories of Japan and the important role the Japanese had once played in Siam remained surprisingly strong. In April 1855, less than two years after Perry's first visit to Japan and before any of the concessions he extracted had borne tangible results, John Bowring arrived in Bangkok to negotiate the first of Siam's "unequal" treaties with the Western powers. Ties between the two countries had been almost non-existent for some two hundred years, but nevertheless Bowring recorded:

> In ancient times, a corps of Japanese soldiers formed the body guard of the Kings of Siam. There are no Japanese now in the country; but the traditions and recollections are many and vivid, and the subject of our commercial and political prospects in Japan was frequently discussed. The prime minister requested that I would allow him to send a Siamese noble to accompany me whenever I should visit Japan ...[7]

Despite this early Thai interest, however, the restoration of direct contacts between the two countries took place only some three decades later, during the nearly simultaneous reigns of the Emperor Meiji (1868–1912) and King Chulalongkorn (1868–1910).

The Meiji era brought a revival in Japan of an interest in the wider world, an interest that had never totally disappeared and that had been fuelled by "Chinese" contacts and "Dutch learning" even during the centuries when Japan had closed its doors to most of the outside world. This renewed interest centred on the West and on the adjacent continental areas of Korea and China. It also included the "South Seas," a term whose definition varied greatly from writer to writer and period to period, but which usually included insular Southeast Asia and often parts of the mainland as well. There was an outpouring of writings about the "South Seas," including both factual descriptions of these lands of tropical exotica and more theoretical discussions of what role they might play in a presumed expansion of Japan's sphere of interest. Some writers saw this primarily in commercial or cultural terms and other in more concrete strategic and political terms.[8]

Siam was somewhat peripheral to the main geographical focus of the "South Seas" concept, but nonetheless often figured in these discussions. For example, in a work published in 1893, the early Asianist Tarui Tokichi urged that Japan and Korea unite to form a new "Great East" state, which, with the cooperation of China, should work to free the "South Seas" area and especially mainland Southeast Asia "from the fetters of the white man." In particular, as parts of his plan to free Asia from Western domination,[9] he envisioned his "Great East" state and China helping Vietnam to regain its independence and working "to unite Siam with Burma."

Nor was this Japanese interest limited to theoretical formulations. In the 1890s particularly, as "South Seas fever" swept Japan, Japanese adventurers and would-be colonists came in increasing numbers to Southeast Asia, including Siam. Often from samurai backgrounds, the leaders of this Meiji "South Seas" movement expounded a philosophy which was Pan-Asianist and implicitly anti-Western. That Siam alone in Southeast Asia remained nominally independent only heightened its importance. It was clear that British influence was great and growing, and that both Britain and France were steadily encroaching on the peripheries of the kingdom with the very real prospect that Siam might soon go the way of the rest of Southeast Asia. Thus, Japanese efforts were directed, as Tarui was urging, toward saving Siam from Western domination. These efforts took the form of both individual enterprise and also larger cooperative schemes for Japanese agricultural colonization aimed, in part, at strengthening the "Asian" element and thus aiding Siam in resisting the Western threat. Poorly organized, underfinanced, and lacking any substantial Thai support, these ventures invariably failed, but the motivations and spirit behind them are typical of this early Japanese rediscovery of Siam and the "South Seas."[10]

Although the Thai showed little enthusiasm for a Japanese presence in Siam, the example of Japan's rapid modernization and rise to a position of acknowledged equality with the Western powers exerted a strong influence on the Thai elite. On the official level, the Meiji-Chulalongkorn eras saw the first significant contacts since the seventeenth century, with exchanges of correspondence between the two monarchs and missions between their governments. A "Declaration of Friendship and Commerce" (1887) was followed by a "Treaty of Friendship, Commerce, and Navigation" (1898), in which Japan's insistence on obtaining the same special privileges that Siam had been forced to concede to the Western powers (although with provision, for the first time, for their eventual relinquishment) did much to dampen Thai enthusiasm for Japan and Japanese professions of Pan-Asian unity. Toward the end of the period, Japanese specialists began to be employed as advisers to the Thai government in legal and certain technical capacities, though their impact was small compared to that of the dominant British, or the French, Germans, and other Europeans, or Americans.

But, even more than within the ruling circles, it was among critics of the absolute monarchy's measured pace of institutional reform that the example of Japan was constantly cited. In 1885 a group of eleven princes and officials with extensive experience in Europe presented a petition to King Chulalongkorn with the first calls for political modernization. Advocating a constitutional monarchy and other changes along European lines, the group cited not only the European nations, but also repeatedly invoked the case of Japan, which, they said, had followed the "civilized" road. They called for Siam to follow the European example

> or as close to the European path as possible, like Japan which is the only country in the East which has embarked on the European path.[11]

The writer and social critic, Thianwan, was another important figure of the period who frequently cited Japan's modernization as a model for Siam. Thianwan had worked for a time on Western cargo vessels that plied routes throughout Asia and the Pacific, and he may well have called at Japanese ports; in any case, he had read widely on developments in both Asia and the West. He was impressed by Japan's successful adoption of Western technology and methods to counter the Western threat, and he cited Japan and the United States as countries that, because of their representative institutions, had efficient administration of government.[12] He strongly criticized French actions in Asia, and, in words reminiscent of those of the Japanese Pan-Asianist Tarui cited above, argued that if Japan, China, Vietnam, and Siam would cooperate, "justice" could be established in the East, and

> If China would follow the lead of Japan, the Europeans wouldn't be able to cross the oceans and exercise their power as previously.[13]

This Thai interest in the example of Japan was, in considerable measure, a response to Japan's growing power and importance on the international scene. The first significant demonstration of Japan's new strength came in the Sino-Japanese War, in which modern arms and efficient organization resulted in a crushing Japanese victory over China's disorganized forces. This coincided with Japan's success in throwing off the restrictions of the treaty system, leading the American Minister in Bangkok to comment upon

> Siam's uneasiness under extraterritorial jurisdiction when she realizes her own progress and Japan's recently acquired freedom.[14]

Then in 1902, the conclusion of the Anglo-Japanese alliance put a formal seal of recognition on Japan's equality with the major Western powers.

But the event that had the greatest impact on Thai and other Asian perceptions of Japan was Japan's generally unanticipated triumph in the Russo-Japanese War of 1904–05. Prince Bidya (better known by the pseudonym "N.M.S.") wrote a contemporaneous account,[15] and, in July 1905, Thianwan published a long analysis of the factors behind Japan's victory, stressing particularly spirit and modern weaponry. The following month, he composed a petition to King Chulalongkorn in which he traced Japan's rise to power. He stressed her selective borrowing from abroad and willingness to abandon outmoded customs, and ended with a call for Siam to "follow Japan's path."[16] The Russo-Japanese War also influenced Thai strategic thinking. In 1928, Luang Sinthu Songkhramchai, who subsequently became a member of the 1932 coup group, a Navy commander and a major "pro-Japanese" figure in governments of the first Phibun era, published what has been described as "the first Thai treatise on modern naval warfare." It bore the title "Modern Naval Warfare: The Japanese Victory at the Straits of Tsushima."[17]

Early in the reign of Chulalongkorn's successor, Vajiravudh, the Thai government uncovered a conspiracy which was the first potentially violent manifestation of the calls for political change that critics like Thianwan or the petitioners of 1885 had long been disseminating. The "R.S. 130 rebellion,"[18] as it has come to be called, involved mainly junior army officers. It was loosely organized (one the group's own members revealed its existence to the authorities), and somewhat fuzzy in its ultimate aims. Its one clear purpose was to bring to an end the absolute monarchy, considered an anachronistic institution hindering Siam's further development. The plotters compared Siam's progress under absolute rule with that of other nations and found it deficient; examples cited included the West and also China, where the recent overthrow of the Ching dynasty seemed to presage a new era. The other case repeatedly invoked was Japan, like Siam an Asian state, but one which, under a constitutional monarchy, had progressed within a generation to acknowledged equality with the European nations.

Informed of the conspiracy, the government rounded up those involved and meted out rather mild and subsequently commuted prison sentences. Vajiravudh, nonetheless, was clearly aware of and concerned by the constant references to the Japanese case made by opponents of absolutism in Siam. He was sure that proponents of representative institutions in Siam would use the example of Japan. Therefore, in an article entitled "Japan for Example," he argued that Japan was in no real sense "democratic," but ruled by a bureaucratic oligarchy, and that, while it was true that Japan had progressed, it had done so in spite of, not because of constitutionalism.[19] Vaji-ravudh thus reversed the conclusions that his critics had drawn. However, the fact that he felt compelled to discuss in print the "Japanese example" is in itself an indication of its significance in Thai thought on the eve of the First World War.

Siam and Japan in the Interwar Period

Despite the restoration of official links between the two countries and the considerable influence the Japanese model exercised over both the Thai leadership and its domestic critics, economic relations between Siam and Japan were relatively insignificant in the pre-First World War period. This seems somewhat surprising, since, elsewhere in Southeast Asia where its economic stakes were much larger, Japanese business faced the restrictions and discrimination that were frequently a part of colonial policy. In independent Siam, the Japanese, in theory at least, could compete on an "equal footing." However, in this early period, neither country had products of vital interest to the other, and Siam's foreign trade was dominated by Western, especially British, interests and by the Chinese. Rice cultivation, the mainstay of the economy, was a Thai preserve, and several tentative Japanese efforts to penetrate it had proved unsuccessful; teak, tin, and rubber production were in British and Chinese hands. The limited Japanese economic role was reflected in the very small size of the Japanese community in Siam. From 1915 onward, what Japanese businesses there were faced the additional obstacle of periodic politically-motivated Chinese boycotts of Japanese trade.

Between 1914 and 1941, three major developments on the international scene greatly enhanced the relative importance of Thai-Japanese economic relations. The first of these was World War I, in which both Japan and Siam were nominally participants but, in fact, largely observers. However, the war diverted European attention and resources to the theatre of combat and completely eliminated Germany (formerly a significant shipper and trading partner of Siam) from the Asian scene. The Japanese were quick to take advantage of the opportunity to increase their share of Siam's foreign trade. With the return of peace, they successfully resisted efforts of the British and others to re-establish the economic *status quo ante*. The 1920s saw increasing competition to supply Siam's import needs as in certain types of cotton goods, "a market where Britain and Japan had been fighting it out since the end of World War I."[20]

Japan's next major step forward as an economic partner of Siam came with the Great Depression. While trade in general suffered, low-priced Japanese goods fared relatively better than the more expensive product lines of their European competitors. A sharply depreciated yen added to the Japanese comparative advantage, with the result that "between 1931 and 1933, British dominance was overturned," and Japan emerged as the largest single exporter to the Thai market. Nonetheless, Siam still constituted a relatively small component of Japan's overall trade with Southeast Asia, accounting for approximately 14% of Japanese exports to the region and approximately 10% of Japan's total Southeast Asian trade; in the same period, figures for the Dutch East Indies were nearly 50% in each category.[21]

The final sharp escalation in Thai-Japanese economic relations came in the special circumstances of 1940 and 1941, with war raging in Europe and Japan herself at war in China. War in Europe again stimulated Japanese exports to Thailand (as Siam had now become), but more dramatic was the tremendous surge in Thai exports to Japan. Faced with a need for greatly increased quantities of food and raw materials and increasing restrictions on trade imposed by the British and Dutch colonial authorities and the United States, Japan turned to Thailand to buy such commodities as rice, tin, and rubber. By 1941, Thailand was the single largest Southeast Asian exporter to Japan and second only to the Dutch East Indies as an importer of Japanese goods.[22]

It should be stressed that this escalating Thai-Japanese economic relationship was confined almost totally to trade. Notably absent, in contrast to such areas as the Philippines and the Dutch East Indies, was any significant Japanese capital investment. Among various factors cited as contributing to this pattern of development were the lack of a plantation mode of production in Siam, the lack of viable cash crops or other resources not already being exploited by well-established interests, and, at least until 1932, the relatively hostile attitude of the Thai government toward Japanese capital investment.[23] The investment that did take place was late, little, and semi-official in nature (in considerable part through government-backed "national policy companies"). It came in the latter part of the 1930s when contingency plans for a possible Pacific war were being formulated and "economic cooperation [with Thailand] was one means towards closer political and military ties."[24]

Growing economic links between Siam and Japan and the intensifying competition of Japan with Britain and others in the Thai market were paralleled by increasingly close political, cultural, and ideological ties. In the latter spheres particularly, the 1932 change of regime in Siam proved a watershed in relations with Japan. Post-1932 Siam and Japan found a convergence of interests that was anti-Western, anti-Chinese, and sought to challenge and ultimately overturn the established order in Southeast Asia.

In the last two decades of the absolute monarchy, it was mainly among various dissident groups that Thai interest in Japan continued to be evident. Official relations had been restored and regularized during Chulalongkorn's reign; they remained correct but somewhat distantly cool. Factors in both Japan and Siam contributed to this situation. On the Japanese side, despite a continuing undercurrent of private interest in *"nanshin ron"* and the "South

Seas," official attention in the years following the Russo-Japanese War focused primarily on the adjacent continental areas to the north and west—Korea (annexed in 1910), Manchuria, and China proper. In Siam, Chulalongkorn's successors, Vajiravudh and Prajadhipok, were both British-educated and, to a considerable degree, British-oriented in their international outlook.[25] As Japan's expanding spheres of activity came increasingly into conflict with what the British empire regarded as its own rightful spheres of influence, the Anglo-Japanese alliance forged in 1902 came under increasing stresses. Added pressure from the United States (whose own relations with Japan were deteriorating) caused it finally to be abandoned altogether in the agreements resulting from the 1921–22 Washington Conference. As British-Japanese tensions mounted in the East, Siam's last two absolute rulers maintained the long established policy of following the lead of the West, and particularly Britain, in international affairs. Prajadhipok, especially, was concerned about any suggestion of Japanese (or other alien, including Chinese or Western) acquisition of agricultural land. The Thai Legation in Tokyo was instructed to keep a close watch on the press for any signs of Japanese economic or political interest in Siam.

A special factor that negatively affected Thai-Japanese relations in the period was Siam's large and economically powerful Chinese community. Japanese actions in China from 1915 onward caused anti-Japanese reactions not only within China itself, but in overseas Chinese communities. Throughout the last years of the absolute monarchy, there was a series of anti-Japanese boycotts and strikes among the Bangkok Chinese that caused economic dislocations and political problems for the government, which was balanced uncomfortably between the conflicting pressures of the local Chinese (Siam had no diplomatic relations with any authority in China) and Japan's official representatives.

The coup of 24 June 1932 that ended the absolute monarchy also had a profound effect on Thai-Japanese relations. The question of possible Japanese contacts with members of the coup group prior to the coup is uncertain.[26] However, one goal of the coup group in overthrowing the power of the largely anglophile princes was to reduce foreign, and particularly British influence in Siam—a policy which coincided closely with Japanese aims. Fearful of the possibility of European intervention, the new government went to lengths to assure the West that foreign rights and interests would be respected. Nonetheless, it continued the process already initiated by the former regime, for both economic and ideological reasons, of reducing the number of foreign advisers. It also accelerated the drafting of the new law codes whose promulgation was a prerequisite to the final abolition of Western treaty privileges. In the late 1930s, it took a series of measures to curtail the activities of both Western and Chinese businesses operating in Siam. On the international scene, the most visible sign of a new orientation in Thai policy came early in 1933 when Siam refused to go along with the rest of the world in the League of Nations' vote condemning Japanese actions in Manchuria.[27] Japan was effusive in its gratitude for the Thai action; the West and China were alarmed at what they saw as evidence of an emerging Thai-Japanese entente. In fact, the Thai vote had been intended simply as an impartial refusal to take sides in a dispute between Asian neighbours. But, under the circumstances, it was a "neutrality" which favoured Japanese interests.[28]

The months immediately following the League vote were a period of intense factional manoeuvring and conflict within the new government, at the root of which were both policy differences and personal rivalries. After various upheavals, the end result was the "second coup" of 20 June 1933. This coup ousted the government of Phya Mano, who was British-educated, conservative, and not a member of the original coup group. It brought to the prime ministership Phya Phahon, who alone of the important leaders of the 1932 coup group had direct experience of Japan. (He had spent a year there in military training in the early 1920s.) It also brought to prominence Phibun and a group of his close associates, who had already been in touch with the Japanese Legation the previous month and who again met privately with Japanese diplomats on the day of the coup.[29] For the next decade, Thai-Japanese relations would move erratically but inexorably closer, with Phibun playing a key role in the process.

A number of figures outside official circles were also important in the development of Thai-Japanese relations in the 1930s, of whom perhaps the best known was Phra Sarasas. Phra Sarasas' career was one of vicissitudes. He had been an instructor in the Thai military academy and, as he later claimed, the intellectual father of the abortive 1912 plot against the absolute monarchy. In the 1920s, he was living in exile in Europe, where he circulated anti-monarchical tracts among Thai students and was in contact with Pridi and other early members of the coup group. Under the pen name "555" he also wrote political and social critiques in the Bangkok press. After the 1932 coup, he returned to Siam, and, early in 1934, became Minister of Economic Affairs. Despite his oft-proclaimed "socialism," he was soon involved in a dispute with striking railway employees, and then in an even more serious controversy over a draft treaty fixing quotas for rubber production. The rejection of this treaty by the National Assembly in 1934 led to the resignation of the Phahon government and the subsequent formation of a new Phahon cabinet. Phibun, for the first time, became Minister of Defence, while Phra Sarasas, who as Minister of Economic Affairs received much of the criticism for the treaty fiasco, was dropped from his post. The following year, citing "political dangers" in Siam, he left clandestinely for Japan.

Phra Sarasas spent most of the next decade in Tokyo, working unceasingly to promote closer Thai-Japanese relations. He delivered lectures and made radio broadcasts, wrote for both the Bangkok and Japanese press, and was associated with a culture centre called the "Thai Room."[30] He wrote a substantial work in English entitled *Money and Banking in Japan*,[31] for which he received a degree from a Japanese university. Then, in 1942, he published in Tokyo another work in English, *My Country Thailand*, the outcome (according to the preface) of lectures he had been asked to give during his stay in Japan. Dedicated "To the Nine Nippon Heroes of Pearl Harbour," this work consists of a lively, rather iconoclastic history from earliest times, followed by sections on various aspects of Thai life at the time of writing. The last of the historical sections, on the reign of Prajadhipok, was not by Phra Sarasas but by his (second) wife Claude. According to her introductory note, this was "in order to relieve my husband of the difficulty he encountered in chronicling the change of events in which he was one of the principal actors."[32] And, indeed, in this impassioned and highly subjective account, Phra Sarasas does emerge as "the man behind the first revolution of 1912" and the main instigator of the 1932 coup.

In addition to its florid prose and highly personalized perception of modern Thai history and the author's role in it, *My Country Thailand* is notable particularly for the rather critical view Phra Sarasas takes of the Thai monarchy. This includes not only such expected targets as Vajiravudh and Prajadhipok, but also, to some degree, "hero figures" such as Chulalongkorn, of whom it is said

> ... he was all the time haunted with the problem of how to perpetuate his despotic rule. This nightmare made him advance the civilization of his country only when such advancement would help and not hinder absolute kingship.[33]

Many earlier kings are subjected to similar criticism, although Taksin is somewhat rehabilitated at the expense of the Chakri Dynasty. In contrast, the Japanese imperial line is described as "holy and everlasting,"[34] and there are lengthy sections on the early period of close Thai-Japanese relations in the seventeenth century. On the Chulalongkorn-Meiji periods, Phra Sarasas stresses the similarities but also the failure of Siam to follow the Japanese model:

> As mentioned above this King [Chulalongkorn] had many characteristics in common with Emperor Meiji of Japan. By virtue of these qualities of her ruler Thailand should have been on a level with Nippon, and she surely would, if the King had but turned his eyes to the East. It was a misfortune that Thailand at that time was far from intimate

with Nippon as she had formerly been in the time of King Songtham [1610–1628]; for she failed to profit from the experiences of Japan which ran exactly parallel to her own.[35]

Rather surprisingly, given his supposedly socialist views, Japanese official sources indicate that during his years in Japan, Phra Sarasas was financed by one of the companies of the Mitsui *zaibatsu* group and particularly the Pan-Asianist Mitsui director and subsequent governor of the Bank of Japan, Ikeda Seihin.[36] The volume *Money and Banking in Japan* was dedicated to Ikeda, "[whose] unfailing co-operation and assistance have made possible the fulfillment of my desire."[37]

Though living mainly in Japan in the decade after 1935, Phra Sarasas visited Bangkok a number of times, where he gave interviews, lectured, and wrote articles on Thai-Japanese relations. These activities and his broadcasts over Radio Tokyo made him perhaps the most visible Thai spokesman for Japan. At the end of the war he was arrested along with Phibun and a few of his close associates, and charged as a "war criminal."[38] Ultimately freed on a legal technicality, Phra Sarasas eventually disappeared from the Thai scene to live quietly in Europe. But he remains a paradoxical figure—a key actor in Thai politics of the early twentieth century, a proclaimed socialist who found refuge in Japan at the height of the militarist period and a long-time critic of the monarchy who admired the Japanese imperial system.

While Phra Sarasas was working in Tokyo to promote closer Thai-Japanese relations, Thai interest in Japan was also being stimulated by the publication in Bangkok of a large number of works dealing with aspects of Japan's modern experience. These included the growth of the Japanese military, economic development, and the influence of the *bushido* code and other uniquely Japanese cultural components and institutions. An example of these works is the account of an official mission around the world in 1936 and 1937 written by Luang Katsongkhram. The author was a member of the 1932 coup group and subsequently a cabinet minister and a leading figure in the military's postwar return to power in 1947. The first volume was subtitled "A Discussion of Why Japan Has Progressed." In much the same way that Thianwan had done a generation earlier, Luang Katsongkhram attempted to analyze the causes of Japan's rise from isolation and obscurity to a position of recognized equality with the major Western powers. His conclusions were also similar; they stressed bravery, group unity, self-sacrifice, and selective borrowing from abroad. In the introduction, Luang Katsongkhram implied that the Thai should study and follow the Japanese model of national development; the work ended with a call for Thailand to become a great power.[39]

The rising Thai interest in Japan subsequent to the 1932 coup coincided with a renewed official Japanese interest in the "South Seas," and especially in Siam. This was because of Siam's strategic location in the centre of mainland Southeast Asia and because dealing with a sovereign government allowed a freedom of action impossible in the remainder of Southeast Asia under Western colonial regimes. Through diplomatic and other channels, Japan sought to loosen Siam's traditional political, cultural, and economic links to the West, and, in so far as possible, to replace those links with links to Japan. Trade between the two countries was promoted (though, in the later stages, Japanese "economic" enterprises sometimes became little more than a cover for espionage activities directed both at Siam and the neighbouring states), and various cultural and educational organizations were established. A variety of Thai delegations was invited to Japan, including a naval mission headed by Luang Sinthu Songkhramchai, a rising figure in the new government, who had written the 1928 volume on Japan's naval victory in the Russo-Japanese War. Japanese propaganda stressed traditional affinities between the two countries—the Yamada legend and a history of purportedly cordial early relations, supposed shared "Asian values," and the Buddhist religion. Even the Japanese admitted privately the somewhat distorted and artificial nature of some of the claimed links. Japanese Buddhism, for example, differed greatly

from the Thai Theravada doctrine, and played a much less important role in Japanese life than Buddhism did in Thai life. In 1934,
when a group of young Thai officials with seemingly promising
career prospects was invited to Japan for a "Pan-Pacific Buddhist
Youth Conference," Japanese official documents conceded that the
conference was only the "ostensible" reason for the invitation.[40]

Politically, the Japanese concentrated on cultivating Thai government leaders thought to be favourably inclined toward Japan.
Above all was Phibun, who, after his appointment as Defence Minister in 1934, clearly emerged as the real power figure in the Phahon
government, and who, in December 1938, himself became prime
minister. Dealings with Phibun were handled especially through
Wanit Pananon, a close Phibun aide and confidant. Wanit held relatively minor official positions, but served as a go-between in secret
dealings between Phibun and the Japanese, without the knowledge
of most of the Thai government leaders. Wanit's early relations with
the Japanese were primarily in the economic field. These continued
into the wartime period, but from the time of the Indochina crisis in
1940–41 he also began to play a major political role. He was a key figure in the conclusion of the Thai-Japanese alliance in December
1941.[41]

But the Japanese "net" was cast surprisingly widely. In the
immediate postcoup period, they had hopes that Pridi, the leader of
the "liberal" civilian faction, might be induced to lean towards
Japan, and it was only in the late 1930s that attempts to win him over
were abandoned as a lost cause. And the effort to promote Japan's
interests extended beyond official circles to a wide range of Thai
"opinion makers." One such was Kulap Saipradit, a leading jour-
nalist and writer, who in 1936 undertook a "study tour" of newspaper operations in Japan, presumably with official sponsorship. The
immediate result was a rather atypical romantic novel with a Japanese setting. However, if the Japanese had hoped to sway Kulap's
political sympathies, they were notably unsuccessful. He was and
remained an outspoken critic of Phibun's pro-Japanese policies, and,

in the postwar period, became a prominent popularizer of Marxist thought. Ultimately he died in exile in Peking.

This concerted campaign to increase Japanese influence in Siam was accompanied by a steadily growing diplomatic and commercial presence that included the opening of Japanese consulates at Chiengmai in the north and Songkhla (where Japanese troops were soon to land) in the south. In 1941 relations were raised to full ambassadorial status—the first in modern Thai history. Earlier, the Indochina crisis of 1940–41 had provided an opportunity for Japanese diplomatic initiatives, though the end result of Japanese "mediation" and the Tokyo negotiations was a settlement which, in the Thai view, awarded Thailand less than Thai historical claims or feats of arms deserved, and which was accepted only after strong pressure was exerted by Japan. This and concern over the ominous advance of Japanese forces into southern Indochina where they faced the new Thai frontier combined, in mid-1941, to produce a temporary setback to the developing Thai-Japanese relationship. But the events of December 7 and 8 and the weeks that followed were to show the success, albeit against a backdrop of *force majeure*, of Japan's long campaign to cultivate the sympathies of elements of the Thai leadership as well as segments of the Thai public.

Conclusion

Thailand's rapid march into the Japanese camp—from the troop passage agreement of December 8 to the alliance of the 11th and the ultimate step of the declaration of war against Britain and the United States on January 25, 1942—surprised not only many in the West and Thailand, but also the Japanese themselves. However, while formal Thai-Japanese relations had never been closer, it soon became clear that the appeal of Japan's example had been greater when observed from a distance. In sum, "the intensive contacts of the war years strained rather than solidified Thai-Japanese relations, while the outcome of the war virtually severed them"[42] until the 1960s, when a

Japanese presence reappeared in a new, more subtle, and ultimately more entangling economic guise.

The interwar period had been marked by increasingly close commercial relations and, in the later phase, a new political dimension as well including Japan's use of "economic" links to pursue, both overtly and covertly, political and strategic objectives. The 1932 change of regime in Siam provided the Japanese with new opportunities to expand their interests and influence, which they were quick to seize. The parallels in the political development of the two countries in the 1930s are striking—intensive promotion of government-sponsored "official" nationalism, rising militarism and an increasingly direct military involvement in the political process, and an accelerating drive toward expansionism abroad. In their anti-Western, anti-Chinese ideological orientations, the two regimes also found a convergence of interests.

Thus, it is hardly surprising that the two countries should find themselves moving toward closer relations—economic, cultural, and political—even without the deliberate efforts of a few Thais and many Japanese. That such efforts did take place, particularly on the Japanese side, only accelerated the process. The end results were quite different however: for Japan a shattering defeat; but for Thailand, once it became clear that Japan was not the wave of the future in Southeast Asia, a deft realignment of foreign policy to conform to the perceived changes in power relationships in the region. How successful this "opportunism" was is illustrated by Phibun's return to the prime ministership in 1948, to remain for another decade as the staunch ally of countries upon which only a few years previously he had declared war. Thai admiration for Japan from the Meiji era onward was real but pragmatic, for it was admiration of Japan's "success," and it lasted only as long as that success could be sustained. If Japan were to falter, the Thai elite would turn their attention elsewhere for other, more promising "models," either abroad or within their own traditions.

Notes

1 Eugene Kamenka, "Political Nationalism—The Evolution of the Idea," in *Nationalism: The Nature and Evolution of an Idea* ed. Kamenka (Canberra: Australian National University, 1973), p. 3. Nonetheless, Kamenka adds, "... nationalism, as a political ideology, as an 'ism,' is above all a specific historic phenomenon to be distinguished as such from the much more general sense of patriotism or national consciousness."

2 See for example Benedict Anderson, *Imagined Communities: Reflections on the Origin and Spread of Nationalism* (London: Verso, 1983), chapter 6; Eiji Murashima, "The Origin of Modern Official State Ideology in Thailand," *Journal of Southeast Asian Studies*, 19:1, March 1988, pp. 80–96; Kullada Kesboonchoo, "Official Nationalism under King Chulalongkorn" (Paper presented at the International Conference on Thai Studies, Bangkok, August 1984, and based upon analysis of late Fifth Reign school textbooks).

3 David K. Wyatt, *Thailand: A Short History* (New Haven: Yale University Press, 1984), ch. 8, "The Rise of Elite Nationalism."

4 This expressive phrase seems to have been used first by Chatthip Nartsupha, Suthy Prasartset, and Montri Chenvidyakarn, eds., in the Introduction (p. 24) to *The Political Economy of Siam 1910–1932* (Bangkok: Social Science Association of Thailand, 1978). The traditional Thai *sakdina* system of manpower control had been based upon a social hierarchy which was strictly ordered and fairly rigid (excepting in times of dynastic or national upheaval, when there could be spectacular cases of upward or downward mobility); indeed *"sakdina"* in its narrow sense was simply a numerical rating assigned to everyone from slave to heir apparent (the king alone having a worth beyond reckoning) which determined his position in the hierarchy.
   Sakdina, in the formal sense of awards of numerical rankings, disappeared with the 1932 coup. The term however has recently been much in vogue with social critics, applied to the present as well as the past, with a range of meanings such as "old-fashioned," "conservative," "reactionary," "royalist," and (frequently, if somewhat inaccurately) "feudal."

5 The treaty system was launched in Japan by Townsend Harris, who had come directly from Bangkok where he had concluded the American treaty with Siam; Harris' Thai treaty in turn was closely based upon the earlier Bowring-Parkes treaty. Harry Parkes, after being involved in the opening of both Siam and China, subsequently represented Great Britain in Japan.

6 The question of fact versus fiction in accounts of Yamada is discussed in Yoneo Ishii and Toshiharu Yoshikawa, *Khwam samphan Thai-Yipun 600 pi* [Six Hundred Years of Thai-Japanese Relations] (Bangkok, 1987), pp. 49–53. This work surveys a wide range of aspects of Thai-Japanese relations, particularly of the late nineteenth and early twentieth centuries.

7 John Bowring, *The Kingdom and People of Siam* (London: J.W. Parker, 1857) (Reprinted, London: Oxford University Press, 1969), vol. I, p. 438.

8 These early discussions of Japan's relationship with the "South Seas" area— known collectively as "nanshin ron"—are described in detail in Shimizu

Hajime, *Southeast Asia in Modern Japanese Thought: The Development and Transformation of "Nanshin Ron"* (Canberra: Australian National University, 1980).

9 Quoted in *ibid.*, pp. 8–9.

10 The activities of Japanese adventures in Siam in the 1890s are examined in detail (primarily on the basis of Japanese sources) in E. Thadeus Flood, "The *Shishi* Interlude in Old Siam: An Aspect of the Meiji Impact in Southeast Asia," in *Meiji Japan's Centennial: Aspects of Political Thought and Action*, edited by David Wurfel (Lawrence, Kansas: Regent's Press, 1971), pp. 78–105.

11 Chai-anan Samudvanija, *Phaen phatthana kanmuang chabap raek khong Thai: Kham krapbangkhomtun khong chaonai lae kharatchakan hai plianplaeng kanpokkhrong R.S. 103* [The First Proposal for Thai Political Reform: The 1885 Petition of Princes and Officials for a Change in the System of Government] (Bangkok: Aksornsamphan Press, 1970), pp. 66, 69; Niphon Insin, *Naew khit choeng totan rabop watthatham kao: Syksa chak wannakam khong chon chang klang nai samai Phraphutthachaoluang* [Intellectual Opposition to Traditional Culture: A Study from the Literature of the Middle Class in the Reign of Chulalongkorn] (Sakol Nakorn, Thailand: Teachers' Training College, 1978), p. 30, and see also p. 20.

12 Niphon, *Intellectual Opposition*, p. 83, with attribution to Vella via Thamsook in an article in the journal *Chulasan...* January 1975.

13 Niphon, pp. 85, 86. The latter passage is quoted (p. 93) from the text of a petition from Thianwan to Chulalongkorn dated August 1905, reproduced in Chai-anan Samudvanija (ed.) *Sanniphon khong Thianwan* [Collected Works of Thianwan] (Bangkok: Students' Association of Ramkhamhaeng University, 1974), pp. 185–231; see also, for example, the reference to Japan in line 2 of the Thianwan poem which prefaces this work.

14 Quoted in Benjamin A. Batson, "Siam and Japan: The Perils of Independence," in Alfred W. McCoy (ed.), *Southeast Asia Under Japanese Occupation* (New Haven: Yale University Southeast Asia Studies, 1980), p. 271 (the Minister's despatch was dated 21 December 1899).

15 Wibha Senanan, *The Genesis of the Novel in Thailand* (Bangkok: Thai Wattana Panich, 1975), p. 146.

16 Chai-anan (ed.), *Sanniphon khong Thianwan*, pp. 144–48, 190–229.

17 Kasem Sirisumpundh, "Emergence of the Modern National State in Burma and Thailand," Ph.D. diss., University of Wisconsin, 1962, pp. 210, 371 (n. 10).

18 "R.S." denotes a year system dating from the beginning of the Bangkok period; R.S. 130 is the year from 1 April 1911 to 31 March 1912. The conspiracy was revealed and the plotters arrested in February 1912. For details of the affair see Thamsook Numnonda, *Yang Toek run raek: Kabot R.S. 130* [The First "Young Turks": The 1912 Conspiracy] (Bangkok: Ruangsin, 1979); and Walter F. Vella, *Chaiyo! The Role of King Vajiravudh in the Development of Thai*

Nationalism (Honolulu: University Press of Hawaii, 1978), pp. 53 ff.

19 Vella, p. 70. The article was published in 1912.

20 William L. Swan, "Japanese Economic Relations with Siam: Aspects of Their Historical Development 1884 to 1942," Ph.D. diss., Australian National University, 1986, p. 45. The discussion of Thai-Japanese economic relations given here is based largely on this study.

21 *Ibid.*, pp. 67, 54, 68.

22 *Ibid.*, p. 111.

23 *Ibid.*, ch. 7.

24 *Ibid.*, p. 100.

25 Unlike Chulalongkorn, both did visit Japan: Vajiravudh in 1902/03 when as crown prince he returned from his studies in Europe, and Prajadhipok in 1924 and again in 1931 en route to the United States to receive medical treatment for his failing eyesight.

26 There is some discussion of this question in E. Thadeus Flood, "Japan's Relations with Thailand, 1928–41," Ph.D. diss., University of Washington, 1967, ch. II, "Japan and the Rise of the Siamese Military."

27 The vote was 42–1–1; only Japan voted against the critical League report, and only Siam (of those participating in the vote) abstained.

28 The "neutrality" policy had, in fact, been formulated some months earlier, in the last days of the absolute monarchy, in part because it was feared that possible League sanctions against Japan might affect Thai rice sales (already severely depressed by the economic crisis) in the Japanese market.

29 For details of Japanese contacts with the "second coup" leaders see Flood, "Japan's Relations with Thailand," ch. II.

30 Presumably this is the same as the "Mitsui-Thai Room" Swan mentions as a "research organization" (p. 90).

31 Phra Sarasas, *Money and Banking in Japan* (London: Heath Cranton, Ltd., 1940).

32 Phra Sarasas, *My Country Thailand* (1st edition, Tokyo: Maruzen, 1942), pp. 219, 223. This work, in substantially revised form, has gone through a number of postwar republications in Bangkok (6th edition, 1960). Needless to say, the later editions no longer bear the dedication to the "Nine Nippon Heroes of Pearl Harbour," and the section on the Seventh Reign has also been much rewritten and is no longer attributed to Claude Sarasas.

33 *Ibid.*, p. 123.

34 *Ibid.*, p. 63.

35 *Ibid.*, p. 126.

36 Flood, "Japan's Relations with Thailand," pp. 124–25.

37 Phra Sarasas, *Money and Banking in Japan*. "Preface," p. 12.

38 When Phibun resigned in 1944, the now-dominant Pridi faction was said

actually to have considered making Phra Sarasas prime minister because of his obvious acceptability to the Japanese, who were still militarily in control. See Pridi's testimony at Phra Sarasas' trial in Thak Chaloemtiarana (ed.), *Thai Politics: Extracts and Documents 1932–1957* (Bangkok: Social Science Association of Thailand, 1978), pp. 370–404.

39 See Batson, "Siam and Japan," pp. 273–74, and n. 28 (pp. 291–92). Although the author's trip had taken place several years earlier, the account was apparently written in 1940 and was published only in October 1941. Note 28 continues:

> Luang Katsongkhram, like Thianwan before him and a number of writers since, tended to assume that Siam and Japan had begun their quests for modernization from roughly the same "starting points," and thus to seek causes for Japan's relatively greater "success." This approach tends to ignore the fact that the traditional social structures and value systems of the two countries were vastly different, and that the economy of Tokugawa Japan, if not "modern" in a Western sense, was extremely sophisticated and highly developed.

The frequent comparisons of Chulalongkorn's Siam and Meiji Japan have also been criticized on the grounds that the two countries' relationships with the outside world, particularly the Western powers, were not really comparable, and, most importantly, that the changes effected in Japan were fundamental while those in Siam were not. The first of these points is stressed in Ian G. Brown, "The Siamese Administrative Elite in the Early Twentieth Century and the Historical Origins of Underdevelopment in Siam," in J.H.C.S. Davidson (ed.), *Lai Su Thai: Essays in Honour of E.H.S. Simmonds* (London: School of Oriental and African Studies, 1987), especially n. 55, pp. 182–83. For examples of the latter argument see Norman Jacobs, *Modernization without Development: Thailand as an Asian Case Study* (New York: Praeger, 1971); Benedict Anderson, "Studies of the Thai State: The State of Thai Studies," in Eliezer B. Ayal (ed.), *The Study of Thailand* (Athens, Ohio: Ohio University Center for International Studies, Southeast Asia Series No. 54, 1978), pp. 193–247; and Chatthip Nartsupha and Suthy Prasartset (eds.), *The Political Economy of Siam, 1851–1910* (Bangkok: Social Science Association of Thailand, 1978), "Introduction" (pp. 1–31), pp. 30–31.

40 Flood, "Japan's Relations with Thailand," p. 103.

41 On Wanit and his eventual fate see Asada Shunsuke, "Wanitto no Higeki" [The Tragedy of Wanit], English version in Benjamin A. Batson and Shimizu Hajime, *'The Tragedy of Wanit': A Japanese Account of Wartime Thai Politics,* (*Journal of Southeast Asian Studies,* National University of Singapore, Special Publications Series No. 1, 1990).

42 Batson, "Siam and Japan," p. 287.

9

Some Closing Remarks: An Agenda for Further Research

IAN BROWN

It is an excellent principle that a gathering of scholars focused on a single theme and the published papers that emerge from such gatherings should concentrate less on reaching settled answers than on refining existing questions and developing new, more insightful ones. Certainly that was the principle that was applied at the workshop held in Shimoda in April 1988 that formed the foundation of the present volume, and that has been applied in the preparation of the volume itself. It therefore falls to these closing remarks not to draw the preceding papers into a firm, rounded concluding statement, but to propose an agenda for further research. I must emphasize that this is *an* agenda, not *the* agenda; for inevitably it must reflect mainly my own interests as an economic historian of Southeast Asia.

The preceding essays have clearly demonstrated the extraordinary complexity of this subject, but it would be valuable as a preliminary exercise briefly to explore further the origins and nature of that complexity. Two broad arguments are important here. The first—a rather elementary observation—is that the three principal political blocs involved in this subject—Japan, Southeast Asia, and the western powers—each embraced highly complex and frequently contradictory interests and ambitions with respect to the other two. Thus, as the papers by Shimizu Hajime, Hatano Sumio and Kokaze

Hidemasa make clear, in Japan there were complex divisions within the military as well as between elements of the military and parts of the civilian administration in this period with respect to the importance of Southeast Asia for Japan's continued economic advance and with respect to the prospect of serious commercial confrontation in the region with the western powers. There were comparably complex divisions within the western bloc, notably between those administrators and merchants who were determined to preserve Southeast Asia as a market for western manufactures and those administrators and traders who saw benefit in the massive influx of cheap Japanese manufactures into the region—in that it would, to some degree, protect the material welfare of the indigenous populations and maintain the buoyancy of commodity markets during a period of severe depression. In this broad context, there were also major contrasts within Southeast Asia itself; and as these regional contrasts have not perhaps received sufficient emphasis in the preceding papers, it would be as well to dwell on them here. Some of the basic data relevant to the argument are set out in the following tables.

These tables suggest that in the interwar years, Japan was a far more important trading partner for Southeast Asia (taking the region as a whole) than Southeast Asia was for Japan. It need only be noted that in 1935, a year in which Asia absorbed 52.2 percent of Japan's exports and was the source for 35.18 percent of its imports, the five Southeast Asia territories together accounted for only 11.35 percent of Japan's exports and only 6.6 percent of its imports. However the tables also suggest that, within this overall pattern, Netherlands India was, by a substantial margin, Japan's most important trading partner in Southeast Asia in this period; and that, in the mid-1930s, Japan was a very important trading partner for Netherlands India and Siam (for both territories, over a quarter of imports were of Japanese origin), a markedly less important partner in the case of the Philippines and British Malaya, and less important still for French Indochina. But it must quickly be added that aggregate figures

Table 9.1 Japan's foreign trade with selected countries: percentage of Japan's total foreign trade, 1910–1940

	Straits Settlements		Netherlands India		French Indochina		Philippines		Siam		Asia*	
	Export	Import	Export	Import	Export	Import	Export	Import	Export	Import	Export	Import
1910	1.43	0.99	0.68	4.07	0.07	0.95	0.96	0.17	0.12	0.57	40.63	48.69
1915	1.78	1.00	1.19	3.06	0.09	0.69	1.10	1.37	0.11	0.53	48.22	56.70
1920	1.83	0.73	5.50	2.94	0.18	0.88	1.76	0.70	0.21	0.14	51.24	40.34
1925	1.95	1.44	3.71	4.02	0.17	1.89	1.27	0.65	0.34	0.92	43.40	47.18
1930	1.83	1.87	4.49	3.88	0.16	0.51	1.93	0.69	0.64	1.22	47.90	40.91
1935	1.94	1.64	5.72	3.16	0.16	0.61	1.92	0.97	1.61	0.22	52.20	35.18
1940	0.64	1.55	4.74	3.63	0.07	2.83	0.73	1.76	1.35	1.53	68.22	43.84

* Includes China, Kwantung, Hongkong, British India, The Straits Settlements, Netherlands India, French Indochina, The Philippines, Siam.
Source: Calculated from *Japan Statistical Year-Book 1949*, Nihon Statistical Association, pp. 474–77.

Table 9.2 *British Malaya: percentage of trade with Japan, 1915–1939*

	Export	Import
1915–18 average	3.1	7.4
1919–23 average	6.3	4.2
1924–28 average	3.4	2.9
1929–31 average	6.4	3.2
1932–36 average	9.0	6.6
1937–39 average	8.0	3.5

Source: Lim Hua Sing, "The Value, Composition and Significance of Japanese Trade with Southeast Asia, 1914–41." Ph.D. diss., University of London, 1981, Appendix H.

Table 9.3 *Netherlands India: percentage of trade with Japan, 1910–1939*

	Export	Import
1910–14 average	3.95	1.39
1925–29 average	4.72	10.25
1930–34 average	4.25	18.63
1935	5.37	29.71
1937	4.4	25.4
1939	3.3	18.2

Source: Lim Hua Sing, Appendix I.

provide only a very rough indication of the varied importance of the commercial relationships between Japan and the countries of Southeast Asia; indeed, in some respects, they are misleading. The analysis needs to be refined, most notably by considering and weighing the trade in individual commodities—textiles (a task undertaken in this volume by Shinya Sugiyama), rubber, tin, petroleum, iron ore,

Table 9.4 *French Indochina: percentage of trade with Japan, 1913–1938*

	Export	Import
1913	6.0	1.5
1925–29 average	9.4	2.3
1930–34 average	4.9	1.5
1936	4.6	3.6
1938	3.1	2.9

Source: Lim Hua Sing, Appendix F.

Table 9.5 *The Philippines: percentage of trade with Japan, 1914–1940*

	Export	Import
1914–18 average	6.7	10.8
1919–23 average	6.1	10.0
1924–28 average	4.7	9.2
1929–31 average	3.8	9.7
1932–36 average	4.3	11.4
1937–40 average	5.9	8.5

Source: Lim Hua Sing, Appendix E.

and possibly abaca and rice.[1] This refinement will show that, in the 1930s, Southeast Asia (or, it must be firmly emphasized, parts of the region) was of major importance to Japan as a market for certain manufactures (outstandingly, textiles) and as a source for certain raw materials (including petroleum, rubber, tin). And, of course, it was over these *specific* markets and resources within Southeast Asia that there emerged the commercial confrontation with the western powers in the region. But, as a final point here, it might be added that even a focus on the individual commodities traded fails to convey fully the nature of the commercial relationships between Japan and

Table 9.6 *Siam: percentage of trade with Japan,*
1910–1939

	Export	Import
1910/11–1914/15 average	0.4	2.8
1925/26–1929/30 average	4.8	5.4
1930/31–1934/35 average	4.0	11.7
1935/36	2.0	25.6
1936/37	2.8	25.7
1937/38	3.5	19.8
1938/39	1.2	14.8

Source: Lim Hua Sing, Appendix G.

the individual countries of Southeast Asia in this period, for it is clear that there were also important political dimensions. As the papers by Milagros Guerrero, Benjamin Batson, and Anne Booth make evident, the ease of Japanese commercial expansion, the severity of the rivalry that it provoked, and the nature and effectiveness of the local administration's response were markedly different as between the Philippines, Siam, and Netherlands India. This was in large part a reflection of the sharply contrasting political circumstances of those three territories in the 1930s: the Philippines achieving internal self-government and an assurance of full political sovereignty within a decade; Netherlands India held very firmly by a colonial administration determined to defend its dominant economic and political position; and Siam, politically independent, adjusting to Japan's rapidly growing power in eastern Asia.[2]

The second argument may be noted more briefly. The complexity of this subject also reflects the fact that it can be discussed in a number of important, but distinct, contexts. It can be considered, for example, in the context of the origins of the Pacific War. In this case, the commercial confrontation between Japan and the western powers in Southeast Asia is seen either to have made war virtually inevitable, to have been a contributory element, or to have been of relatively minor significance in the growing tension between Japan and the western nations at the close of the 1930s. It can be set in the context of the impact of the great interwar depression. Here, Japan's remarkable export expansion is related to the Japanese financial and economic crisis of the early 1930s; the wide availability of cheap Japanese manufactures in Southeast Asia is seen to have mitigated, to an important degree, the impact of the collapse of primary markets on the material welfare of the indigenous peoples of the region; and the determination of the western powers to defend their markets in Southeast Asia can be seen to have been heightened by the serious economic and social distress in the metropoles. And finally, this subject may be placed in the broad context of the changing structure of the Asian trading network—the processes, underway before the first world war and clearly continuing long after Japan's defeat in the second, by which Japan has emerged as the dominant force in the Asian economy of the late twentieth century.

It is now appropriate to outline three possible areas for future research. It must be said again that this is a personal agenda, for the extreme complexity of this subject makes a wide range of new approaches and perspectives feasible, indeed imperative. The first proposal concerns the Japanese retail networks that were created in many parts of Southeast Asia in the interwar decades. It was the effectiveness of these networks that secured the remarkably rapid penetration of the region by Japanese manufactures, notably in the face of the boycotts of Japanese goods by Chinese merchants in the 1930s. Milagros Guerrero and Shinya Sugiyama both make a number of important observations on the extent, structure, and practices of the Japanese networks, but several questions remain. The success of such networks required traders to be fully familiar with local custom, fluent in local languages and, of great importance, to have had long experience of local market conditions and requirements. The Chinese merchants who dominated retail distribution in the region at the beginning of this period had taken many decades to establish their trading networks. By the early twentieth century many, if not most, were local-born and, in certain parts of Southeast Asia, had achieved a marked degree of assimilation with the local population. How had Japanese retailers acquired their familiarity, fluency, and experience in such a short period of time? What indeed was the geographical extent of the Japanese retail network; to what degree did Japanese retailers work through local traders; to what degree were Japanese manufactures retailed through alternative, but not Chinese, networks, for example, in the case of British Malaya, through Indian networks? To confront these questions would require a number of detailed local-level studies.

The second proposal concerns the impact of cheap Japanese imports on the material welfare of Southeast Asians during the 1930s depression. The assertion noted earlier, that the wide availability of Japanese manufactures mitigated to an important degree the impact of the collapse of primary markets on the real income of local producers, needs to be subjected to rigorous statistical examination. That examination would have to be sensitive to the contrasting economic circumstances of the principal export-dominated districts of Southeast Asia; and it would have to recognize that the sharp influx of Japanese manufactures into many parts of the region may also have had damaging implications for indigenous welfare—to the extent that it created unemployment in competing cottage industries or denied an opportunity for modern industry to establish itself.

This last observation leads to the third proposed area for further research. It is important that Japan's commercial expansion into Southeast Asia in the interwar period and the fierce rivalry that it provoked with western interests be set in the broad context of Southeast Asia's modern economic experience. For most of the nineteenth century and for the first half of the twentieth, economic change in the region can be said to have been provoked primarily by the intervention of western industrial capitalism. In the second half of the twentieth century, to an increasing extent, the most dynamic influence has been the industrial capitalism of Japan. This has come to have an impact, notably through direct investment in the manufacturing and service sectors, perhaps comparable to, although in markedly different directions from, that exerted by western capitalism in the earlier period. Seen in that context, the 1920s and 1930s become a major turning point, the point at which the influence of Japan's economic might on the course of economic change in Southeast Asia first began to be felt seriously and when western capitalism was pushed into retreat, the point at which the structures which were to be prominent in the economies of Southeast Asia in the late twentieth century first began to take form.

Notes

1   A wealth of statistical data on Japanese trade with Southeast Asia in the interwar decades can be found in Lim Hua Sing, "The Value, Composition and Significance of Japanese Trade with Southeast Asia, 1914–41," Ph.D. diss., University of London, 1981.

2   Reference should be made here to the work of William L. Swan on Thai-Japanese relations at the end of this period: "Thai-Japanese Relations at the Start of the Pacific War: New Insight into a Controversial Period," *Journal of Southeast Asian Studies*, 18, 2 (September 1987), pp. 270–93; "Thai-Japan Monetary Relations at the Start of the Pacific War," *Modern Asian Studies*, 23, 2 (May 1989), pp. 313–47. See also his "Japanese Economic Relations with Siam: Aspects of their Historical Development 1884 to 1942," Ph.D. diss., Australian National University, 1986.